F

Integra

Stories of Home and Displacement

Ciara Ryan-Gerhardt

Ilona Press

Integra

A percentage of the profits from the sale of this book are donated to Woodlands League, an independent, not-for-profit Irish NGO whose aim is to restore the relationship between people and their native woodlands, and the re-forestation of Ireland; they hold walks, talks and trainings throughout the country promoting native woodland heritage and actively lobby to change Irish forestry policy. For more information see: http://www.woodlandleague.org/ and www.ciara-ryan-gerhardt.com/offset-ecological-costs

More about the author: www.ciara-ryan-gerhardt.com

Dedicated to

my homes around the world

and the people who have helped me find my own;

to all peoples,

in need of a home, inside or out,

who yearn to be treated with dignity and respect;

the nomadic soul who wonders and wanders,

never finds rest,

and knows the road;

the indigenous peoples who live close to the earth,

who know and hold deep planetary wisdom.

and the earth:

the seas that roll and crash, the skies, grey and blue,

and the land, green and fertile or dust-red and arid.

"The Office of the United Nations High Commissioner for Refugees was established on December 14 1950 by the United Nations General Assembly. The agency is mandated to lead and co-ordinate international action to protect refugees and resolve refugee problems worldwide. Its primary purpose is to safeguard the rights and well-being of refugees. It strives to ensure that everyone can exercise the right to seek asylum and find safe refuge in another State, with the option to return home voluntarily, integrate locally or to resettle in a third country."

UNHCR website

"Over half the world's refugees are children."

UNHCR website

"Asylum is a right, not a crime."

No One Is Illegal - Toronto

Contents

Introduction

Integra: a Latin word meaning "something which is whole."

What kind of home do we want to create, and where and how will we create it? These questions, at the root of this book, are becoming increasingly important for us—personally, collectively, politically and ecologically. It's something I've wondered about since I was a child. As I travelled I heard stories, I picked up and absorbed ideas about ways of life that sparked my wish to write *Integra.* I loved and still love listening to stories; as a child I was blessed to have a mother who read or recited poems and novels to me at night.

    Integra is a story of finding and losing and coming home. What we share across cultures and the seas, what links us across the globe, is important for our and the planet's present and future, which are of course inextricably intertwined. Stories of our humanity, of shared loss are timeless. Some of the stories in *Integra* span continents I have not been to, though each person, except my late uncle Kurt, is someone I have met during my life. Home, to me, is not simply a building or geographical place, but is where we encounter a living and breathing experience of being ourselves. Warmth, love, freedom to express ourselves, fulfil our needs, and security. And then collectively, home as the sanctuary of "not just one person but of a whole people, utterly integrated with their environment."[1] What I look for when I enter a home, any home—mine or another person's—is shelter: *asylum*. Somehow, the word "migrant" has become nameless, faceless; a cold and unforgiving word. It is my hope that *Integra* will create greater understanding, respect and integrity in ourselves and between cultures, and in our relationship to the natural world around us, which is not separate from us.

I wrote *Integra* because of my childhood, how I live my life, everyone I had met where I've travelled and the current crises in the world, led to *Integra* being written and my running after it, trying to keep up.

We stand now at a crossroads, and I wonder which way we will turn. So many in this world are homeless, stateless, orphaned and lost, abandoned, disowned, marginalised and deemed illegal by a system that forgets our shared humanity, criminalises compassion, and forgets that each and every one of us has the basic right to exist, and to belong.

A correspondence with Jen Christion-Myers about her PhD thesis, while writing *Integra,* helped me form a way of thinking about my overarching question for the book: How do we live in the world? How do we create ourselves and our homes, whether they be inside or out? Our relationships? What do we do when we are forced to move?[2]

Confronted by the forces of modernity, the connections between humans and the places they live are increasingly fragile. "How do people maintain this vital connection to place in the face of ecological deterioration and systemic injustice?"[3]

Her PhD was an enquiry into the resilience of place-based connection in the face of collective trauma by the small island community of Vieques, Puerto Rico. "The way in which you are and I am, how we humans are on the Earth, is [in German] *Buan*: dwelling... The old word, *bauen*, says that man *is* insofar as he *dwells*."[2] We engage with what's around us, she wrote, "through concernful involvement." And this she explained, "is always already in the world. Heiddeger calls the human condition being-in-the-world."[4] In this way, place becomes "integral to the very structure and possibility of experience."[5]

Although *Integra* is written for anyone, anywhere, much of the book was written in Ireland: I am Irish and the heart of *Integra* lies here, as well as on another small

---

[2] Emphasis my own.

island—Malta, where much of the first draft was written and where the performance that lead to the creation of this book, took place. It was in a small alleyway in Valletta, for the opening of a photographer's exhibition on intercultural dialogue and inclusion. That night, on the makeshift stage I sang and read poems I had written in both anger and love: anger for the regime of border control and abdication of responsibility for people who are forced to leave their home countries, who are "greeted with folded arms and documentation enquiries."[6] Love, because it breaks down barriers and fear and an unfortunate idea of "them" and "us." And, it is the basis of friendships and connections that are made and held across continents.

At the National Integration Conference in Dublin, awaiting the arrival of a great friend of mine whom I met because of this book, one of the key speakers said something that has stayed with me ever since: "We have always moved," he said. "Humanity's history is one of movement, of *migration*. Movement *is* migration. It is how and why we're here as a biological species." As a young woman with an Irish mother and German father—at a time of unprecedented intercontinental flows of people, culture, ideas and information—sense of place has always interested me.

Home, to me, was about many things: lineage, love, connection, community, engagement, art, friendships, family. I haven't often experienced homesickness, but when I leave and I *do* miss home what I miss isn't something I can describe in a practical or tangible sense; nevertheless the ache is there. Perhaps this is like *home* itself: something we know intimately, yet cannot describe. There are words and feelings associated with it, a house, a place, memories, but does this really describe what it is?

I do not mean to romanticise the idea of home, in this book. Toward completion of *Integra,* I visited the exhibition "HOME/SICK" in the National Science Gallery in Dublin, and it reminded me how our homes can be idealised: they may be a place of abuse, neglect, fear, mistrust, toxins, or distraction. Several days later, I passed a homeless couple lying in a doorway. They had created a kind of sanctuary behind sheets and bags they'd hung up and lay behind it, in sleeping bags beside each other. I was reminded of a story Keith, a young man from Rhode Island, had told me. "The homeless people I met in California everyday described themselves as houseless, *not* homeless," he said, flicking back the brown curl that fell across his eyes, at our restaurant table. "We are from *here*," they emphasised, whereas Keith described *himself* as homeless—but with loads of *houses* he could go to.

Because the place of his childhood has been taken away, destroyed—the trees cut down, the quiet replaced with shopping malls, and the dunes where he used to run and roll, levelled with concrete. The philosopher and professor of sustainability, Glenn Albrecht, coined the term "solastalgia"—that particular form of psychological distress that sets in when homelands we love and knew which we take comfort from are radically altered, rendering them alienating and unfamiliar. He went on to describe it as "the homesickness you have when you are still at home," and one that is fast becoming a universal human experience. Not only local and regional transformation, but "it is the big picture, the Whole Earth, which is now a home under assault."[7]

I asked an old friend, Martin, from the Camphill community in which I spent many of my childhood years in Ireland, why he uses the name "NoWhere Boy" on Facebook. (It is taken from the name of the movie of John Lennon's early life, before he joined the Beatles). He wrote back: "Because I feel like I am nowhere at home and therefore everywhere... does that make sense to you?"

It did. "Remember," he continued, echoing JRR Tolkien, "not all people who travel are lost."

I understood what Martin said.

He explained to me that, for him, home was not about a place or things he takes with him, but instead is wherever he *is*. I began to think that home is created from our experiences and can be taken with us wherever we go; in fact, a security and belonging in the world was created, for me, *from* my travels. To me, it had always been somewhat of a necessity to travel, to see, learn and be challenged—and because I was curious about the world. Iranian writer and professor, Azar Nafisi, writes in *Reading Lolita in Tehran*, "most great works of the imagination were meant *to make you feel like a stranger in your own home*.[3] The best fiction always forced us to question what we took for granted," she told her students on the first day of term and her first day of teaching. "It questioned traditions and expectations when they seemed too immutable."[8]

Many travel the world through books and literature, and there is an idea that this is only an "escape": that we "retreat" into books and fantasy worlds. Nafisi said that a novel is "the sensual experience of another world" and, if we don't become involved in our characters' worlds, their destiny "you won't be able to empathize."[9] Speaking at the launch of her latest book, *Republic of the Imagination*, at the International Literature Festival in Dublin, she

---

[3] Emphasis my own.

described fiction as inextricably linked to what we call "reality." She used the analogy of a spider-web, and said that the edges of its web—I would even say its *centre*—is attached to the world as we know it. And, fiction, then, as a gateway between two worlds: the one where we can imagine, where we can extend ourselves beyond what we previously thought possible, and the one that *is*. Art, literature; each exposes society to itself, and makes change imaginatively then visibly possible, and it allows us to empathise, allows us to feel.

In this book, the stories are real, they have happened, and they are an invitation to step into another person's world.

From an ecological perspective, place—an eco-system—is dependent on symbiosis and connections in a *healthy* environment. Roots, flora, bacteria, insects, animals, water, air, soil, organic substances and other chemical elements all combine in fluctuating yet always present cycles. This as an idea fascinated me, and in practice even more so. Balance is in a system precisely because of its changing form, its interdependence, and relationships with what lies around it.

And then, there is *integration*. A mathematician friend, reflecting on this, wrote to me about how a new idea arises unexpectedly, "Is this something magical?" he asked. "It looks like the brain has unconsciously synthesised a solution, come to a holistic understanding of the problem, while prior to this experience there were only disjointed glimpses which were obscuring the way to the solution."[10] This holistic understanding is the way we need to address the current crises that we face: political, ecological, economic, war, migration, inequality, all of which we cannot afford to consider as separate.

Integration, in the cultural, social sense of the word, invokes another, urgent question: what does integration mean? What is one integrating into? A fixed society? Probably—hopefully—not. A society is never the same as it was before another person from another culture and country, joins it. It is not static because *we* are not static, and it's precisely this notion of a static nation state, with fixed borders and high fences, that is a crux of the problem. So, it is not integration, only, but something more than that that we are looking and fighting for. Perhaps *adaptation* is a more appropriate word; in any case, we must examine the language we use in our international humanitarian efforts, and uncover the hidden prejudice it often holds.

With forced migration, we must also remember the circumstances in which people left: with little or no choice because we live in a world in which geopolitics and our economic system are rendering many innocent men, women and children unsafe. However, in the immediate circumstance of their being a refugee, both the individual who has left their home country and the country that receives him or her has the potential for enriching their community and their life, for adapting, and changing a previously fixed idea. (As for example, there is a Syrian man who has been feeding the homeless in Berlin to show his gratitude to Germany for taking him in, in a time of need. This goes against many people's perception of refugees, and the idea that in a time of crisis, we cannot *also* give).[11]

Admittedly, this approach of adaption requires massive changes in political will and international agreements, structures and facilities, and avenues of communication and outreach. The work on-the-ground during 2015 has shown tremendous capability for change and a compassionate approach, and refugees are organising many acts themselves, throughout Europe. There have been rallies, demonstrations and volunteers co-ordinating help. Banners made, organisations set up and money collected all across Europe, and, in many cases, refugees themselves asking for and demanding better conditions. Yet still, every day people attempt perilous journeys across the sea in overcrowded, unsuitable boats, travelling underneath lorries from Calais to the UK, are trafficked across borders, in fear and desperate circumstances, and still they are met with hostility and worse.

I am not an expert on migration. I wrote this book because the opportunity to arose, and I couldn't turn it—or the people in it—away. And because, to put it simply, I understood in my heart what my head could not.

In the immediate present, where humanitarian help and compassion is needed, we need to look beyond this for longer-term solutions, and consider where we are now from a deeper, and historical point of view: *why* are people fleeing their countries *en masse*? Is it possible, as political analyst Gearóid Ó Colmáin says, that migration is an "engineered" process, a geopolitical "tool used by nation states to intentionally destabilise another?"[12]

What is our responsibility toward solving the cause of forced migration, because we in Europe and in the West certainly have one, given our role in the creation of destabilised nation states and inequality? Political powers, international (dis)agreements and corporations that allow for the current situation to continue must be dismantled, or at least decentralised, to begin to solve the *cause* of the crisis. If we want peace, we cannot allow imperialism and military expansion in the name of "the war on terror" to continue, nor for the oil-hungry geopolitics of our times to

11

continue its reign, rendering many millions homeless, displaced, injured or killed. The numbers of displaced persons has increased more than ever before in 2015 and projections say that this will continue for the foreseeable future.

We must ask ourselves what are we doing to embrace inclusivity and solutions on a local, national and international level? How can this translate and extend to our international agreements: climatic, social, economic, political? How will we prevent the widening of the inequality gap, radicalisation and polarisation; and the detention of innocent people, held without a charge for indeterminable amounts of time, in horrific conditions, and no option of bail?[13]

Which choices will we make, as we stand at a cross-roads? Did we choose war, or did we choose peace? Did we choose compassion over politics?

I let the book and its stories and people speak for itself.

Ciara Ryan-Gerhardt

Tuitestown, Ireland, January 2016.

Part I

"I do yoga to find a way to always feel safe
and at home within myself.
Because I can never rely on a physical place."
- Emma Watson, actress, activist and yoga teacher

1.

Origins

I would like this story to be inter-hemispheric, like when a lady named Fiona introduced the two sides of my brain to each other. I wanted my art and my activism to begin from a place of integrated thinking. That is, the more creative *and* the more logical side, fond of reason and deduction. First, nothing—no, not nothing, but neural networks are strong—then, the following year, 2014, all hell broke loose. Or heaven, it depends on your perspective. But, slowly, the two sides saw how this could work, how each can be given its own time and eventually communicate. I wanted my humanitarian work not only to be political, nor solely artistic, but to combine thinking and study with dialogue and simple acts of kindness.

My friend Ingram wrote to me from his desk in Leeds University where he is studying for a PhD in mathematics, saying, "The Maltese *Integrazjoni* refers mostly to the operation of integration. When I think of integration in this sense, it means making the social body one, as opposed to some minority being outside of it."

I closed my eyes and thought for a moment.

Integration. *When the inner and outer world is in harmony.* These words had stayed with me, haunted me almost, since my friend Fiona Lyndley had said them. *Given* me them, as a question. I had gone to her for cranio-sacral therapy, a form of body (re)alignment, because of an injury. *When the inner and outer world is in harmony.* So... simple yet profound? Something I could spend the rest of my life searching for, making, remembering.

And this was funny because at the beginning of my writing *Integra,* in the beginning of summer 2014, my heart felt as though it was still at Flat No. 5 across from Hampton Hotel where Dave, my boyfriend, slept. The bus drifted slowly through a sleeping Dublin and I was returning to Malta, where I studied agriculture and focused my thesis on agro-ecology and biodiversity with small-scale farmers. I was twenty-three years old and I'd come to Malta from Spain where I'd worked for one year as a gardener in an eco-village. I liked the Mediterranean, and at that time wanted to learn more about growing food in hot climates; I had previously an incomplete BSc degree in International Development and Food Policy from University College Cork, Ireland, and had felt the need for something more practical and immediate.

With Dave and I, it felt like we were always saying goodbye, what with living at different ends of Europe for most of our relationship, and one month later he came to Malta to do just that. He stayed one week, but this would be a different kind of goodbye; we needed closure in our relationship.

On the morning before his departure, in Sliema, on the east coast of Malta where I lived, I sat on the white-yellow rocks looking into his eyes, and it was like they were magnified: remembering all the times I'd done so, all at once—everything I'd ever seen I could see now. Then I stood up, pulling him with me. We stared out into the sea, then walked towards the bus and laughed at our definitions of relationship and friendship. "Like close friends walking very close together," he said, when we tried putting our hands in our own pockets, to see what that was like.

It was ironic our playing with words at the disintegration of our relationship. He had been my first mentor and coach for creative writing and performing; as a poet, writer, spoken-word artist and public speaking coach. During the nine months we were together, I had watched him grow and share his passion for creativity and performance, authenticity and magic on stage with so many people. My singing and performance poetry at the mixed-media exhibition, *f'Darhom,* on home and intercultural dialogue at this time marked the beginning of *Integra.* Our relationship was the beginning and foundation of many important and beautiful things, for which I am grateful.

Malta is a small island in the Mediterranean, between Europe and Africa, though it lies on the African tectonic plate, off the coast of Tunisia; the closest European country is Italy and its island Sicily. Malta receives many refugees, and has a coastal watch on alert all the time. Usually, people want to move on further into mainland Europe from Malta. Culturally, it is both an Arabic and a Catholic culture, and usually, at student events and Mediterranean dinners, there was an eclectic mix of cultures and languages. Its language is complex and particularly unique, in large-part derived from Arabic and Italian, but also entirely its own, and only made a written language in the last century.

Malta's strategic geographical location, political and otherwise, made for uneasy reading at the time I lived there: there were articles written in *The Times* that had sparked my writing responses to the depersonalised accounts of "migrants" making their way across the Clandestine Strait by an EU border agency. These statistics resulted in my writing a piece called *Migration Pressure Ballistics*. They were *people*, and they were looking for a place they could start their lives anew because of war, political upheaval or persecution. Yet, following horrific treatment or trauma in their home country, and after a perilous crossing of borders on land and/or sea, they were greeted with *"Ihre Papiere bitte"*—Your papers please.

Growing up as a child in Ireland, I was very lucky to have a very multi-cultural dinner-table and schooling that involved foods, smells, travel, and stories from around the world. This always meant as I got older that I had friends all over the world. In a very real and tangible way, I knew something about a country and its people that was far away geographically, but not far away in my mind—like the Chinese artist, Ai Weiwei, on Lesvos, Greece, who said "the border is not really in Lesvos, the border is in our mind and heart."[14] In this way, I didn't fully understand the meaning of the term "foreigner," or at least I did not apply it to my understanding of people, as I grew up. I always smile at how Becky Thompson (poet, activist, yoga teacher and professor) describes a local man in Lesvos who said "the Greek word 'sano' means foreigner and guest. For us, they are one and the same." The people there have welcomed refugees for thousands of years, she wrote.[15]

About the time I performed in Valletta at *f'Darhom*, I briefly stayed in a hostel while searching for a new apartment after my lease finished. While there I met *Akeem, a man with jet-black hair, and he asked me to sing for him on the stairs early one morning. He was hung-over because he hadn't finished his yesterday and had not yet gone to bed; I was starting my day having just woken up, before I would go to university.

"I want peace," he said, looking up at me from his step at the bottom of the long, winding stairs. Apparently my singing brought him this. I stood there, holding a tall glass of tea, and thought for a moment. That morning I had in fact finally turned Akeem's literary piece into a song and so was happy he'd asked. It had always been a song, really, from the beginning, and that's why it hadn't worked on the page.

At *f'Darhom*, I adapted Akeem's song again. My voice husky with tiredness as I had not had more than a day's notice that I would be performing, I sang: "There is a particle in you that holds peace. Its very centre is peace, and it is the seed for it, always. There might be a particle that wants to destroy it at the very same time, but it is there. Can you feel it? Can you hear it? Do you notice it?"

The DJ, the people, the compassion that was at the same time draining my heart and opening it, and my anger at a *Times of Malta* article and its objectification and "othering"—all resulted in my doing something resembling hip-hop on stage, though afterwards I couldn't understand or remember how. I had a lot of energy, a lot of anger, and I wanted to do something creative with it. The statistics of people flooding European waters, and all that Akeem had clearly seen and was traumatised by in Libya—though he never disclosed actual experiences, but more generally the life in Libya that he'd left behind which he had hinted at, had all come together in mind.

I had been delighted when a photographer and anthropologist, Pietro Bonacina,[16] contacted me through a mutual friend of ours who had said that I might be the person to ask to a mixed-media exhibition on home and intercultural dialogue. It was a fascinating mix of video footage, and "homes" that had been re-created in the old building where the exhibition was held. These were the seven homes that Pietro had visited and the families and individuals he had met. Objects that represented home to the participants had been collected and organised: a dog that, on closer inspection was a (very-realistic looking) teddy, lying near the heater, coat hung behind the door, a large and comfortable, homely couch, a teapot, personal prayer items, a Catholic cross necklace, a jumble of shoes, etc., etc.

But to me, what was most interesting was where these homes overlapped. What a young family, an older woman, a child, and people of different cultures and religions had chosen were essentially the same. What was also beautiful was that it felt like I *had* just been invited to a number of people's homes: Pietro had done a very good job of making it realistic, and the objects come alive. They were arranged in an easy, and personal way with the uniqueness of each home, each person, still intact and visible; and yet, which transcended time and place and cultural upbringing.

That night in a small alley-way in a cosy street in Malta's capital Valletta, I spoke about peace, and how intercultural dialogue was in the small things. It was not only an international concept with political and economic dimensions and we cannot leave it to the responsibility of our governments; it is too precious and too urgent for that. It began in our gathering together that night, in extending ourselves and our definitions of home, of family, recognising our different backgrounds and celebrating them.

2.

Two crumpled sheets of paper

"Hello," someone said as he passed in front of me.

I looked up, and the man smiled. He was tall, and had a wonderful smile with deep brown eyes. I answered him but continued walking—it was late, there were no buses now and I was tired.

I was on my way home from Valletta where I'd been with two friends and was walking from the harbour to the shortcut to my street in Sliema. I now lived in a shared apartment two streets from the hostel I had stayed in briefly. I enjoyed walking at night; it was cooler now, though still warm. The buildings on the back streets were older, made with the same limestone that is used throughout the island—a light yellow-gold, or paler beige. I was reflective, thinking back on memories of my two friends, as one had left Malta that year and had been back for a visit.

Five minutes later, again, "Hey!" from behind me.

I jumped.

"Sorry. I didn't mean to frighten you."

We fell into step together, he had to walk the same way to get to his place. "How are you?" he asked, introducing himself.

We shared conversation until I had to turn left for my street, when I said goodbye.

Some days later, he and I walked across the rocks at Sliema's waterfront in the baking hot sun. He choose the name *Amanuel for this book. "I come from a small country in Africa," he said and as he spoke I continued scribbling on two crumpled sheets of paper I'd found in my pocket. I told him, in a jumble of excitement what I was writing and why I had taken out pen and paper, asking him if he was happy with that, and if so to carry on.

"It used to be part of Ethiopia, now it's not; it's called Eritrea, and it's in the East of Africa. To get out, I had to cross borders. I had to cross as an 'illegal immigrant,' as they say. I am very lucky… the way I had to survive… it is incredible!

"In Sudan, where I came to first, I worked in offices. In Arab countries, it works like this: who you know makes you live or not. Whether you've papers or not, if your boss *wants* to employ you, he will. I worked as draftsman, assistant office clerk and translator: Italian to English.

"My family are Orthodox Christians. In my country, there are four legal religions, the others are banned. If you're Pentecostal, you go to prison; Jehovah's Witness, you go to prison. There's people detained in prison for ten years because of their faith. I know some, my neighbours, school mates, imprisoned because of their faith."

We were now sitting in the shade, as I waited for Amanuel to continue.

"I crossed the border and went to Sudan for two-and-a-half years; crossed the desert into Libya, and spent two-and-a-half years there too. I had to leave then, when the fighting started and the Gaddafi regime was being overthrown. In a boat, I crossed, legally, to Malta. It cost €2000. It was a big boat, not one of the smaller, rubber ones. I guess my story is the typical one of an African immigrant: I was looking to fulfill a dream I had. It wasn't safe, but I had to choose, I had to try. I had studied, before, how to get out of Eritrea. I left my military camp, and walked.

"There are more Russians here in Malta than us Africans," Amanuel continued. "Put all of us immigrants together, and we'd still be a minority, yet all the eyes are against us. I don't feel at home here because people look at me like I am somebody different. Where will be my next destination, my next flight? Because I left home, I am looking for home. I wish I could see Malta as home, but I don't. From the start, I felt that: of being different, prejudiced against."

There was silence for a few moments as I scribbled short-hand.

"When people get off the boat," he continued, "they go for seven or eight months in detention. It's dependent on which country you're from.

"I was lucky, I wasn't dead. Eritreans and Somalians, we are given protection status—'refugee status'. But West Africans, like those from Ghana or Nigeria, for example, are given only temporary humanitarian protection. For one and a half years they put you in a cell. Then they give you temporary papers; they let you go." There was a silence for a moment. "You come back then, every three months or so, to get your work permit renewed. For this you have to speak Maltese, and your employer needs to issue a new employer permit."

As I listened to Amanuel, I became acutely aware he hadn't spoken about this before, and much less to someone who was almost a stranger to him.

I struggled to put words together.

"And, during this year and a half, they are... thinking about solutions?" I asked, already knowing the answer.

"Solutions?" he said. "There are none. No. They just spend their time there. You come from your country, imagine. You want, and think about, a brighter future and then they close you in this cell for one and a half years. It makes you worse psychologically.

"Eight years it's been, wow. Sometimes I count the years, where I've gone in the meantime. And I've never been back. Never seen my mother."

"And now?" I said, looking up.

For a moment, I was reminded of Little Bee, a Nigerian girl in Chris Cleave's book *The Other Hand*. It is a phenomenal, dark, yet hopeful story in which Little Bee speaks about her time in a detention centre in London. Though it is fictional, Cleave's one year of research before he even began to write the book results in a shocking and accurate picture of the asylum system in the UK, where, as he says in an interview, innocent people are imprisoned, and wait with the possible threat of deportation back to their home country. In the story, Little Bee visits a playschool where she meets Charlie, four years old: *"I knelt down and looked into Charlie's eyes. 'We are the same, you and me. I spent two years in a place like this. They make us do the things we do not want. Does it make you cross?"*[17]

"It's the same: same politics, same leaders," Amanuel said. "And, if I went back... Well, I left my military unit. Everything, everyone is counted. There are those... *round-ups* by the police. If I get caught, I'm right back to the military."

"You serve indefinitely?" I asked.

"Indefinitely. Compulsory. For men and women—if *you* were an Eritrean girl, you'd be in the military! Except, maybe, if you get married. It's indefinite, yes, but when the government thinks you're not of use anymore, *then,* yeah, you can go home. You're useless to them then..."

Amanuel trailed off for a moment.

"There is no exit visa out of our country," he added, "except for Party members. Our country is divided in two: the 'pros' and the 'cons,' killing each other, and our own country."

The conversation turned toward him and where he is now, how he makes contact with his family back home.

"We cannot Skype. In Eritrea they didn't want to make a world with contact to the outside. The internet capacity is made such that video is impossible, though you can 'chat message' each other sometimes, yes. But the voice or camera, no."

Amanuel told me of something he'd sent his mother last year. "I knew I wanted to send something, you know, a present. Wherever I go (Sudan, Libya, Malta, Italy), I take pictures. I'm quite practical on the internet, looked up video-making programmes, found Windows Movie Maker and downloaded it. It turned into something really quite good, I had to watch it five times!" he said, smiling. "I put it on CD, sent it in the post. And she could see me, her son, that I'm okay. That I'm here in Malta."

Amanuel told me about his family, there are six siblings in all. "For their future, I wish they could be here with me, because in my country, you die. You die mentally, you die morally. You're blind, because you don't see hope. It's a struggle.

"Where will I be in the coming years? Where can I find home? These are questions in my mind. For you, it's easy, you want to go back to Ireland, to your home country, but I don't see for myself, in the long-term, that I can settle in my country. I don't see how I can do that—so I better find my home soon, my *second* home.

"My citizenship is Eritrean, which is useless, right? For me, it just means I have to travel, I have to move. I feel like people don't understand it. You—yeah, I can see you want to listen, you're interested, you know a little already, and you want to know more, you want to understand, but some people have prejudice. It's like when someone says 'I am gay,' and people start looking and saying something, and it's similar when I say 'I am an immigrant.' That feels bad."

Our conversation came to a close and I walked Amanuel toward his apartment soon afterwards and thanked him. We arranged that I would meet him again to see the video he had made for his mother. Afterward, I ran home to type everything he had told me, and continue studying for end of term exams. As it was the second and final year of my diploma in agricultural sciences. Between the genetics and chemistry classes, I buried my head and hands in the ecology of agriculture, or how this could be created: soil systems, horticulture, biodiversity, permaculture etc. Initially, I had wanted to study a BSc degree in Earth Systems Science, but hadn't the relevant subjects from secondary school.

That evening, I did a little research on Eritrea. It turns out that Isaias Afewerki was elected president of independent Eritrea by the national assembly in 1993 and had been the *de facto* leader before independence. Presidential elections, planned for 1997, never materialised. Eritrea is a one-party state, with the ruling People's Front for Democracy and Justice (PFDJ) the only party allowed to operate. President Afewerki has failed to implement democratic reforms and government has clamped down on critics and closed the private press, with many journalists having been jailed, or worse.

Eritrea was an Italian colony for sixty years, from 1882 to 1941; Italian will prove important in Amanuel's story later. Many Italian settlers got out of their colony after its conquest by the Allies in World War II in November 1941. Italian Eritreans (or Eritrean Italians) are Eritrean-born descendants of Italian settlers, as well as long-term Italian residents in Eritrea. The absurdity of the current situation was revealed further as I read that although many remaining Italians stayed during the decolonisation process (after World War II) and are actually assimilated to the Eritrean society, some are stateless today, through no fault of their own. This is because none were given citizenship unless through marriage or more rarely by it being granted to them by the state. Statelessness is when a person isn't considered a national by any state. Although stateless people may sometimes also be refugees, the two categories are distinct and both groups suffer their own unique impingements on human rights. Statelessness can happen for various reasons including failure to include all individual citizens when a state becomes independent (state succession), discrimination against minority groups in nationality legislation, and conflicts of laws between states.

This means we have a system, a world in which the idea of a 'state' is upheld above all else, or the emergence of new states and changes in borders resulted in a person (in fact, many millions of people) being without a country which they could call home. I read about professor Railya Abulkhanova, who had been born in the former Soviet republic of Kazakhstan. She began studying in Russia, but when the Soviet Union collapsed one year later, it left her citizenship in question because papers were granted only to those in permanent residence. (She had surrendered her permanent registration card in Kazakhstan upon leaving to study in Russia.) Following the collapse, ex-Soviet republic countries were in desperate economic crisis, and survival was on people's minds, she said, not citizenship or nationality. Later, a subsequent application for naturalisation in neighboring Uzbekistan, based on her work there as a university professor, failed. In 2008, she applied for papers in Russia but later withdrew those when she married a French national and moved to France.

She is now living in Lille as the wife of a French citizen—but without a passport. She is stateless. Because of her lack of naturalisation papers, Abulkhanova says she has been unable to find work despite possessing a PhD, eight years teaching experience and fluency in six languages including French. The irony was that it was easier for her husband, a Frenchman, to get a visa for Kazakhstan, *and not her,* despite it being her "place of origin" as she described it. "I have no roots, no state, no house, no home, no personality," she said, holding up a "Travel Document for the Stateless" in a Youtube video appeal advocated by the UNHCR (United Nations High Commissioner for Refugees) storytelling campaign against statelessness. She said that one of the worst experiences is, of course, travel: the blank expressions on people's faces, her explanation of the term "stateless," and the ignorance and mistrust she encounters. "It's as if you had to prove your right to exist!" she said. "There is a plant with no roots. In Russian it is *'perekati pole'—tumbleweed.* It tumbles, it rolls—with the breeze it rolls away." With her hands she demonstrated a somersault-motion, a slight smile to her lips, though it soon disappeared. "That is what it is. That is statelessness. And me, I want to put down my roots."

I read that at least 10 million people worldwide are

stateless. Having a nationality is essential for basic human rights, such as voting and participating in work. Stateless people are often unable to obtain identity documents; they may be detained because they are stateless; and denied access to education, health services, and employment. UNHCR has been given a mandate to work with governments to prevent statelessness from occurring, to resolve those cases that do occur and to protect the rights of stateless persons. [18] Given the nature of how "nationality" is granted, some people are born stateless, while others become stateless over the course of their lives.

For example, in countries where nationality is only acquired by descent from a national, statelessness will be passed on to the next generation also. In twenty-seven countries around the world, according to the UNHCR website, women are not allowed pass on their nationality, while in some cases other discriminatory criteria like ethnicity or race, define who and who does not belong to a state.

I was reminded of a day in University College Cork some years before, when I had studied International Development there, and our discussion one morning in a lecture. We had been talking about the long overdue capitalist theory of "the rising tide floats all boats" (also known as the "trickle-down theory" in economics)—the idea that wealth and financial benefit accumulated at the top will be distributed and brought to those who have less: the majority.

The simplicity of this idealism and grandiose promise didn't sit well with us as the International Monetary Fund had just come to Ireland, in autumn of 2010, to decide on our austerity cuts and fiscal planning. We were a burden and thorn in the backside of Europe and apparently needed our belts tightened; certainly our banks and many of our politicians did.

We sat in class both angered and slightly bemused, students and professor alike. "Free market ideology may still bind the imaginations of our elites, but for most of the general public, it has been drained of its powers to persuade," as Naomi Klein says in her book *This Changes Everything,*[19] and which most of us have become familiar with, now that the more ugly sides to our "progress" have become apparent. It seems more like not all boats are carried equally on our seas, nor is everyone given a boat, or even allowed on board.

3.

Integra Foundation and a
Mediterranean night

"When you're a famous author, you'll remember me: the lady who gave you lettuce leaves," Stella said, laughing, after she'd taken away the little translucent plate I'd been preparing my sandwich on. It incidentally turned out to have been the cat's plate; I am quite minimalist when it comes to eating and kitchenware, and had grabbed the nearest and smallest.

I looked up to see Stella's infectious yet reserved smile, her short red hair. We laughed.

"Make yourself at home," she said. "It's not much, but you're here for two days, make the most of it and enjoy your stay. I give you the peace and quiet of my home; I like it like that." She walked out and back to her settee and the World Cup—England vs. Uruguay.

Stella's house was my third home that week, granted out of generosity of heart, in Malta, during my last week there in June 2014. As I was going back to Ireland I had asked some friends to host me since my apartment lease had finished one week before my flight. Stella lived in a beautiful old Maltese cottage, complete with wooden doors and bolted latch handles, and a flat open-air roof. Maltese houses, like those in Morocco and other hot climates, have flat-topped roofs to allow for socialising and enjoying the sun or meals with friends and family, and for the thermodynamic cooling effect.

Stella and I had met at an intercultural poetry and storytelling event held by a mutual friend of ours, Censu Caruana (who, at the time, was also my thesis supervisor as assistant lecturer in the Centre for Environmental Education and Research). This event, *Hwawar u Fjuri*,[20] was held in collaboration with Integra Foundation, and was a space where local Maltese and refugees could meet each other and set-aside cultural, religious and ethnic differences, through stories on the use of herbs and flowers in one's own country and culture and cuisine. Integra, a non-profit organisation founded in Malta, advocates and works toward the vision of an inclusive, non-discriminating and non-disabling society, where all individuals have the right to human dignity, freedom, respect and social justice.[21] They facilitate space for marginalised individuals or groups to be listened to, and to have an active and meaningful say in their lives and well-being, on their own terms, through community development, research and advocacy, and supporting events such as *Hwawar u Fjuri* and others. Stella's best friend, Maria Pisani, was the founder of Integra, a lecturer in youth and community studies, and a former Head of Office for the International Organisation for Migration in Malta. I had wanted to meet her for a number of weeks, but somehow we'd always had to reschedule and now it was too late.

That night, I wandered round the living room—where I was to sleep—after Stella had gone to bed. There were paintings on the walls: two were of cats; one of flowers; a green lady with eyes unseen and her mouth open, a whitish grey-green light framing her face; the naked bust of a man, his ribs peeking out like fish-scales, his eyes were also unseen. Next to him, and above my head when I lay down on the settee, was a lady's naked bust, her eyes open and clear; a pale beauty hung beside her, a red ribbon fastened in her dark hair above her ear, looking away into the distance, a curl framing her face.

Early next morning, out walking at Hagar Qim, one of Malta's ancient temples, I found out most of the paintings were by Stella's daughter. Stella spoke with nostalgia, of "the days when I was young," of rich boyfriends, America, and travel. I smiled to myself, as I'd met Stella only six weeks before and didn't know anything of her past.

"You must meet my friend, Maria," Stella said as we clambered down the rocky hill. "She's in Geneva at the moment, it's the World Refugee Conference. She's a very good friend of mine. In fact, she even has a key to my house."

I knew that I would be returning to Malta in September to do exams I had missed while I'd been ill in January, and suggested that we would meet then.

I walked that evening and ended up at the playground. I was still trying to get rid of belongings before I went back to Ireland and took a half used bottle of children's bubbles with me. I found a little girl, five or six, who was happy to take them. She did not have much English, and I not much Maltese, but she came back twice asking, "You want bubble? You want bubble?"

"No, they are yours now," I said. "They are for *you!*" I smiled and waved toward where she had left them, and made hand gestures. "I have to go in an airplane soon. They won't let me take the bubbles."

She smiled and asked more questions. I could guess at their meaning, though I couldn't understand each word.

She had an older brother. "He not here, homework," she said, and pointed in a direction away from the playground.

When I returned to the house soon afterward, none other than Maria Pisani was seated in the back courtyard of Stella's house.

I was delighted! I'd wanted to meet Maria ever since I'd heard about her work. I'd also tried to visit the Integra organisation but their office had been closed that morning. And now, here she was at the table in Stella's courtyard!

Maria and I talked about migration policy, the ethics of qualitative research, and other legal aspects of writing the book I'd just begun. We talked about the Conference she'd just come from for the World Refugee Day; Eritrea, Libya, the Congo—I told her about my uncle Kurt and his work there in the 80s, in former Zaire, as UNHCR. We admitted there is a lot to be concerned about, but there is also the hopeful situation of those who are advocating for respect and dignity and rights. We also spoke about social media, and how it has helped to raise awareness and spread news faster than ever before. Networking is possible and easier than before, and is useful insofar as it doesn't promote complacency (or Facebook likes). Maria's account of her time in Geneva, having landed back at home in Malta only the day before, was very interesting. One man, whom I'd met at a workshop with my thesis supervisor, also a friend of Maria's, had gone with her to Geneva as an advocate, and had told the story of how he had reached Malta. He was a very confident man, and liked to do outreach work: advocacy and storytelling came easily to him, as I'd seen in the workshop. He was humourous and good-natured, approachable and kind. All of this meant that, alongside his interest in fashion, he was great with publicity and campaigns for promoting awareness of refugees and the current migration crisis.

There was an interesting time-warp: I had so many questions and anecdotes and a deep curiosity for Maria's work as it had built up in recent months in Malta, and since I'd begun writing *Integra*. I remembered my first year there, which I'd spent closer to University, in Msida, right around the corner from the Refugee Commisioner's Office and the obvious racism that I'd seen there. So, that night, as Maria, Stella and I chatted, I had no idea how much time passed. Or, afterwards, the details of what we'd really spoken about.

We drank wine into the late hours of the balmy Mediterranean night, in Stella's backyard, and told stories about poetry, and what it meant to us to be a woman. They had the kind of friendship that went back many years, to when Maria had been in her teens; a friendship that was raw and deep and real. I loved hearing this, it was one reason I was going back home—I was tired of goodbyes, and had friends all over Europe and further afield. I wanted to work with the land in Ireland and in community development, and I was becoming acutely aware that this required my staying put in a place for a number of years at least: in Ireland, *home.*

4.

"What is your name, in your own language?"

That week, my last in Malta, Amanuel invited me to see the video he had made for his mum. I stood in the living room of his apartment, a ten minute walk from where I had lived in Sliema. It was bright, large and airy, simple, with white walls and some paintings that caught my eye: landscapes, trees, a lake.

Amanuel had two Italian flatmates, one of whom emerged to say hello, and the other was at work. We made ourselves some tea and then, "Look at what I have," he said suddenly, smiling. I looked down at his hand: 50+ sunblock. "My Italian flatmate laughed at me. He said, 'What you doing with that? That's for albinos!' I don't want to get any more tanned though," Amanuel said as we both laughed.

We cleared the table and sat down. A video was open on the laptop screen in front of us. Amanuel pressed play and the Eritrean capital, Asmara jumped to life before my eyes. There were Catholic churches and institutions, palm trees lined the streets, beside large hotels, high-rise buildings and other signs of colonial wealth. Elsewhere were traditional mud-brick African houses, "*Medeber,* made of recycled tin," he said. Then, the outskirts of the city, "the poorer areas," he said, pointing.

Tigrigna music was the backdrop to the video: "*Asmara, we can never get enough of you/You are in my heart/One day things will change...*"

"Our region and our language, it's called *Tigrigna*. All my story was around this neighbourhood," Amanuel pointed to the screen. "See this 'airplane building' and the way it's shaped like it has wings? I was born here, five minutes from it, and stayed here almost twenty years. It's so wide that it's surprising it can stay up like that. It's designed well—you see?"

"Yes," I said. I'd never seen a building like it before.

I asked Amanuel again about his family and siblings. He has one brother and four sisters, he tells me, and is third in the family. "In Eritrea, we have both our own and our father's name, even our grandfather's name too.

"My mother is a very strong woman. Six children." He paused. "My father and mother gave me the chance to learn Italian. You had to pay to go to this school—the others went to government school. They had dreams for me..."

Amanuel showed me photos of his sister's wedding. Marriage in Eritrea is a week-long celebration, both sides of the family need to party and be involved.

"We like dancing and food, we *really like* dancing," he continued, laughing. Then, about his brother he said, "We Eritreans are not happy with our current situation. My brother, he's bored you know. He cannot be in the military because of his eyesight, and he cannot leave his country. We do not have a future.

"For sure life is stressed there: the fact that you don't have hope, the fact that your dream is crushed, and you cannot leave. 'Girls,' I say to my younger sisters sometimes, 'you cannot leave—not like I did.'" He paused. "Girls get raped, lose a lot of money. I would like to help them out, take them out. But in a *safe* way."

I nodded, "Of course."

"We are family, a community, we help each other out. Not like Europeans, where government looks after the old people. I help my sisters, my sisters help the family."

Amanuel arrived in Sudan after fleeing the army in Eritrea, and stayed there until November 2008. The video opened with the writing: *You never know how strong you are until you have no choice but to be.*

"In Sudan, I worked as an assistant draftsman, even though I was illegal. It was miraculous, really. A blessing. I taught Italian, too. In Sudan, the law is not very strict. ID and you can start, legal or not."

An image of a very clouded, sandy, Arabic city came on screen: "*Kamsing*; it's Arabic for sandstorm," he said.

"The police can imprison you for being an illegal immigrant. They bribe you, and if you pay, you get out. It's a business there. I, luckily, did not get caught and imprisoned, but it *was* a danger that was on my mind, yes."

"Now is the third phase of my life since leaving Eritrea," Amanuel continued. "It was November 2008; I was headed for Libya. To cross from Sudan to Libya you have to go through the desert. You use jeeps—you have to choose the safest one."

"How do you know which...?"

"Word of mouth... The desert, to me, was like a sea. There's no direction. I don't know where it starts, where it ends. Sometimes your jeep breaks down. The drivers say they will be back to you in a week, but it might be a month, or not at all. They might have got lost, or the truck might break down. And nobody comes...

"I was safe though," he added, "I chose the safest one."

There were images of men dressed for sandstorm weather, not much of their faces seen, but guns ominous and obviously present; the backdrop was sand, sand and more sand. "The Libyan patrol forces," Amanuel indicated. "They are waiting. They know about these illegal transitory movements, of course. If you get caught by them you're in one of those containers," he pointed toward the computer screen. "Like animals. And detention, that lasts one, two or maybe three years. Misrata prison, that's a common one. Families, children, everyone, anyone."

Words were scrawled across the screen some minutes later: *Don't say why me, but try me.* "I had to be strong, like a lion, morally and psychologically," Amanuel said.

An arrow is only shot by pulling backward; it's going to launch you into something great.

"Faith," he said, "means that you first go forward. It gives you the strength.

"We crossed in one week, with these... human traffickers. I paid US$800 to a US$1000 for the fare. They are the only channel, only way out, only way across. For me, they are *criminals*. They don't care about people, only the money.

"In Libya, I looked for Italians. I went to the Catholic Church in Tripoli. There was a man outside, smoking. 'I am Eritrean,' I said to the man, 'I need a job.' 'Good. What are you doing here?' he asked, handing me his business card. 'My story is a long one,' I told him. He was happy with my level of Italian. He told me to send an email with my CV, then asked me did I have a work permit. 'Come to my office' he said, 'and tell me everything.'

"I did, I told him all of it. He was very nice," Amanuel continued. "He spoke to his accountant, and somehow it was made possible for me to work there. In the Arab world, if they want you, they'll do it, whatever it takes. If they want you, they'll protect you.

"God made great things for me, I got some kind of divine help; I can explain it only that way. I was working in this prestigious place," he gestured at the photo of the outside of an office building. "I had no visa, no working permit, and I was an irregular immigrant, illegal.

"I remember the floor I worked on: the eighteenth floor. I worked as a translator, Italian to English; I had a contract, I was an office clerk! 'Why these good things?' I wondered. I am not special. I seemed to be *protected*. Others were in detention, with the same situation, same irregularities, and the police were chasing them all the time."

There was a photo of Amanuel at his desk, and another with some of his office mates. I could see the faith he'd spoken about: he looked hopeful and there was a sparkle in his eyes.

"I stayed in Libya until February 2011," Amanuel continued, "when I had to leave because the uprising, the revolution, started."

We arranged to meet once again before I left, later that week, back to Ireland: there was still the story of how Amanuel had come to Malta.

I had one more thing to ask, however, before I left. "Your name," I said, handing him my pen. "The one you chose for this book. Can you write it? In your own language."

He took the pen and drew characters I could not read on a page in front of us, carefully printing the pronunciation underneath each.

"What does it mean?" I asked.

"It means, 'Comes from light. *Represents* light,'" he said.

I arrived at Amanuel's apartment four days later, his laptop open on the table again. He told me to go ahead and begin the video where we'd stopped it last time. I pressed play; we were coming to the last part of his time in Libya: the words *Tripoli always* flashed across the screen while Enya's *Carribean Blue* made the sound backdrop. The sky there was grey however: it was winter.

"Every day I work, I came here," Amanuel said pointing to an office building. "In fact, this is the area where they capture many people. But you know, they didn't get me. It's a nice feeling. There are spots I avoided though, because I knew I should.

"In those two years, I never spoke to any Libyan women, because it's illegal. They, the authorities, can catch you anytime; their brother could see me in the street; you cannot hold their hand."

Amanuel had collected and put together various clips and videos to show what he had seen on his journey. In one, a man on the screen pounded clay, glanced briefly toward the camera, then returned to his potter's wheel. A woman, all in black, entered from the left and stood in the corner, and still the wheel spun. Then there was blue: the coast, the sea.

"Bahari Sea, many drowned here," Amanuel indicated. "A lot of my friends crossed this sea. I was the first one on a legal boat from Libya to Malta. It was a ferry. It was overcrowded. That's why they drown sometimes, the refugees."

He pointed to a photo on screen of himself, tired and en-route in the boat. "I was wondering am I going to make it. In Libya, it had not been secure. I'd been working, yes—but now to Europe, and risking my life to do so. But when you don't have an option, you risk it.

"The captain took the money from the five of us who were illegal; we did not have visas: US$2,500 we paid. The rest were legal, with visas. It was thanks to those five I got here, because I was sharing a flat with them. It's a life of community, we are very connected, we help each other. The rest, they were workers and employees of companies. We were all different nationalities and it was a Maltese boat, going from Libya to evacuate us!"

On arrival in Malta, Amanuel and those who had been on board without a visa were detained by the police, and then brought to the "open centres."

"I was safe, out of Libya, safe from the war, and also not in shitty detention. 'If you want your papers,' the Immigration Officer said, 'If you need sleep, go to Hal Far,' the container they're given is now better. There were tents there too but they were broken and ugly. Marsa is better."

On arrival in Malta, migrants have to go through a detention centre, of which there are three. There, they are screened by authorities who register them in the EU Eurodac database of fingerprints of applicants for asylum and "illegal" immigrants. If they are granted asylum (a lengthy process in which it is determined if a migrant is entitled to asylum), migrants are relocated in open centres, where they are provided with daily meals and someplace to sleep. If they are not, they remain first in a detention centre. This is a harrowing experience and process that *is* improving, though painstakingly slowly. Marsa and Hal Far are "open centres" which Amanuel referred to. The site at Hal Far was originally part of the Hal Far airfield that saw intensive air combats during World War II.

"But ninety percent of people end up in Hal Far, Marsa cannot take everyone—it's packed," Amanuel continued. "Hal Far is where the fresh ones or their friends end up. If you don't have friends who can help you, you get a kind of pocket money. In Marsa and Hal Far there are the open centres, and in Safi, there is the detention centre."

One of the videos embedded alongside Amanuel's own showed up now. There were many men behind a barbed wire fence. *Hoping for a better future in Europe* was the name of the YouTube video. *"A brand new—"* I did not catch their words or their hopes, as the narrator spoke too quickly.

"Eritreans and Somalians get out first from detention. We have priority somehow, are recognised—the case-workers start ours first; asylum will be granted. Now, you stay two to three months, do interviews and get out, it's good; but some years ago, it used to be one year."

It broke my heart to hear this—that it was "good" to stay only two or three months. Certainly it was better than one year, but even one day is too long, in conditions worse than the prisons of many countries around the world, for not having done anything wrong. The circumstances, the state of the buildings, the months and years spent waiting. Detention for the lack of a piece of paper.

Next was a collection of media interviews and YouTube shorts of which I caught only snippets. *"Their arrival often crushes hope—Few that make it are—5, 000 euro cash-drop to leave—And the volume of numbers—Some go back home."* Carmelo Mifsud Bonnicci, Maltese

Minister for Home and Parliamentary Affairs, named Malta's limited resources as reasons for the current situation and emphasised Malta's provision of (what he considered to be) humane, international protection.

Amanuel continued with his story. "I got a job as interpreter for the government, for refugees, so I could get a flat," he said. "It's sad, the stories people tell, of how bad things are. And, I'm a sensitive person. Each day, I listened to two stories, three times a week—six stories per week, for six months."

"It made me stronger, my trip," Amanuel said then. "But sometimes I wondered, 'What would I be doing if things were different?' I don't have a regular life. I want to be where I can be stable, integrated. I'd been raised in a well-educated family: my mother was a teacher, my father a taxman. I can't complain. I got good marks, I won my Italian diploma.[4]

---

[4] It was not until I read and re-read many times Antoine Cassar's *Passaport* some months later, when we began corresponding regularly, that the injustice really sank in: *The Universal Declaration of Human Rights* states that those who are persecuted are granted the fundamental right to leave their country or to return home (Article 13), and, Article 14, the fundamental right to request asylum from persecution in another country. Amanuel had been given no choice but to leave, nor about joining the military before that—though it was clear what would have happened if he hadn't obeyed. Or what would happen now, if he went back, if he *could* go back.

"Then, our government passed a law not to allow anyone leave," he said. "There were *entry* visas, but no exit visas, so I lost the scholarship to study in an Italian university. I had to join the military. That was one heartbreak for me and my family. But I had to go through, one way or another.

"In our country we are not supposed to show emotions," he said. "They teased me, acted like it was wrong if I did. And, as a child, you know, these things have a big impact—you believe, then, that it's *true.* I remember when we had to go to school I cried, I didn't want to go. I wanted to take my father with me—I used to take him by the hand."

"And now?"

"Now, I find it difficult to feel, to cry," he said. "A few times, I have cried as an adult. Once, in the military, I was so down. It was not a good time for me. We were two hundred to a bunker: one here, one next to him *there,*" he gestured, showing how they were like sardines—packed in right next to one another, in metal containers and sweltering heat." And at night, Amanuel and his comrades were locked in.

"Six weeks, they'd said, was the time we students who had scholarships would do in the military. We were waiting and waiting. Two months. Three months. Finally, after about six months, we knew: we knew the Italian school reps weren't coming, and we knew why. And our families, well, the whole time they were enquiring, trying to find out what was going on. They were told, 'No more exit visas are being given. This is the current situation, and you will be informed when it changes.'"

"So how long were you there, in the military?"

"All in all, four years. From the Italian side," he continued, "everything was fine, everything was ready: I had all the documents. There were two hundred of us supposed to go. They'd started writing, asking why the boys from Eritrea hadn't arrived yet. They knew nothing—they were wondering where we were. And, of course, *we* knew nothing of it all either, at first."

I asked Amanuel whether any of the same boys from the Italian school were in the same military camp as him.

"No," he replied, "we were separated. Of course, they did that on purpose.

"Since then, I began thinking how to get out, making a plan. I had to do things on my own: you change when you face difficult challenges, you get in touch with real life *on-the-ground*, not imaginary. It's different. I knew I needed to study because the world I'm facing needs educated people. Engineering was not possible, now.

"We need a purpose, a strong one. What am I here for? Purpose makes the difference, a whole difference. 'I need to sort it out,' I said to myself. I never give up. I trust myself, my instincts, my personal intention. I know my potential. I always try to..." Amanuel paused, "*upgrade myself to face challenges: to boost myself, my energy. I knew that the potential is there, I just cannot avail of it where I come from. I've been believing in myself to live this life.*"

He turned his attention back to the computer screen.

"So, after detention, you live here—if you are lucky," he gestured at the container houses that came after detention, in an open centre. "For many years."

Angelina Jolie appeared suddenly on the screen, it was a video of her paying a visit to one of the open centres as part of her UNHCR Goodwill Ambassador work. A woman on the other side of the bars was crying out, "*Freedom!*" I could hear only two words Angelina said in reply, as she gripped the other side of the bars: "*You will...*"

"For centuries the Valletta harbor has provided protection for seafarers," DeutschWelt TV said next. "Its high-fortification made it one of the safest harbours in the world. Yet, at Valletta Military Harbour, the coast guard is always on alert. Nowadays being 'rescued' in Malta can mean months behind bars in a reception centre, and they must stay there until a decision is reached about their status."

Ahmed Bugri, a Ghanian-Maltese pastor and coordinator of the Marsa open centre spoke next. Bugri was invited from Ghana by a Catholic prayer group to study and work in Malta in 1990, at the age of twenty-four. He planned to stay a while before moving on, but a wife, and later, three children meant that he made the little island his home. He made me think differently about why people have left and still leave their country. "In full knowledge I have a fifty percent chance of survival," he said, "what would make me take that risk? What kind of state would I be in? What would I have witnessed? What would make me risk everything? If I can understand that, I can understand why these people leave."

In 2011, Amanuel took his first plane: to Milan from Malta.

"All my trips before, they had been on the floor."

"On the ground, you mean!" I said, laughing.

"Oh, yes," he smiled. "It was my first time in Italy, and even I was fluent. In Italy people asked me, 'Where are you from in Italy?' From Milan, I took the train to Zurich. It was a cold Christmas."

"Where is your, where is—no, you weren't together yet?"

"I was single-mingle," Amanuel said, laughing, as he went out to buy food and I carried on alone, watching and scribbling what I could hear and see.

Welcome to Switzerland.

The video now showed a very pretty landscape: trees, lakes and mountains whizzed by the train's window and a pair of hands were visible, holding a camera in the reflection.

Next was Amanuel in Malta, smiling next to the paintings on his wall. The same apartment where I was, two years later, watching his video. I skipped ahead to 1:43:40. There were words above his bed, I couldn't read the print, but the music and his girlfriend's smile and green dress gave something away of his happiness. I smiled.

Next, they were in the kitchen, cooking, and in the last moments of the video I read: *This is your life. Do what you love and do it often.*

.

5.

Toward Home?

I thanked Amanuel and we walked to the bus-stop together, where we talked about his sisters, about how to get them out of Eritrea and whether there was anything I could do to help or speed that up. As we said goodbye, I knew that I'd be back in September for exams, but that was it after that—I was returning to Ireland after almost five years abroad; a huge change for me.

I boarded the bus and became acutely aware of the "privileges" I had as I entered the airport building. *Flight cancelled? Know your passenger rights*, it said outside Luqa's airport entrance, and beneath it was a number to call.

I'd connected the last dots: I'd sat in Amanuel's sitting room for almost four hours that day, watching the last half of his video, listening, writing, scribbling. His story made more sense in my mind now. The harshness and reality of his video was still raw in my mind, having finished it only two hours previously. I felt disconcerted passing through airport security with such ease and no second looks at my passport, because I am European.

At Luqa airport, the nondescript Immigration Control office had an open door and I stared in as I walked passed. The lady looked at me uninterested, security handed me back my passport, the men at the screening area smiling and wishing me a good flight. I almost tripped over a little white, transparent something on the floor and bent down to pick it up. It was a bouncy ball, broken in half, and unnoticed. I handed it to the security man beside me, he took it and I left. A loudspeaker called a man's name, en route to Tripoli: please come to gate number thirteen for immediate boarding. I ran to a table, sat and began to write about my afternoon with Amanuel. Passenger Maliq to Tripoli was called again on the loudspeaker. *To Tripoli, to home,* I wondered?

I felt confused about going "home." I'd spent the last week in four different houses and they had all been welcoming and homely. It felt different, strange even, to be going to Ireland not on a visit as I'd done for years, but for good this time. Was I going home or leaving home? Malta had, in a way, felt like home, though I knew I didn't want to stay there. The extended urban zones where I had to live as a student and lack of greenery made me long for Ireland again. If I hadn't lived there, I would have lived on Gozo, the smaller and quieter of the two islands.

On board the plane through the little Ryanair portholes, there were spider-like web trails of light scattered across the night and tiny island that had been my home for the past two years. I taped pages from Amanuel's interviews and video on to the seat in front of me and continued to type. Three hours later, we were over the west coast of Wales. There were little icicles on the windowpane and more spidery light-trails—homes, 35,000 feet below—and the red horizon of the sun as far as my eyes could see.

In Dublin, I was to stay with Mags. We'd met as fledgling storytellers under Dave's instruction some months back, at *The Art and Heart of Storytelling* in Galway. In the arrivals hall, while I waited, I wandered round in circles, thinking, as it helps me when I write. Suddenly, I heard, "Hello!" and there was Mags.

We headed up to the top floor to see if there was any tea available. It was late, and *McDonald's* being the only option, both of us pulled a face and instinctively moved toward the exit.

"This *is* your bag, isn't it?" she asked as the metal steps rolled us down to the ground floor. "I didn't think, I just pulled along whatever was near you."

This was testament to the hour and to our tiredness. "Yes, that is mine," I laughed. "Oh, it's good to be home!'

At the ticket machine, Mags rooted through her handbag and found a two euro coin, which she dropped into the machine slot. We were off then for home, for sleep—but not before stories over tea in the kitchen, in hushed voices.

Next morning, I woke early to the sound of birds, with sunshine streaming in through the curtains. Sunshine! And in Dublin! I ran downstairs, happy. It was quiet and still; nothing was stirring and nobody was up yet.

Later that morning, we went to Mags' parents' house, a short drive away, where I watered the roses and other plants in their garden, planted sunflowers, and tidied up. "Home-help had forgotten to help the day before, while another carer cut scallions in the kitchen with blue plastic throw-away gloves on"—these were the words that would become the bones of the comedy skit that arose in our minds as we tried to make light of the situation later. One carer not turning up previously had resulted in her father not receiving his medication following an operation.

Mags' mother followed me out to the front porch as I went to and fro from the tap, filling the watering-can.

"People ask me what's wrong with me, and that's the thing, I don't know," she said, looking at me. "It's old age you know, it's like that. It's... I find it difficult to let people *do* things for me, though."

"Yes, my grandmother, she said something similar to me," I said. "She is two years younger than you. Eighty-eight."

"Oh, and where does she live—Malta?"

"No, no, I'm Irish. I don't look it, nor sound it, but I am."

"Well, I don't mind where you're from. You don't bite." I smiled, and with that she turned round and went inside the house.

Mags' father then said he thought I was an orphan. I thought it funny but a little disconcerting—to be consistently asked where I was from in the country I'd been born in. It happened every time I came home.

"Well, you know, there's always a certain look about orphans," he said.

I smiled, thinking how strange a thing it was to say as I stood in the doorway to his room; I had come upstairs to ask him if he needed anything. "Maybe. I don't know what an orphan looks like…"

There was, of course, no "look" to an orphan, but it seemed he was referring to my childhood—which I had lived almost all of, until eighteen, in county Kilkenny. It had been a very stable time; I had moved three times, each time within a short distance from where I'd been before. When mum was pregnant with me, her and dad had moved out of a Camphill community near Poulacapple, Callan, which they'd begun some years previous. Camphill is a world-wide charitable trust working with people with intellectual disabilities (based on Rudolf Steiner's philosophy of anthroposophy). Pioneered by war refugees in Scotland almost seventy years ago, there are now over 100 intentional communities in twenty countries. My sister and I grew up around and went to school in one, in south County Kilkenny. When my parents moved out, we'd then lived in a cottage just outside the small village of Kells, overlooking the King's River—in fact, the back of the house sat almost right on it and flooded most winters, though luckily not the winter we lived there. We were there only until I was seven months old, and during that time dad and some friends renovated another old cottage (about three miles from Kells) into a two-storey house which we moved into, where we lived until I was fourteen years old.

Here, we'd had about two acres of land, much of which had been given over to growing food, with vegetable beds, fruit trees and bushes, a large polytunnel, and wild grassland and trees, especially toward the back. As a child, it was a small forest to me and my friends, and became a place of underground dens and hide-outs, especially at the time I read *The Famous Five*. Later, dad tells me we replanted our own Christmas tree each year, back into the ground here. We had animals: chickens, a goat called Freddy, pigs, ducks, and dogs—Murphy grew up alongside me, and died one year before we left Caherleske, at thirteen. There were other properties built over the years for the many people who came to live or stay with us, and there was the Kindergarten that was begun on the top floor of one of the sheds, and later moved to another location nearby (now Ballyhall Steiner Kindergarten). There were also play areas for my sister Liadan and I, and our friends, as well as numerous sheds for dad (for welding, woodwork, and so on). We had climbing frames, a tree-house, grass areas where I could play soccer and other games, and there were apple trees in most parts of our land. The front had a beautiful creeper that covered the front wall entirely, and the windows were painted orange.

As an adult, looking back on this time, I remember certain specific details, though I am not sure my memory of this time can be said to be complete, having lived there as a child. What seems to have stuck is the memory of a happy childhood, though there were times such as my transition from Steiner school to national school that were not easy, and were darker; times of being misunderstood and severe adjustment—far less freedom and a lot of rules to remember that I didn't understand, but which I was to obey. I remember many people, usually in flashes of memory: a face captured with a background or something they were saying at that moment, almost like a photograph. I remember feeding Freddy in the field at the back where the grass was let grow wild. Eating raspberries while reading *Harry Potter*. And some of my jobs, which included picking the apples or peaches, and mowing the lawn. Climbing the straw bales in the farmer's field next door with my friend and neighbour Rachel; the parties we had each year in the autumn, when we didn't know what to do with all the peaches anymore.

I had free reign of the surrounding fields and lane-way beside our home, and when I was a little older, would pack a bag and leave for an afternoon, often on my own or with Rachel, as an "explorer," or later, a "detective" (this came from being particularly good at sports, liking mysteries, and, admittedly, detective novels). We would bake something to take with us, and then leave, sometimes on our bikes to a village nearby. The land that Rachel's family owned was right next to ours, across the lane, and had a quarry in it. Inevitably, we spent much of our time in there too, climbing around its sides, through brambles, or squelching along the bottom of it, in the marsh grass.

As a child, I felt there were too many years between Liadan and I to consider ourselves friends and not only sisters, until we were much older—in fact, until I turned nineteen. At four-and-a-half years younger than me, and being very different, Liadan and I fought a lot, though I doted on her in her early years. Liadan liked dolls and clothes, and had only one boy in her class at school. I on the other hand, liked rugby, soccer, running, helping dad in the garden—I even had my own "workstation" in the wood shed, where I carved things—and had only boys in my class for the first year-and-a-half of school. My mum and I joke now about the times we went shopping, which I hated, where she would insist that for each blue, black, or green T-shirt, I had to buy a red or purple one, too. That was the first part of the battle, the other was getting me to actually *wear* it. There were two things Liadan and I both shared a love of, however: reading—we were both avid book-worms—and music. I played harp and piano, Liadan sang, and still does beautifully, and played the flute and tin whistle.

Eventually, at fourteen, we moved from Caherleske to a rented bungalow very close to Callan—I could now walk to school. Though we were not Catholic, or religious, I attended the local Catholic convent, as did some others like me from Camphill school—we simply sat out of confession and mass etc. Dad had found the house, its upkeep and the garden too much work as it mainly fell to him; mum had been the full-time earner while dad worked part-time and night shifts as a care worker and several other odd jobs like plumbing and electrics. We rented for two years, while we built the house where my parents still live now. It is a beautiful, L-shaped house with a half-acre of land by a wood, between three small villages, one of which I'd been to national school for two years in.

This house did not feel like home to me until recent years. I am not sure why, but perhaps because I had seen and helped it being built; I'd seen it as nothing, before: a plot of land, in a field that I was told would later be where

I'd live. This was, of course, not very interesting to me at the age of fifteen—it was rural and I would have no access to public transport, to my friends and parties. (And besides that, many friends couldn't even find the house because it was so rural.) After that, there were the foundations, and it began to take shape.

That summer, I'd gone to Tanzania to see my godfather and go to school, as he worked in two schools there. Before I'd left, I'd packed my things into black sacks so my parents could bring my things with them when they moved. When I came back... it was all done. We had moved, but I'd had no part in it. It didn't feel real. I didn't give it much thought, but the feeling of it being *home* wasn't there, yet.

Apart from my time in Tanzania, our holidays or visits to my German grandparents, and a winter when I'd gone to New Zealand and Australia with my dad when I was eight (where I'd also briefly gone to school), this was my life until eighteen: in south County Kilkenny, rural Ireland.

After I'd turned eighteen I had moved a lot, and had left Ireland. I didn't *look* Irish, people said, and my accent was a confusing mix by the time I arrived at Mags' house so I understood her father's confusion.

After we left Mags' parents, I met Dave and we lay in the grass at Trinity College, both of us weary but happy to see each other. The future held something very different for both of us, but we had a friendship that carried on. The tiredness after three weeks of little sleep, a lot of moving around, exams, deadlines for my dissertation, an upcoming project with the National Women's Council of Ireland, and the end of our relationship, were all starting to catch up on me. And as for Dave, he had just finished a month's tour of storytelling in sitting-rooms in Ireland with comedian Aidan Killian, and was also tired.

Dave looked different to me now. I lay and watched him, and saw how peaceful he looked, the most I'd seen him in a long, long time, in fact. When I told him this, I realised how hard our break-up, and our relationship, had been for him, too. Our falling in love at a time when he wanted to explore his sexuality meant that neither of us had known how long we would be together, but it was clear that we *would* be. In the end, we spent nine wonderful and heartbreaking months together. "It has only been beautiful what we have shared, what you've given me," he said quietly.

That night, we went to Blanchardstown, for our friend Leslie's birthday. It is a beautiful home, with lots of light. We were three hours late as we'd gotten lost en route, and laughed about all the times it had happened in our relationship: wandering streets in London, Dublin, Galway or Malta.

I knew some of Leslie's friends: Mags winked at me in a motherly way from across the table, laughing at our being late. Many of us were creative/performance progeny of Dave's and Aidan's, and some were from Leslie's LGBT circles. I saw Leslie's flatmate, a dark and handsome man with beautiful green eyes. As he passed behind the table and Dave's chair, he laid his hand briefly on Dave's shoulder. It was a normal gesture, as anyone would do when they want to pass between chairs or a narrow space, but it made something visible and real for the first time where I'd only been able to imagine it before. Though we had talked it through—we had to, or we could never have been in relationship—the fact that Dave wanted to explore his being with a man, until that moment at the table, I somehow hadn't fully realised it, not in the way that I did then.

I was reminded of what a friend had said the week before on Sliema's waterfront, "When you meet a person behind a label, the statistic, suddenly you understand a little more of this person. You understand a little more of their life, their desires, their soul and their path. Don't you think?" Amanuel, who had been there too, said, "Not in Eritrea, but in some countries in Africa, we just don't even *know* about the option of being gay. We have no exposure to such things. We come to Europe, and some, for the first time, start to find out that it's possible."[5]

---

[5] According to The International Lesbian, Gay, Bisexual, Trans and Intersex Association, there are eight countries in the world where homosexuality is still punishable with the death penalty; in another sixty-seven, citizens can be imprisoned because of their sexual orientation. There is an excellent book, released this year, *Queer Wars,* which deals with the growing international polarisation over sexual rights (see Further Reading).

6.

"We've got dreams:
something beautiful is emerging"

From Dublin, I soon made my way back to Kilkenny and Waterford, where I visited my grandparents and went to the Book Centre in Waterford, to type. I had interviewed *Amal, a University of Malta student, one week before I'd left. We'd met almost two years previously, when I'd first arrived in Malta, at a youth entrepreneurship training. The name she chose, Amal, means "hope."

"Home..."

I watched her, in bright orange and white, as the word lingered on her tongue for a moment, her dark hair hidden neatly behind her headscarf. Amal has big, round, dark eyes and beautiful skin, and always spoke eloquently. She is also an excellent public speaker, at the entrepreneurship training we had worked together as a team. We sat together, on a bench by the students union building in the shade by the olive trees. It was busy at the University as it was the end of term. Amal and I had both just finished our exams.

"Home changes," she said. "It's different now, and more detached the farther I am from Libya. In Libya, the *concept* of home in my country was family, it was smaller. Now that I'm in Malta, it extends to the city, Tripoli, the whole nation and country. I've been thinking about this a lot, been struggling with it recently. My memories, they are here. I've friends here, and school, but it's always felt temporary. Like we're not *staying* here, we're going to go back.

"We have a 'little Libya' inside our house: we speak our own language, have our own lifestyle, cuisine, rules. We wouldn't change that. Whenever a friend comes to my house, they feel like they've stepped into Libya. I feel protective of who comes in, whether they're from Libya or not. It's our sanctuary; it's the only place where I can be who I want to be.

"Malta is my place, my *home,* now. And I go home to Libya, and I defend Malta because it's something that is part of me, too. But I don't *feel* part of Malta. Citizenship: yes or no? That's one of the questions in our family now. More Maltese, less Libyan if yes, if we go for it. I've been in Malta for eleven years now. I've lived here all or most of my adult life, yet I still defend Libya, too. All I have is my nationality, yet it hurts when people back at home say, 'Oh, you're not Libyan.' One time, I had applied for a funding application and I was refused, despite all the application process leading up to it. I was considered 'less Libyan' than others just because I'm not there now.

"As we grew up, it changed, though, to the point where on a daily basis I wondered, 'Who am I?' It was like I was between two worlds. I always *felt* more Libyan: it's who and what I am. I want to defend my nation, I need to dress, and talk in Libyan, and yet, all I have is my nationality.

"When I was in first year in Junior College here, the Revolution broke out in Libya. I felt useless, helpless. It was a new era, a revolution for Libya, and I couldn't do anything. I felt excluded being here in Malta—they were so a part of it.

"My schoolteacher told me—and I still remember to this day: 'Your role is later. Focus on education and you'll have more to do later, you'll be *able* to do more later.' It stuck with me. I need to study and learn. I'm getting education and experience, and then I'll go and I'll give back."

We spoke about Gaddafi and his "law," and the role of education and women in Libya.

"After the Revolution," Amal said, "I decided I'd do law at university. Not court law, but law to understand the workings of government: constitutional law, history, administrative law and the development of law. There are a lot of people who speak about change, give lectures. I want to be in the centre, where it's all happening and *make* it happen.

"There is a lot of ignorance of law in Libya. I see many who don't understand anything about the basics of it, on TV. There was a sole legislator, a sole concept. Now what's developed is a *detached*—objective or external— form of legislation. It's no longer about what someone—a dictator—wants, and us having to follow his every command.

"The role law plays in education is very interesting to me. The lack of knowledge people have really reflects how people react to it. Laws are being issued and people are not able to follow—to relate to—them. They don't understand the *weight* of the law, they always think they are, or there are, exceptions.

"The people who're closer to power, wealth, and political power, those were the ones who could get something done in Libya, in the past. Regulating education with law, this is something I've been thinking about: how much freedom should be given to institutions? How to legislate education with law, and how much restructuring to the schools should be done by the law? I'm thinking about doing my thesis on how to develop laws to regulate schools.

"What's happening right now in Libya is so interesting," Amal said. "I wish I was an anthropologist; it would be a perfect chance to study the development of a society. It's in a state of weak government, no army, the development of armed groups. Interestingly, there are two different sides to this: there *is* the freedom to do everything, yet many are not doing it—they are not using their full freedoms. I think we are so used to being regulated that we are afraid and won't use them even if the law *doesn't* exist to stop us. This makes me think about our history and how things develop over time. There's mafia, there's the army, terrorist groups, and no-one stops them. They've merged into society.

"With kidnaps, recently, they're held ransom: old men, young guys, but not as many cases with women now. Still there are women that are kidnapped, but they're *not* raped, now. So, these groups are doing certain things, but they're not breaking *all* societal rules. It's like there is a line, and it's not being crossed. In other words, with rape for example—*she's a woman and you just don't do that*. But this is in contrast to when that has happened," she explained. "But I can't help thinking, 'There's nothing stopping them, so why are they stopping?'"

I'd seen a post on Facebook that Amal had written two weeks previously, about female Libyan activists, her role models, which was what had prompted me to speak to her.

"Regarding women," she said, "some say it's worse, some say better... On the one hand, it's *very* bad: there's no army, no police force, nothing to stop the terror and violence continuing. But on the other, the empowerment—I've never seen it before: so, *so* many women, now that they are not scared of being killed or molested, of Gaddafi and his law, of not being allowed to go in the street, they can take their veil off. There are many more women working. And they've got dreams. They really want to do something. I think it's really, really great. They are eager for change, to make a difference: in Gaddafi's time, you could be a teacher or a nurse. You *could*, but it wasn't encouraged!

"Now there are organisations, so many more, and being *started* by women. But there is also bribery, and threats made to women in the courts. There *are* women speaking about policy, in the elections the percentage of men is really still much higher, but the women are ready to take that step. The second time, they go again—I can see they want this. There is so much potential, but with the backdrop of political tension.

"Now that it's after the Revolution, the problem is ours. It feels like it's our responsibility. We can no longer blame others, but we are putting ourselves down for the same reason. There's fighting, no constitution: we are the problem, the problem is not the country—*it's us.*

"Libya feels like a person," Amal said then, "like a relative. I often think of whether what I'm doing will benefit; what will it do in the future? Will this be productive or useful for Libya? It's like a measure. I really want to help. I want to know, mingle, connect with others, and I see this happening there too. This is different to the past. Now there is sincerity, where before we were scared of 'the other.' Under Gaddafi's rule, if we were with someone, maybe they would report us. Now, though, we know if someone wants to speak to you it's because they really do *want* to.

"I would say there are four categories of Libyan people migrating to Malta," Amal continued. "It's shocking to realise there are Libyans who have to run away from their home! The first, they are young men who are so fed up with the situation there. They come mostly from the rural areas. It's close, they've connections, it's easy to get a visa. They come here looking for a job. But then they get lost in all of this—you see them in Paceville, the party zone, you see it in their faces. And unfortunately, there are a very big number of them. They're running from one place to another and they're trying to live, they're getting money just to spend their days.

"The second group, they are here to 'learn English,' though actually I think they are running away from the reality of Libya. And then they have to go back. They get lost here, too. They're young and they're away from home for the first time: lost between two cultures. They have grown up in a culture not open to the world, and their parents were so scared that they'll do something—join some sort of gang or group, so they send them here to Malta.

"The third category are families, families that have truly left. They want a better future for their kids. There are a lot of these groups; for example, just recently I found out that one third of the class in a school nearby were Libyan. They want a better life, they have seen too much. But they left with a mission, to do something, and that's something I really admire: leaving because of wanting a better life for your kids—there is a sense of responsibility.

"The fourth group are those who have been here in Malta for over five or six years—and this includes me. I think that we are the most open to other Libyan migrants. We are nostalgic; we want to help. Sometimes, within migrant groups, there is this tension: who came first? So many people are flooding out of Libya. So, I and others, who have been here for a long time, try to be open to meeting other Libyans and to showing them around. They want to feel their home country. They—*we*—cling to our culture, our identity and who we are. Even in their kids, I see the parents instill their values from back at home in Libya. The opposite, of course, is the adapt method: '*Come on, let's go out and become European.*'

"All four groups that have migrated often end up bringing their sense of home and culture, what makes us Libyan, here, and move *back* to their culture, in a sense, even though they are in Malta.

"My parents are very conservative since a very young age," Amal said. "I went to Islamic school when I was young; they always wanted me to remember. 'You are Libyan,' they said, 'there are things you can and cannot do.' However, it was easier for me, with older siblings. My parents were very open-minded with many things. They were supportive, yes, but they demanded respect, for example, with following house rules. When I went to secondary school, and I'd question something, my father would say, 'I know what's best.' We've never minded, it's not extreme. I was always told, 'You can go out, but not drink.' They sacrifice for us and we for them.

"My parents are really in love with going back home," Amal continued. "They dream of 'All the things I'll do when I go back home.' Or I often hear, 'When I go back home I'll...'

"Now, when they go back, they keep extending their stay. Our being here is a temporary thing from my parent's view. They'd always said, 'Five years. Oh, maybe five *more* years...' My mother, now, when she goes back, she keeps extending her stay. My brother recently got married in Libya, so now my mum feels like she has a second family, and is preparing to go back. I guess she feels like, 'Oh the kids are having families, and so on.' Somehow, sometime, hopefully, we will go back. As a culture, though, we don't make plans.

"It's easier for us to go from Malta to Libya than for some Libyans to see each other in their country. Sometimes we just go for two days. Sometimes, in Libya, people might not see each other for a year, even though it's not far.

"We feel less restricted—we can just go and leave. Now, we go and come back whenever we feel like it. It didn't used to be like that, though—we used to have to be so careful about what to say, at the airport especially.

"There are Libyans who'd never left their country, and now, every summer, they go abroad. There is so much movement now, it's escalated. Within their country, with friends—they just want to travel. There is this feeling of being so much more open to the world—even travelling for no reason, that it's normal. You used to always have to have a reason. There are also many going back to visit. They owe it, somehow—they've had the education, the right training. These are the people starting projects, new organisations. Most of our politicians, in fact, used to live abroad.

"The whole situation there is very temporary. We've had the current government for one month now; we've no constitution, there's a lot of confusion. Now, we don't know what will come next, or who will take over. The political experience has been a negative one. It's quite normal not to know which way to vote, and what's happening now is like a normal experience of political development. Like me for example, I don't know who to vote for, what to search for, and sometimes there's a really good person, but they're just not right for the job. It's not strategic thinking, intellect or studies that's important, but capability, and the ability to achieve results. There's this lost feeling in what to fight for and what to look for," she said, pausing for a moment.

"There's this activist, Mejdeline. A feminist, too, very opinionated, provocative even. She spoke out about Libyan Jews having the right to return. She was kidnapped and tortured, but they didn't rape her. In Gaddafi's time, a woman would definitely be raped, or subjected to sexual molestation. We never, until now, had a Libyan woman to look up to, but now there is this feeling: she made it and so can I! As a Libyan, there's so many women to look up to, it really inspires me!

"We used to get told, 'Look around you! See, *because you're a woman* you cannot do what you want to do!' Now, for the first time, we know that it is possible.

"There's this Libyan lady, an engineer," Amal said excitedly, shifting in her seat on the bench in front of me. "She studied in Canada and started a new internet and phone service. It was an idea first, only. *Aljeel Aljadeed,* it's called. She and other women used to make and sell bracelets in Canada; the money went to Libya, toward fighting injustice, and to families who needed it.

"After the Revolution, she came back to Libya. I worked with her once—we organised a conference. She'd started a centre, a group for women to gather, it's called *Phoenix*. She'd said, 'How can we make a place where we can meet up and do things together?' At Phoenix they hold trainings, preparing women for work. Women were saying, 'We want to have a religion that facilitates empowerment, and we want to discuss this.' We needed a place, and she said, 'Use the centre.'

"Us women had to start from nothing in Libya, there were no rights for companies. No commercial framework existed—it's different to here," she gestured, with a small laugh. "It was difficult even for *men* to do it!

"We are rising from and through the Revolution's ashes and remains. Something beautiful is emerging," she said, looking up, her beautiful eyes smiling.

Part II

"Not all who wander are lost."

\- JRR Tolkien

7.

The border at 18,000 feet

At home in my parents' house in County Kilkenny, I set up a desk upstairs. This became my office, and I really enjoyed having a physical space to write and research. My parents began, slowly, to take my writing "seriously"—in other words, not ask me as many times when I would go and get another, "real" job. From here, I researched and wrote. By my desk was a Velux window that looked out on the field behind the house. It was the end of June, the grass had grown high before it would be made into silage bales in the beginning of autumn. It was so quiet here that I felt I could hear my thoughts and gather them, after the busyness of Malta and city life there. I stayed one week before I left to a camp that I volunteered at each summer in County Tipperary, nearby.

I wrote to Richard, who had organised the *Learning from Ladakh* programme I'd interned on with the International Society for Ecology and Cultures (ISEC) the previous summer.

Ladakh, or "Little Tibet" is one of the most sparsely populated regions in Jammu and Kashmir, India, in the

Himalayan mountains, with the famous Karakoram Pass to the far north. Its culture and history of Tibetan influence is visible in Ladakhi language, folk art, religion, medicinal traditions, and architecture. In between guitar lessons and cooking in the *Amale*'s (Ladakhi word for mother) house where we stayed, I remembered Richard telling me something very interesting about Ladakh's politically strategic location. It borders Pakistan, Tibet and China, although geographically part of India. The partition of India and Pakistan in 1947 was a brutal and "colonially created border that displaced between twelve to fifteen million people within four years," I read in Harsha Walia's book, *Undoing Border Imperialism*.[22] Richard wrote back to me, reminding me of his friend Babaji's stories about the Indian-Pakistani border, high up in the Himalayas:

> I remember the late-night conversation with Babaji, whose uncle had served up there, on the border. According to him, the state of tension on the line of control was to a certain extent at the whim of the officers in charge. If they were friendly types, both sides would chat to each other on the radio, maybe even meet up, if not they'd relieve the boredom by taking pot shots at each other. It is a sort of phoney war, with a lot of posturing, but it can turn deadly serious at the drop of a hat—as it did in the Kargil war

in 1999 (and towards Kashmir, it's always serious). In Ladakh, up on the Siachen glacier (18,000 feet plus, at its source), the mountain and the altitude are more of a hazard than the opposing army. In April 2012, when an avalanche killed over 130 Pakistani personnel, the Indian side offered humanitarian assistance. When an Indian helicopter got lost and came down, both sides co-operated in its recovery. There is, in theory, a permanent military presence up there on both sides, but in the winter it's so cold it's more about survival than fighting, so there's a sort of truce, and I think the higher military outposts are abandoned by both sides until the spring. Earlier in the year, the Indian army allows its Ladakhi scouts soldiers to go home for a while to help with the harvest, I don't know if perhaps the Pakistanis do the same?[23]

While reading Richard's email the absurdity of the situation struck me: soldiers at 18,000 feet plus, guarding a glacial-ice border. In India, while travelling the perilous journey by jeep into the mountains and on into Ladakh, from Srinigar to Leh, I'd written *Stately Cows*, a long and rambling poem as we crawled along the dusty roads, deeper and higher into the Himalayas. The journey hinted at all that Richard wrote, and soon I observed "An arm raises/A hand waves/And we drive on," [24] as we navigated the numerous checkpoints, and carefully negotiated the passing of another long, dark-green army truck, often on little more than a dirt track.

The largest social disturbances in Ladakh's history have come from outside its borders, writes journalist Julia Harte.[25] Over the centuries, Muslim armies from Baltistan and then Indian Mughal troops weakened Ladakh to the point where, in 1846, it was formally incorporated into the state of Jammu and Kashmir. Though it has maintained that status ever since, Ladakh has gained degrees of autonomy in recent years. In 1995, a community-based, democratic governing system called the Ladakh Autonomous Hill Development Council was set up, and its leaders granted the right to make (some) decisions affecting Ladakhis. Here, as author Janet Rizvi states, were only the simplest of technological devices, yet "an extraordinarily delicate balance operates between man and his physical environment and the rhythm of the seasons." [26] The decentralised structure allows for traditional Ladakhi governing bodies (councils of elders in each village) to maintain considerable power; however, there is still much work to be done. Ladakhis are still eager to split from Kashmir altogether, and become an Indian Union Territory of their own.

Since Ladakh was opened to tourism in 1974, a rapid influx of cash and Western cultural influences, on an economically-poor but spiritually-rich people, brought changes to the entire region, though particularly Leh, the capital. It is alarming how sudden the changes took place, and the loss of knowledge in Ladakhi's youth, that had previously been carried from generation to generation for centuries. [27] These changes were also plainly visible in small villages like Likir, at 3,800 metres above sea level and 30 miles northwest of Leh (a bumpy three hour ride by bus climbing higher and higher into the mountains). This was where I stayed with other interns: Jen, a PhD student, and Felicity, a mother and farm-owner with her husband. We stayed with local families to help with the local barley harvest, the quickest and most efficient harvest I have ever seen—no "technology" *per se,* but bare hands and a method tried and tested over centuries; later, the staggering loads were carried on our backs, though the locals made it seem effortless as they manoeuvred the tiny, uneven paths. Here, they will make their crop last throughout the harsher months of winter, when it's not possible to grow anything due to the ice and snow. In fact, their four- to five-month growing season makes their survival truly remarkable; the other eight months of the year the high ground is frozen. Just six inches of rain fall on these parched peaks each year, although recent climate change has resulted in increasingly unpredictable precipitation and the melting of glacial water from which Ladakhis find their water source, in addition to underground springs.

In an attempt to temper the effects of cultural transition, anthropologist Helena Norberg-Hodge launched a project which sends volunteers to live and work with a rural Ladakhi family for one month, and sponsors various local renewable-energy initiatives. I had come in contact with Helena and her work because my father had ventured into the Himalayas some years before with a guide and donkey, and later, in Leh had encountered the *Women's Alliance of Ladakh*, created by ISEC. The *Learning from Ladakh* programme also sends Ladakhi community leaders to cities in the West, encouraging appreciation for their own culture by exposing the more undesirable aspects of Western culture. Such information is often, unfortunately, otherwise left unknown or unsaid; considering the messages and advertising the Ladakhis receive of idyllic American life, it is perhaps no surprise. The project also discourages Ladakhis from using chemical fertilisers or pesticides, or growing cash-crops, on their exceptionally desolate and beautiful land by way of explaining the detrimental effect they can have on soil and water.

During workshops with ISEC (held by local activists, farmers and educators, Helena, and renowned scientist and author, Vandana Shiva) we explored different initiatives that aim to create and deliver Ladakhi versions of educational materials that are more relevant and meaningful to Ladakhi culture, as unfortunately the national Indian curriculum seemed despairingly inadequate and inappropriate and is rendering a wide and perhaps irreparable gap between generations. One such initiative was the *Students Educational and Cultural Movement of Ladakh* (SECMOL)[28] founded in 1988 by a group of young Ladakhis. They focus on activities that empower Ladakhi youth, and I was delighted to see that students take part in the running of their school. On our visit, we found them in large part in charge of the basic day-to-day necessities: cooking, feeding the animals, checking the solar-powered technology, giving tours to those who were interested. There was an air of responsibility and ownership I'd rarely seen in youth; yet, they certainly knew how to have fun also—groups of young people sat around playing music, sports, chatting to visitors, sharing skills. The students rotated their shifts every few weeks so that they had an holistic understanding of their environment and school and what was involved in its running. Classes were held independently or in groups, with students meeting teachers to organise days and times for their lessons.

In one of the workshops we had on the *Learning from Ladakh* programme, we were told that, in the Himalayan wilderness people in one community had wanted to be able to communicate, they wanted to be heard. They were given telephone lines—perhaps not what they'd meant. Similarly, they wanted *access*, so roads were built—again, perhaps not exactly what locals had asked for. The more wary tourists who come to experience this wilderness and culture, notice this anomaly: exactly what they came to see, has been or is now being destroyed in order to be more like tourists from the West. "Like America," the family I stayed with near Likir, often said.

In another workshop, an eco-tourist guide told us about a monastery which had a road built right through it! He was interested in what tourists—without whom he would not have a job—thought about this. Of course, when they realised the road was built (almost excusively for them) they cried out at the poignancy.

In Likir, the local *gompa* (or monastery) is distinguished by its leader, the Dalai Lama's younger brother, and a 30-foot statue of the Buddha. A tributary of the Indus River runs through the steep gorge through which Jen, Felicity and I made our way on a trek, taking off our shoes. The mix of old and new—what had interested us and brought us from our homes in Arizona, Tasmania and Ireland/Malta respectively—was brilliantly, if somewhat poignantly, visible in Likir: the telephone lines strung at funny angles to the steep inclined hills; the monks in traditional maroon-wine dress robes and nearby prayer wheel; the local monastery "shop" selling Snickers bars; the occasional Coke bottle now strewn across the landscape as, with it, came no instructions about recycling, or plastic not being biodegradable; and the dusted-yellow JCB digger outlined against the dusk.

To reach Ladakh, I had travelled from Srinigar by jeep, where I met Mark and Michael, brothers from Chicago, Illinois. There were not many tourists in Srinigar, so they were easily noticeable—particularly Mark with his light-blonde hair and green eyes. He had worked for a human rights NGO as part of his law-school internship, in India. His brother Michael was in the process of setting up a philanthropic organisation, its aim to link donors more closely with their chosen charities, and to promote further engagement and thought with the issues concerned.

I'd enjoyed our conversations about our experiences of India, and how living in a different country helped us understand our own country in a different light, when we returned. We had plenty of time to talk as we got stuck at landslides and wound the perilous corners, in the back of two jeeps. Our journey, in total, had taken two full days leaving early each morning—though we had been delayed by a hold-up with rock and scree that had fallen on the narrow road, right before a sharp bend. Soon traffic of all kinds (jeeps like ours, large trucks carrying goods and fuel, army vans, some local families, traders) had piled up in a resolutely stubborn traffic-jam in which no one wanted to move first, and instead preferred to beep their horn at regular intervals. Mark, Michael and I spent two hours reading, talking and watching from outside the jeep, as it was decided what would happen next. Eventually, the rocks were moved: dropped 100 feet below, near a small army-base cabin with only a small path leading toward it where presumably, later, it would be someone else's problem and might all begin again.

It had been almost a year since we'd met in India, when we arranged to Skype. I smiled as Mark appeared in my webcam and began speaking from his desk in St. Louis, Missouri, where he studies. I asked Mark to tell me about his experience working in India.

"I was working for an international NGO with locations all around the world, fighting injustice," he said.

"How did you begin this work?"

"I was in a desperate place in college: I wanted to get away. Both my friend and my father had died, and then my girlfriend broke up with me. I was... directionless. My aunt had said she knew about an organisation that was concerned with anti sex-trafficking. Given that she knew I had an interest in international stuff, a desire for meaning and purpose in my life, a Christian faith, and absolutely no direction whatsoever, she figured this would be perfect for me, and she was right.

"I was always interested in international issues, in cultures. The training was a really good experience. It was a year before the end of my studies, and I had no idea what I was doing with my life: I volunteered and I got asked where I wanted to go. The last place I ever wanted to go was India," he laughed.

"So, why *were* you in India then?"

"Remember, I was totally directionless," he explained, still laughing. "I just said, 'Okay, India it is then'—almost *because* I'd said I'd never go there. The whole thing seemed foreign, at first. I was in India for a total of ten months.

"During my time there, I saw that it's so difficult to get convictions—real prosecution is *extremely* hard. The Indian justice system is overwhelmed with cases, and there are very few judges. We want to get more, of course, but it isn't as simple as that: they have to be qualified, for a start.

"The work that I was involved in dealt mainly with individuals or families that were trafficked to different parts of the country and forced to work in various industries. This allowed us a lot of chances to interact with clients who came from a completely different world than what I was familiar with. I remember once a friend and I gave a medley of *Les Mis* songs for the kids before they boarded the train, when their time of aftercare was finished." Mark said. "It was nice to interact with them. They loved to play with whatever was around. We didn't get to speak long, but enough to show communication. Kids always want to play, throw a ball around or something like that. And of course, there was the novelty of my looking different: my white skin and blond hair. It was limited, what I could do and say with them because of the language barrier, but even smiling can go a long way, and I *could* speak through our translators."

"And are there certain places more likely to be keeping bonded labourers than other ones, in India?" I asked.

"Yes," he said, "there are certain areas where we keep tabs on groups, like in north-eastern state of Orissa, for example. And companies that might've been let off innocent, but get repeat claims made against them."

"What do you think are the main problems that are preventing justice, or bonded labour from being stopped?" I asked.

"Thinking that it's a systemic problem, and that there's nothing we can do about it, like it's only on a macro level. Maybe it's just me, but, the micro is so important: the people around you—you can control how you act and treat the people around you. It might take years and years, and yes, it's going to be hard, but... In history, take for example the Civil Rights movement, there were sit-ins and protests. It took so many years, it was small and they were *local* battles. And, in India, bonded labour exists, and this is a problem, but it needs to be solved in a similar way!"

"I know your brother is involved in the social media side of activism and NGOs," I said, "connecting donors to their causes, and has set up a business of his own doing that. He spoke at a conference about philanthropy, last year, if I'm not mistaken? How do you see the media being useful to raise awareness about modern day slavery and the forms it takes?"

"It makes it accessible. About its effectiveness, that depends on whether there's support being given actively or not: does it emancipate or not? It's good if it leads to action, but it *can* lead to complacency as well, the bumper-sticker mentality, or an 'I've-done-my-part' kind of attitude.

"I remember on the plane to Kashmir," Mark continued, "before I got into Srinigar, there was a Kashmiri girl sitting next to me, in a hijab. It's Kashmir, and I'm an American: I'd thought, you know, that she wouldn't speak to me. But then, she leaned over to me and said, 'Excuse me, but it's a long trip and I see you've got two books. Can I read that one?' I had two books in my hand: One was *The Cost of Discipleship* by Dietrich Bonheoffer and the other was *A Clash of Kings*, the second in the Game of Thrones series by George R. R. Martin.

"Now, I figured there'd be no chance a Muslim girl would be interested in reading Christian theology so, I instinctively handed her *A Clash of Kings.* Almost as soon as the book left my hand, I suddenly realised I'd made a huge mistake. *A Clash of Kings* may not contain Christian theology, but it does contain a lot of gratuitous sex and violence. Immediately I tried to persuade her not to read it. I said, 'Oh, well you may not like it because it's not well written.' She just smiled and said she was happy to read something to pass the time on the flight. Defeated, I waited for the inevitable gasp in horror that might come from her. Thankfully, however, after reading about three pages, she agreed *A Clash of Kings* was badly written and so stopped reading it!

"We talked, though, and she was friendly and engaged with me, and it showed me the bias I'd had and how I'd placed all of that on a certain person. The cool thing about travelling is you have these expectations about people and places and then they don't always fill them. People often say, 'You're being so prejudiced.' But everyone has these: you carry them around, and that's the good thing about interaction because then they change.

"We re-engaged in conversation, she actually *wanted to,* and not only in small talk. When we passed over the Himalayas, she pointed them out to me. 'Oh, Mark,' she said, 'Look! Those are the *Himalayas*!' I'd had this idea that it was dangerous, volatile, that I was going into this hostile kind of territory, in Jammu and Kashmir."

We laughed, on my part remembering the hairpin bends, and the speed at which the jeep drivers maneuvered them, as we climbed, while, in the back, Mark, Michael and I had to trust the driver and the universe—especially the time the seatbelts hadn't worked. I also remembered the innumerable army vans, trucks and bases: both the landscape and the military could be considered difficult terrain to cross.

"Our office when I first arrived, was in a house," Mark continued. "On the weekends, the people I was with were the same as in the office. It felt like community: the integration of your life, when your work and leisure is one and the same, seeing how it all ties together.

"I feel, now, like I see the culture in the US very differently than I did before I went to India. When you live and work in a different country like I did in India, you grow closer with those whom you share similar experiences, and you're on the same *level*. Back here, they don't understand, they haven't had those same experiences.. You see some people would much rather fill their time with celebrity gossip or listen to mindless EDM DJs, like, *Skrillex*, That's not everyone, but those things are definitely on *some* people's minds in America!" he laughed.

"Yes," I agreed, "I can distinctly remember that feeling when I got back from Tanzania, even though it's a long time ago. I didn't know what to tell people, what to say about Tanzania and the experiences I'd had there. It was one of the best times of my life, and that was probably the hardest part to communicate, it was what people at home couldn't understand. They had this image of Africa from the TV: poor and in need of 'help.' And that made me so angry because that wasn't my experience."

"Yeah," Mark said. "I relate to that!

"I noticed the family unit is small in India," he added. "It's ultra-communal—everything you do is reflected in the community. In its worst form, they are 'slaves' to the family. In the West, we have the direct opposite: extreme autonomy, we don't invest in our family, there isn't the same valuing of family as there is in India. We've lost things that maybe we shouldn't have."

Mark paused for a moment, reflecting.

"Kirkegaard wrote about purity of heart... It's really hard to stay integrated in both personal and exterior life. But, as a Christian, I am called to do this," he added, coming to a close, '*To seek justice, rescue the oppressed, defend the orphan and plead for the widow—Isaiah, 1:17.*' To risk sounding fatalistic, even if it were to be a *losing* battle, we, as Christians, still believe it's something we were called to do," he said quietly.

8.

There are no tigers in Tanzania

My conversation with Mark sparked some deep thought in me, especially about my time in Tanzania with my godfather, Reinhold. After my Junior Certificate exams at sixteen, I'd spent my summer there. Back in Kilkenny, many people were curious and interested, of course, but what stands out in my memory is a friend commenting on my being back from "the jungle with tigers, lions, and elephants." He'd asked how all the animals were doing. The people who understood a little more of what I'd seen were my father and other adults who'd been abroad, to Africa, or out of Europe. To the young man that enquired about the jungle, I smiled noncommittally and muttered, "There are no tigers in Tanzania. Or even Africa." Anger simmered inside me, but I couldn't articulate why.

Many things continued as they had before, however much had changed since my going to Tanzania, though I didn't realise it at the time. I found out as an adult that mum and dad had decided it was best for me to go there and keep me "out of trouble" that summer, as the previous one I'd been a nightmare for them. I'd had no idea and was happy to go—to see Reinhold and his family, and a country and continent I'd never been to before. I had always been curious and enjoyed travelling. And so, I just... *turned up.*

My going there affected me and how I thought about the world after that, though it was not immediate and was a more gradual process. I realise, much later, when I came back and couldn't answer the young man in Kilkenny, that I didn't have the language to explain how it was that I felt I'd fitted into a culture that wasn't my own, better than the one I grew up in. Perhaps no one did. Thinking about it now, I'm not sure that it's possible when the educational basis of learning about another continent is on how *different* the people are there: their belief systems, their worldview, skin colour, wealth. How foreign, or far away, or judged to be "behind" in economic progress.

There were innumerable simplifications and stereotypes, including the obvious one: many people my age didn't even know that Africa is a *continent*, made up of over fifty countries, for a start, and thought of it as having the same problems—poverty, starvation, drought—and people. There are differing schools of thought on the exact number, though fifty-three is considered the correct number by the African Union (AU), while the UN's membership roster lists fifty-four states. This is because Morocco is not part of the AU, and further, should the Sahrawi Republic (or Western Sahara) be considered a country, this number would change again. The Sahrawi people were briefly independent in the 1970s, but have since been controlled by Morocco, and to this day still endure political deadlock and terrible displacement with "the longest unbroken stretch of wall on our planet... one of the most hidden, unpublicised and unrecognised barriers to a people's unity." The Berm, a three-metre high wall, "divides Western Sahara into free and occupied territories." With a "400m wide minefield, the wall stretches more than 2,400 km through Western Sahara and has driven families apart for more than a generation"[29] as researchers Mike Fitzgibbon and Mirjam Hirzel write. The wall has driven the Sahrawi people apart for over thirty-five years, who have lived, their existence unknown to most Europeans, either as refugees in southern Algeria, or in fear, in the occupied territories. Meanwhile, Morocco has prevented external investigation, and restricted international travel for the Sahrawi at critical times, despite the presence of the national government-in-exile: the Sahrawi Arab Democratic Republic (SADR) proclaimed in 1976. Since its inception, the SADR has been recognised by over eighty states.[30]

My Tanzanian friend and classmate Franky had written a page-long essay in the back of my notebook, *Karibu (Welcome) to Africa!* In the last paragraph, he'd written: *European who have fear to come. Don't fear, it's just a wonderful continent which will wake you. Enjoy here, because there are a lot of wild animals, a big mountain, and one of the seven wonders in the world. Beaches which will make you happy. I'm sure you can tell others.*

You are welcome again Ciara, welcome again in Tanzania.

Franky.

Though I did not want to, the day, of course, came when I had to go back to Ireland.

This memory had been buried, but I recalled it in later, adult years: on my flight back home, there was a stopover somewhere. As I was on my own, it was, theoretically at least, entirely possible for me to get off the plane and not go home. To stay in Africa. It wasn't a romantic notion, it was a deep yearning to stay.

I'd felt at home there. Comfortable, happy: there was a lot of fun and less pretences. There were less appliances and technology that made life easier (as it's usually assumed it does)—but this was exactly what I'd loved. And most importantly, there was *community.* And because there was less material things, there was more of what mattered, in my experience: people helped each other out and had *time.*

I began to realise, later, that I was missing the *vocabulary.* How to explain a continent, a river, a country, a people, a way of life so entirely different to my own in the Western world?

In my late teens, when I'd finished school, I was aware my choice of study, International Development, was definitely not to go over "there" and "help," but beyond that, I didn't know why I'd chosen this field of study. I thought it had something to do with grassroots solutions and growing food, and critiquing the Western model and idea of progress and what "quality of life" meant. A good enough start, I thought, and with that in mind, I went to university after a gap year travelling.

Very quickly, as soon as I began studying, I began to learn about the complexities of poverty, and its geographical proximity. It was not something "out there" anymore but was in Cork city when we walked out of our lectures. The question of how outsiders can ever know how to solve the unique problems of a place they don't belong to both fascinated and perplexed me; it often seems to fail miserably, the Millenium Development Goals villages being just one (costly and, in some particular villages, deplorable) example,[31] unless great humility and local expertise can be combined with long-term pragmatic thinking and relevant skills, alongside micro-finance.

I can see now how innocent and naïve I was: full of energy and goodwill. I still smile when I think of the first time I met my friend Thomas, from Germany, one year before I'd started university. We were in New Zealand, it was my gap year, and we had just met at an apple orchard where we would work together for the next six weeks. Thomas had just arrived, and meeting him that first day was good for me: it was the first time anyone had challenged me and my wish to study Development—my father knew that I would come to my own understanding, but needed to do so on my own. Thomas began to unravel my basic (mis)understanding of the Westerner who leaves home, and arrives elsewhere with basic, unexamined assumptions and privileges.

"But what will you do there?" he'd asked, as I washed the dishes under our make-shift kitchen roof in the orchard in Hawke's Bay and he began unpacking his things.

"Well, I will do something... to make the world better..."

I was quite stumped for words. I continued washing dishes, and tried to figure out what I'd meant by this. What exactly "better" meant.

I still smile to this day at his answer.

"I've thought about that too," he said, "but I didn't really find any answers. That's why I'm becoming a gardener."

Soon after speaking to Mark on Skype, I visited my grandparents again. My grandfather had recently been in hospital, and I was glad that I was in Ireland now, and could spend time with him. We sat in their bookshelf-lined apartment, chatted and drank tea. Later that evening, I went out for a short walk. Within ten minutes, I stood outside Bolton House Hostel. Through the window I could see into the office: coloured papers, folders, documents, several filing cabinets and a desk. The blinds were half-drawn, a door and cupboard open. *South East Refugee Information* was written across the window pane, a red dot beside each of the services the centre offered. It seemed a great synchronicity that I was here and I needed more information; it was so close to where I spent my time in Waterford: both the museum where my mum worked and my grandparents' home. It didn't seem like anyone was there, but I was too excited to have discovered the centre.

I'd just jotted down the first line, thinking I'd come back another time to speak to whomever worked there when a man, perhaps in his early sixties, stood before me. "You alright?"

I introduced myself, "I'm a writer, I'm documenting the information on the window here. I've been collecting refugees' stories for a book."

"Come in, come in." He introduced himself as Reverend John Rochford.

"I wasn't expecting to find this place," I said.

"I started this work in February of 1997 with the Refugee Integration Agency. The first who came here to Ireland, they were Liberians, nine of them. I was there; they were to be sent back. But the Minister for Justice, Nora Owen, gave an all clear: that meant the cases were examined. Well, after that we got Romanians and Africans in their thousands.

"Then, there was the Irish Born Child (the IBC) Scheme, in 2005. That meant from the 31st March 2005, everyone had to apply or reapply for citizenship. There were 18,000 in residence here," he said.

Later, when I met the members of Anti-Deportation Ireland (ADI), Joe Moore, ADI board member explained that in relation to the IBC, "Irish-born children are still being deported to countries they have never seen. So many children in Ireland are denied recognition as fully human through economic injustice, racial and ethnic exclusions, and the 'migration management' apparatus."[32]

"I offer legal information and help," Reverend John continued. "The Immigration Act in 1999 meant that the power to invoke a deportation was created. But under Section 3.6, about the Welfare of the Individual (concerned with health and employment), I can appeal to the Ministry against these deportation orders; I've stopped hundreds.

"I deal mostly with 'illegals': those with no status of any kind, and with 'alleged scam marriages.' They're only 'scam marriages' if there isn't one doubt about it; until then, in the law, they are only 'alleged.' That's just the way with law—everything has to be proven. They call sometimes, a month after the marriage saying, 'Oh, you know, it's just 'not working.' And I have to find out, you know, what's going on: was this a 'scam marriage,' a way to get out of their country, to Europe?

"I'm a jack of all trades, but I've studied law," he said, in answer to my question. "I like to combine it with a Christian sense: We're doing something for the individual, because God would want us to. There's a social responsibility: respect for the immigrant. If we all had this..." The Reverend paused. "But people don't see it in that way—they see it in a different light.

"Everyone thinks I'm the key man; people think I've *brought* the migrants here," he said on the way out, laughing at the impossibility of this.

I thanked him, as he locked the door and we went our separate ways. He had invited me to come to the centre for more information or ask him any questions I had.

I walked around the People's Park, and found a large tree with a hole in its middle, where I sat for a while, and thought about all Reverend John had said. How the same problems arose in patterns of policy and treatment for the very people the policy was supposed to protect. Was it policy to protect a changing world, and those made most vulnerable by it? Or, was it policy to protect agreements between certain, wealthy countries and brutal governance? Didn't these certain agreements create the very vulnerability and displacement, in the first place?

I was in Waterford, where twenty years before there was little variation in diversity of skin colour or place of birth. Even fifteen years before, as a child in rural Ireland, growing up with a father from Germany, not far away, I was considered to be "different." What was different now was that *everything* was different; diversity had become more normalised, more accepted, largely, in Irish society, though there was still much to be done.

I looked around the park at how many people or their parents had other traditions and ways of life that they'd brought here, and now called Ireland "home," whether by chance or by choice. I knew that, in large part, it was different to the 90s, when there were so few foreigners that, between 2000-2003, Abbas Ghadimi (a local Iranian man living in County Kilkenny since the mid-80s) had helped and accompanied Fr Bobby Gilmore, who was educating children of all ages about asylum seekers, non-national migrants, and refugees.

"I prefer to say Persia is where I come from," he said, "it reminds us of the history of the country."

Abbas is a storyteller, and reminded me of Iran's rich history of poets and storytellers. Fr. Bobby Gilmore, founding member of Migrant Rights Centre Ireland (MRCI)

and lifelong President of the MRCI had heard Abbas'
presentation, and invited him to speak in schools.[33]

I stayed a while longer in the park, looking at the
trees and climbing over the fence and railings toward
where there was a little stream that ran by a large and fine
house that lay on the other side of the water, dividing it
and the Park. Meeting Reverend John had given me a lot to
think about, and reflect on: Ireland's history of emigrating,
of leaving when things get tough; and the first asylum
seekers in Ireland, and how it had changed since.

9.

Earthsong

Soon after seeing my grandparents, I left for Earthsong in County Tipperary, in the beginning of July. I was excited because it was the first year I could network and meet friends outside of Earthsong afterwards. I'd soon be living in Ireland again. Earthsong is a family-friendly camp in rural Ireland each summer in a beautiful secluded location. Its aim is to create a space in which one learns to be sensitive to the needs of the environment. There are also creativity, music, song and dance workshops and events, as well as creative writing—this was where I'd met Dave and begun writing, years before. There is a strong ecological ethos to the camp, with recycling, no littering, compost toilets, and fresh organic produce available to cook with from the shop on site. It is a kind of hub for like-minded people and those interested in sustainability, permaculture and other alternative ways of living; many from Cloughjordan ecovillage in Ireland go to this camp. To keep the community aspect alive, camps are made in smaller circles of about twenty people around the field, with only about 450 people at each of the two camps per summer.

Some days into camp, there was a meeting for people interested in community living, or creating it in our everyday life. It was here I met Rudi, a young woman about my age in her mid-twenties, who had grown up as a Traveller in Ireland until she was seven years old. I spotted her near one of the large yurts soon after the meeting, asking if she would be happy to answer my questions.

The Travellers are a traditionally itinerant ethnic group in Ireland; in Irish: *an Lucht Siúil*, which literally translates as "the walking people." Travelling by horse and cart was particularly common (far less so now, where caravans have largely replaced wagons, though there are still some to be found). There is a wide range of theories speculating on Travellers' origins, such as that they are descendants of the Irish who were made homeless by Oliver Cromwell's military campaign in the 1650s, or due to eviction by landlords when poverty struck with the famine (1840s and thereafter). According to some Celtic language experts, the Shelta language existed as far back as the thirteenth century, 300 years before the first Romani populations arrived in the British Isles, challenging the theory that the historical origins of Irish

Travellers are Romani. There is evidence that Irish Travellers are a distinct Irish ethnic minority, who separated from the settled Irish community at least 1000 years ago. Some researchers say that even though all families claim ancient origins, not all families of Irish Travellers date back to the same point in time; some families adopted Traveller customs centuries ago, while others did so more recently. For his book *Irish Travellers, Tinkers No More,* Alen MacWeeney photographed Travellers, spending countless evenings in their caravans and by their campfires, drinking tea and listening to their tales, their troubles and their music. His photographs are considered to be essential records of a vanishing culture, and I would recommend this book to anyone who wants to know more. [34]

The Travellers have endured ethnic discrimination and many injustices by the Irish government and society. In recent years, there have been attempts to reconcile this—though this is sometimes not with the most appropriate means. Perhaps because their lifestyle is poorly understood, and therefore measures taken to address discrimination are insensitive to the needs of the Travellers themselves; perhaps because there's fear of the unsettled nature of the Travellers' lifestyle; perhaps because of a lack of political will. Attempts are made to house the Travellers and their lifestyle is curtailed by stricter regulations and increasing bureaucracy, all of which makes it difficult to continue an itinerant lifestyle. Those Travellers who go to school, oftentimes endure bullying and other forms of discrimination. In the book *Rural Racism*, edited by Neil Chakraborti and Jon Garland, they indicate that Travellers are often unjustly blamed for thefts and other local crimes; racial stereotyping is sometimes made explicit: who they are is the reason they've been singled out, in some cases.[35]

"As Travellers, we had a community," Rudi said, sitting in front of me on the grass. "But it was always changing, it was so transient.

"There were a lot of children. Whenever I think of my childhood, I am reminded of how free it was, always. I appreciate it immensely, and I feel really lucky—I was on the road until I was nine, then we were semi-settled. It was hard work, though. We had to pack and move. There was a lot to be unsure about: who would be at the next camp, so-and-so might be and so on...

"There are two kinds of Travellers, if you like, in Ireland: the first, the Irish Travellers—'knackers' or 'tinkers' as they're unfortunately often referred to as; and the second group, the hippies. Atheist, and pagan, Buddhist, whatever, they came from England when Maggie Thatcher made the laws on common land and free, vagrant lifestyles so strict that people could no longer live in this way easily. These people wanted to live outside society, and couldn't live freely: they wanted 'common land.' My mother and father were first generation travellers from England—so I am a second generation, settled traveller!

"The first group, the Travellers in Ireland are, you might say, the *indigenous community of Ireland.* They have lived outside of society, as rejects mostly. To me, when I was younger, children who lived in houses were a totally different thing. I felt like they didn't understand us, and like they thought of us as being less than them, probably. We were more open.

"Now, it's great because I am re-making my connection with the land, with the wild. I can go for a walk in the woods and nibble my way around. That's just so amazing! And it's such valuable information, I don't ever remember being told that. The memories of my childhood are coming back, like with horses for example: I connect and the memories become stronger.

"At Earthsong, it's very different. Back in our life on the road, there was a lot of drink, smoke and other drugs. Most people on the road were genuine and were on the road for genuine reasons, but there were also a lot of people who clung on—*leachers*—or they were just there for the parties. But now, here, I wonder about my life in Ireland: how I'm going to function without the music, without the support, openness. A lot of people in my life are lost, and smoke a lot. It's hard to feel fulfilled in those environments.

"I can sometimes be scared about being vulnerable, about opening up, so I put Earthsong off for years. But I have a really lovely circle, there are people my own age. It's a really lovely experience. If it wasn't straight away, it was quick: I fell in love with the beauty of so many people here. So many cultures, homes, and explanations for these. It really opens people's minds. And if your book helps that, too, I think it's great," she smiled.

I asked Rudi to tell me more about her life as a child, how her life had been on the road?

"There was the community and the family level," she said. "So we'd come together, and we'd separate off— that was how it worked. There were certain rules, and if you didn't like it, you could move off a bit or to a totally different part, or place, in Ireland. And those morals and rules had to be there because we were individuals living together; they were a kind of mutual agreement for the time we were together. Respect for the fire, the children, and animals, that kind of thing; because it's what good people do, isn't it? We help each other out! It's so amazing to be here at Earthsong, to have that similar feeling.

"My brothers were my main friends as a child. The other children came and went, and the parents we 'clicked' with we travelled more with. We went to Ballinasloe and other horse fairs, and we had illegal raves, where we'd see the whole community. There might be eight on a piece of land in a community later, when we moved less. Usually though, we had to move because the horses had to have fresh grass. We had horse-drawn wagons, goats, chickens, dogs, horses. I sometimes call it *the Travelling Circus Farm*," she said, laughing.

"It's hard to explain where I come from. We used to be round the fire, cooking; we camped our wagons in circles, we'd no electricity or running water.

"The first time I 'moved out' was when I was four years old," she laughed, "to some people who were just down the road, apparently. I'd packed my bag, saying 'I'm going.' We were independent children, and very free. We'd such support in the group, the community around us, which was great!"

Rudi spoke animatedly about her life and seemed to remember more as we spoke. I think she noticed this too, as I was invited to visit her home in County Clare so that she could tell me more as we could not continue speaking this time.

10.

Alfie and the Lucozade bottle

Still at Earthsong some days later, we stood in line together before the teen boys came back: men, women, and then teens after their elders. (When it was the teen girls' turn, women were first.) The boys walked between us, in the middle, and there we encircled them. I couldn't hear their words, but the *feeling* was there: of presence and courage in the vulnerability of being seen, of male meeting female. Of boys meeting men, becoming men themselves. I stood, holding the hands of the women on either side of me; my belly hurt, and my body trembled.

There is one day of the Earthsong camp each summer in which time is specifically given to the teen boys and girls in their programme with their respective facilitators/leaders and this was it. Those leaders *guide* this time, and are there in a supportive role; that year was my first working with the teens. The boys came into the middle, before they made a line between us and walked toward the teen venues' large awning tent. Some of the leaders followed slowly afterward, but it was mostly teens: this was their time. Myself and the other women and girls lined up, facing the tent, and sat and waited, though nothing could have prepared me for the beautiful scene that was to come.

"When you are ready, stand up and see your sisters," David, one of the leaders said, when the young men had come out. He stood across from me to my left, with the young men standing in front of us. Both sides looked at each other, down the line. Some were still very young, maybe as young as thirteen, some seemed fully-grown young men, but they all stood together, and they all held the space and our eye contact.

They spoke words that struck them, words they wanted to say to the women or girls in their lives. They moved a little closer, taking steps together until they stood in front of us; we were just two metres apart.

"I have some things I suggest we say," David said next. "Say the words after me, if you mean them. *Only* if you mean them—this is authentic, it's got to be *real*.

"I respect you."

"I'm sorry."

I could feel the fear in me lessening, fear that'd been locked somewhere inside me, for how we raise girls, and how we raise boys to be "men," for what it means to "be a man." I remembered how Eve Ensler described it: "I think the whole world has essentially been brought up not to be a girl. To be a woman means not to be a girl. To be strong means not to be a girl. To be a leader means not to be a girl. I actually think that being a girl is so powerful that we've had to train everyone *not* to be that."[36] She went on to say that this suppression led us to where we are now, which I would agree is certainly part of the cause, and an important one.

What we do with ourselves, with gentleness, with nature, and processes that we do not understand, that work in their own time and cannot be forced, is to me linked with violence against women and girls.[37] In Naomi Klein's recent book, *This Changes Everything,* she refers to "patriarchy's dual war," which some feminist scholars indicate as being against women's *bodies* and against the *body* of the earth. Connected to the "essential, corrosive separation between mind and body—and between body and earth," the premise from which both the Scientific Revolution and the Industrial Revolution began.[38]

We stood up to meet the young men and Ross, David and Gearóid, the male leaders.

"*Thank you,*' David said then, the last of the three things he'd wanted to voice with the boys.

Moments later, Colm one of the young men said, laughing, "I'm gonna stop hugging you now, before I hug you till you're dead!"

He laughed again, but there was a trembling in both of us. It had shaken me, and touched something very deep. I couldn't know how it had affected Colm, but I thought it had perhaps done the same for him.

Later, I noticed the red paint on my neck, arms, and hands. It'd been a warm day, and the young men had had warrior streaks of paint on them. We'd expressed and shared something other than words, something so beautiful it couldn't be described, when we'd stood together. It was the most moving thing I had witnessed and taken part in, in a long, long time. And it had moved mountains inside me—mountains of mistrust, fear, and anger about how boys are raised to be men, and the feminine, repressed in both sexes, regardless of gender.

I approached Colm the next day and asked him if he was happy to answer my questions. Those ten minutes I suggested turned into two great hours spent sitting on the grass in the field listening to him.

"There is this book, *Perfect,* edited by Helen Hines," [39] Colm said, "and it's about..." He paused. "The idea of 'perfect' is cringey. That book taught me that women's self-image is very different than what we're normally told. I think that the image of women is magnified and distorted from a view that's not correct."

I asked Colm about the three things that the young men including himself had said standing in front of us at the teen area, to the women and girls in their lives.

"I could just tell, seeing all of you women in front of me, that there are derogatory things that men had done or said or acted upon, physical or sexual. And, in that moment, the only way I could apologise was on behalf of all of us men, and it just showed me how much responsibility I could embody.

"My mam always made sure I had a healthy relationship with girls," he added. "I couldn't do it for everyone, but I *could* apologise by showing respect. I feel there is a friction, a conflict almost, between men and women, and we almost treat each other as such. We speak about 'the war of the sexes.' *I* think that both sides should lay down their weapon and hug it out," he said, and looked up, smiling.

I laughed gently. "Yes. Go on—"

"I can't know what girls and women are subjected to, but it feels like there is a conflict," he continued. "But our coming together yesterday and the ease that we had is a turn-around based on a portrayal of *respect*, and showing that to each other. A mutual unity. It was like we tugged and tugged at the lines of each other—then came together. It's in the past now, and it felt as though we've turned a new leaf. I apologised by showing respect, and was respected in return. It was accepted. This is about, I feel, showing ourselves to each other without any fear."

Colm continued, "I mean no one should decide whether you are self-confident or not. In our *self*-image, we must have consciousness about what we are doing, about who we are.

"I wish girls' self-image was portrayed in a realistic light, and that women would remember how powerful and beautiful they are. Women are sexualised and objectified, it's so distorted. Like the music videos where they're dancing around. That idea of beauty is so wrong, so distorted: 'sexy,' not *beauty.* An image of sexiness—of women crafted by *men*. Women are then led to believe in a different kind of beauty that's *outside* of them. Beauty is perceived through the media, and negative attention is magnified through this.

"Your piece, *Mirror Image,* in the Cabaret, made me appreciate beauty in a way I'd never thought of before. I think young girls strive to go on in a way that isn't right for them, to be something they're not. That they're not *going* to be. I'd never taken a look at this before, but now I've actually made a conscious decision in the last few days, to stop watching porn. We've to lead away from the emphasis on the physical, which takes away from everything else. I think women have endless, endless compassion and ability to give and nurture life. Sexiness just takes away from that entirely. Your piece made me appreciate this, it was very thought-provoking..."

Mirror Image is a mimed-play narrated by myself, produced by and for teen girls in a body image appreciation workshop I facilitated at Earthsong, the pilot project I'd been working on with the National Women's Council of Ireland. As I'd been on the teen team, it was a perfect place to put my ideas and methodology to use. I used snippets of performance poetry pieces I'd written and garnered from my own experience, observation, research, and questions I'd sent to interested friends of mine. Other than the small amount of narration I used from these sources, I let the girls have free reign of the play to see what would come up as most relevant for them, and this informed my narration which was flexible depending on what the girls wanted.

"Thank you," I said to Colm. "We just did what we had to do. I hadn't known it was going to be so powerful, so strong. The organisers of the Cabaret said afterwards they'd never had the Cabaret so quiet—like you could've heard a mouse. It was hard, holding that space and putting it together in such a short amount of time, but it felt important. The girls were so brave to do it, and I'm so happy they did."

"Yeah, ever since I can remember I've always opened doors for women, for girls," Colm said. "My two best friends are Molly and Lorna," he said with an endearing smile. I thought I saw why Colm smiled: the three best friends, Molly, Colm and Lorna, are inseparable and very close.

"I'm always conscious now of the negative way that women can see themselves, and your piece reiterated that," he added. "The tragedy is that women are led to believe that they are supposed to be, and have to be, something they're not. And the epiphany is this image of a falsely idealistic, 'pristine woman.' It is a double tragedy: for both women *and* us men, that women have been led to believe this for so long.

"I've never been outwardly disrespectful to girls, but *Mirror Image* has really made me take a step back, and, what happened yesterday, really embedded this in me too. I wouldn't have the respect, or the opinions, and be where I am now, if it wasn't for Earthsong. To me there are two perceptions of beauty now—the perception of beauty I learned about at Earthsong is very different. It's like one of them is *here,*" he gestured with his hand, "and that's very 'bimbo,' you know: beauty without intelligence, beauty on the surface only. This is where, to me, the aspects of beauty are about make-up, hair, plastic surgery—ultimately, false. And like, considering what this causes for young girls and women, maybe that's not what women are supposed to look like!"

He paused for a moment. "You know, I'd be very surprised if a man felt happy to make a girl feel shitty," he said.

"Then, there's another one, another perception. Earthsong helped me move that first perception, and the contrast between the two is *huge.* I can see now that this is appreciation of beauty as it should be. It's wonderful to see the comfort and ease in themselves that the girls show here. To me, there's nothing as dreadful, or *disgusting,* than looking into a mirror and to want to cut something off yourself, or not want to be what you see. I absolutely love women being okay in and loving themselves, and I would like to say to women not to do the one thing to fit in, but, instead: *You could just be you.* Otherwise, it would kill me. It's so rare: that appreciation for women in their natural state.

"That state of discomfort that I'm thinking of is awful, I think. We spend our entire *lives* in our bodies and do the utmost wrong things. Yet, maybe it's part of being a teenager to feel not happy in our bodies, in ourselves. Maybe that's somewhat natural, almost? I'd hope that women can tap into themselves, though, and discover and enjoy their own style. It's a rarity: happy and beautiful women. There are forms—levels, if you like—of conformity, and so many that are solidified. Every second person is unhappy with *not* conforming, so they conform. There's this saying, '*What Susie says about Sally, says more about Susie than Sally.*'"

He paused and looked up, to see that I understood.

"The thing is, we're so damn afraid of what people think," Colm said. "I've started dressing how I want to, recently. I *wanted* to—had to, you know. If you walk down the street, you cannot hug strangers, there's no eye contact. It's this mentality of keeping to yourself that keeps us 'in our place.' I think we've got to be genuine and not be afraid to reach out, to come together. And *that's* when society can make things happen."

"It's also fun," I said, "changing societal norms, isn't it? Looking people in the eye on the street, things like that."

"Yes. We can be led forward, back—or maybe *here,*" he said. He looked at me then, "Maybe *that* would suit better. To be visceral and be led into a realm of security and comfort in our skin, that takes bravery."

I thanked Colm and wandered away toward the edge of the field to think about all he'd told me. What would happen if women were really and truly honest with themselves, and to the world; if I was honest about my wishes and desires, about where I'm at with being comfortable in myself, expressing myself?

The deplorable fact is that there are girls younger than ten on diets, watching their calories, worried about being "fat" or not "beautiful enough," and going to extreme lengths and dangerous patterns of self-harm and disordered eating. Many women are doing the same. And, there are also men affected by these same body and food issues. There is little or no correlation or truth in the images of women or girls portrayed in the media or fashion, given the airbrushing, strict and often dangerous diets if we consider healthy weight, fertility, and a comfortable weight and figure that is not made of years of stress, fad diets, external "management" and control. Many, perhaps even most, women know this, and yet I think there's a long way to go before we embrace freedom of thought and expression, food and fashion, body image and beauty choices for women. It takes bravery to be at home in our bodies, I thought, returning to Colm's last words in my mind.

On the last night of Camp I didn't sleep much. At midnight, a heap of us were on the ground laughing, piled up in a sort of goodbye frenzy.

It was starry and bright and clear, with a few scattered and wispy, white clouds, etheric and almost dream-like. A few of us walked the field until midnight or later. The tents, fairy lights, fires and shadows cast on the bell tents in particular, were mesmerising—like a fairytale: a village bathed in gentle light in the darkness of the night. I caught snippets of conversations, and some early goodbyes being said. "I'll walk you to your door," Dave said. I laughed at this—the sense of solidity in my temporary canvas dwelling, the field I knew each summer and the people who lived here too, for this brief time. How portable my home had become to me now my tent entrance had become a door.

As I lay in my tent, my mind had that crystalline kind of clarity that comes from lack of sleep, and excitedness or intensity. I often think of it as a form of madness that can only be found at that time of night, and from heightened levels of awareness—or simply exhaustion.

I woke the next morning at 6.30am to the sound of a baby crying nearby.

An hour later, I'd spotted Peter Cowman across the field, ambling steadily along with his empty water containers.

"Ah, yes, *home,*" he said, "I think it goes everywhere."

I'd introduced myself, as I wanted to ask him about his work. Peter is an eco-architect, and teaches and builds using the principles of living architecture, running his own school and training centre in Leitrim, Ireland.[40] I'd gone to university with his daughter, and my father had been on one of his courses and had immensely enjoyed and learned from it.

When I told Peter about *Integra,* he smiled, saying, "We tend to think of home as our *house*, this thing we can see. But I think we could broaden that concept a bit."

"I understand," I said. "The very same thought occurred to me last night in my tent. Homes that aren't always visible. All of this made me begin to ask the question, 'What is home, in the first place?' There's a simplicity to the most beautiful things in life, but they're often indescribable too."

He nodded, his blue eyes smiling in response. I walked with him as he carried his water canisters back to where he was camped.

Peter told me how he had learned from his clients that a home can be *living:* people built or crafted the homes they *wanted* to live in, and their homes were an expression of who they are. He gave me some of his teaching materials, and said I could visit his home in Leitrim. "That way we'll start at the heart of the matter," he said.

When Earthsong was over, I got a lift to County Clare with a woman called Ziva, who lived very close to Rudi. Dave and another friend of ours also came along, as they lived in Galway, nearby, and we all spent that night at Ziva's. Next morning, Ziva's young son, four years old, looked across the road from the driveway. "It's different now. It's *different*," he said over and over again to Dave and I as we sat outside on a flat-cut tree-trunk table. It was as much a wild and beautiful spot as it was furniture. There wasn't much difference, and that was what I enjoyed about Clare and its landscape: the wildness that felt at once like home.

"The road's changed. Look, the road's changed. That's not good. Pooey," Alfie said. He'd joined us, standing on top of the table, holding his toy airplane. I didn't understand what he meant until I suggested we go and take a look.

We stood at the edge of the road, and then I saw what had upset Alfie. He pointed at a Lucozade bottle, which I picked up. The "pooey" smell was the oil that now lay, seeping into the ground around the trees and debris piled by the side, on the edge of the clearing that had extended the road and a small parking area. "I will tell them, 'Take that road away,'" he said determinedly.

I told Alfie about the wood near where my parents live, in County Kilkenny, and how I'd kept my eyes closed for the first few times we'd driven passed after Coillte (Ireland's state-owned commercial forestry company) cut down almost all of the trees by the roadside, after a storm. "They got carried away with the chainsaws," my mum had said. It'd been her suggestion not to look as she didn't think I'd want any more bad news that month. "Eventually it didn't hurt as much, Alfie, or make me as angry," I said. "You see, I did look once, because I forgot. And now, slowly, the trees are growing back. Though, perhaps, that doesn't make it okay. I don't know."

As we turned round, Alfie said, "I'm gonna tell my mom about this. I can't believe it, I can't believe it, I can't believe it! And I'm gonna tell Tony about it too. He will be very cross!"

Tony was the previous landowner of Ziva and her partner Jack's land. Dave picked up Alfie and we headed back to the house, Alfie still clutching his toy airplane, and now an empty Lucozade bottle, which he held up as proof of his anger at what'd been left by the roadside.

I was struck by how easily and passionately Alfie spoke about and was enraged by the oil spill and the new road, a micro-representation of the reality of how oil spills and environmental destruction affect communities and wildlife around the world. Though we might say it is "out there" far away, in the Amazon or another indigenous land, what happens anywhere on the planet can impact the *whole* of our planetary ecosystem and have unforeseen effects. [41] Our economy, our society, everything we consume and produce relies on, and is nested in, the environment.[42] The lungs of our planet are reduced for *everyone* when a tree is cut down. Each time there is an oil spill, wildlife and marine life, the soil and rivers, are affected, and an indigenous community's staple is killed, and their land destroyed. I thought about how we need to not be afraid to stand up for what we love and what is our home—and not be afraid of taking a few lessons, Alfie-style.

11.

Glendree

Angie, Alfie's grandmother soon came to pick him up, and we drove a short way before she stopped the car. We had arrived at the entrance to Rudi and her mother Deb's house. I thanked Angie and opened the gate, waving goodbye to Alfie. I soon saw Deb standing nearby, her blonde hair and work-clothes visible—there was a lot of work being done on their site, particularly with the new wagon Deb was building.[43] Debbie is an artist and general all-round handywoman; she makes wagons to sleep in out of wood, later painting them.

I was welcomed into their mobile home; it served as their living area, and Deb slept here, but Rudi in another caravan.

It was a warm day, so we spent it outside. Deb was cutting wood from plywood sheets with an angle grinder, for the wagon which was taking shape. I walked around the old house that was originally here with the piece of land she'd bought one year before. A rainbow-coloured umbrella was stacked and propped against piled-up blocks of wood. Underneath it, a toilet, and above, just visible through the broken wood of the floor and the ivy tendrils hanging from the ceiling, a red tarp which the sun shone through. It was a tiled, beautiful, old house, "used, the locals say, for *sessions* in its time," Deb said, referring to the traditional Irish music sessions that were usually held in a local home or pub, involving plenty of drink and dancing. A tree grew on the outside of the old house, from the side of the rafters, one metre tall. It was old, I wasn't sure how old and neither were Deb or Rudi, and so went to John, their neighbour to find out. "He'll know," mother and daughter had said, as he had lived around Glendree (which means *Glen* or *Valley* of the magic, in Irish) all his ninety-odd years.

Deb had a small vegetable patch on her land, and in the evening, after feeding all the plants and edible flowers, I carried a bucket of water from the kettle and mixed it with cold water. I climbed the rockstairs, undid the cable, took off the lid on the small water tank and poured all the water inside. I understood afterward why it was called a "use all the water shower": any water that stayed inside the tank wasn't useful for a later shower because it became colder than it was already. The water was mostly cold, which I like, and I showered with old stone all around me, and moss growing over it.

On my second day, Rudi and I made our way down the back of their land and sat on some rocks. I made sure the Dictaphone was balanced on one, before I asked: "Where is home for you? Do you think it's something you take with you when you travel—did you feel 'home' while you travelled in the last year?"

"If I have my hot water bottle with me or my pillow, my sleeping bag or blankets or whatever, as long as I've got a comfy little nest, I feel quite happy. Apart from that, at different times my car would have been my home, travelling around Australia, New Zealand. And, now, I'm back in Ireland!" She laughed and looked up, smiling, her long blond hair falling round her shoulders, "And that's the country that I would call home, I suppose. I accidentally called New Zealand home the other day, though. To Debbie, as well. *Whoops!*"

"So you think it's become something that's a bit fluid, that comes *with* you, in that sense?"

"I guess when it boils down to it, it's where your family is, isn't it? Because, if something happens where you have to be there to support your family, that's what you do, and there isn't really any question about it as long as you can afford to take that flight or whatever it is. That's what really counts, I suppose; that's what's really important. But, in the meantime," she continued, "I'm quite happy to float around the world, and I feel comfortable and at home in most places. As long as I can find a quiet space, or if I'm in nature, then I'm happy."

"And do you think that idea or feeling," I asked, "of home also being there when you're on the road came *from* being on the road when you left Ireland, or did you always have that idea that it could be found in other places as well?"

"I always wanted to travel," Rudi said, "I think ever since I was aware of the idea of travelling to different countries. And we went to England a lot because I have lots of family in England, so I think we went every year. But when some of my friends went to Australia, I was like, 'Oh, wow, I could actually go, couldn't I?' I'd never thought that I would ever be able to see the other side of the world, for some reason. And when some of my friends went, I thought: that's what I'm going to do. I'll go as far away as I can and travel back slowly and see what's out there and experience other cultures. I didn't really think about home as a concept when I was thinking of that; I just wanted to go away as far as I could. It was to learn, and to explore. To push my boundaries, I suppose, and the excitement of that.

"It's nice to have that perspective. I think I definitely do appreciate the country more now. *This time*, being back in Ireland, has been amazing: I realised how many towns are so cute and beautiful and colourful; how the people are hilarious.

"The last two years—and since I've been an adult—the people I best connected with were other travellers. I made some friendships with Australians and Kiwis, but most of my friendships were with English, Spanish—other Europeans that'd been travelling for quite a while. We seemed to just sink into each other, you know, just get on really easily and we had plenty to talk about. I don't know *what* in particular, but it was just easy."

"Do you think that you don't feel that as easily with people who are settled?"

Rudi replied, laughing: "Yeah, maybe that's something deep rooted with me, from my childhood. I think I relate to other people who travel more easily than people who haven't travelled so much.

"When people are stuck in their ways, and are finding trying new things weird, I say, 'Just do it,'" she smiled. "'You can!' There's no one that wanted to go exactly where I wanted to go when I wanted to, so I've done it on my own. That's normal, isn't it?" Rudi said, laughing. "I'm female, alone, travelling; there would've been a couple of people who told me I'm mad, brave, lucky! I'm not really, I'm just doing it!

"One boyfriend in particular was terrified that I would leave. I did leave, in the end, but probably because he was scared that I was going to leave, so he ended up finishing it because I was too unpredictable, too ready to leave at a moment's notice. So I did, I left."

I asked Rudi about something she'd said at Earthsong: that she felt happy about anything that expanded or changed people's definition of home. "Of course, you may have reasons or motivations for that to be the case as you said that when you were a child, children who were settled related to you differently than children who were not settled. Do you want to say anything about that?" I asked.

Rudi thought for a moment, "So that we can understand other people and cultures and how they live. I don't know how to expand on things very well, I'm usually a woman of few words.

"A lot of people live in fear of the unknown," she continued. "So, it's nice to show people that there are other options, as well. A lot of people feel trapped. Maybe if they can see other options, that'll help them. Like, people that live in towns and don't realise, actually going for a walk in nature will help so much, even if it's unexplainable."

Rudi began to speak more about her life with the travelling community, and her experience of childhood.

"The 'rules'—because there *were* rules—ranged from quite strict, like in my own family, to basically 'run free.' And," she said suddenly laughing, "you don't push your brother in a pram right beside the river! (I pushed my little brother once, *into* the river.) In our travelling community, when I was a child, I don't know if there was a definite decision on the rules. There was just *etiquette*, I suppose, that most people understood, without, maybe, having to always be talked about. And, then, all the small families in the tribe, or whatever you want to call it, would have their own rules, because people rear their children differently. Some parents would have stricter rules for their children, and others would just let them run completely wild. I think, personally, my mum was quite strict—we did have a lot of freedom, but I think we knew what was right and wrong and we behaved ourselves quite well. I hope!" Rudi laughed. "And it was kind of like survival, really, so you don't put your hands in the fire, and, you know, you don't grab the knives, unless you know how to use them—which we probably did quite young, younger than regular children, perhaps."

I asked Rudi to tell me more about the community life that she had had on the road, and how they moved from place to place.

"It was so transient," she said. "And that probably was because it's hard to live with people and it's hard to agree on the rules. Obviously, we were all moving constantly to feed the horses and not ruin the land, so there was a necessity to move, but also people would come and go. But, in regards to communities, I think it's so complex for me, the idea is a bit overwhelming because it's hard. Earthsong is a week, and that's brilliant, that's easy, but long-term, I think it's quite a difficult thing to master."

"Had you friends in houses that you can remember?"

"I have family in England that lived in houses. I know that the first house that we ever lived in was in 1998 or '99 in Galway, when we moved to go to a good school, an Educate Together school. And we were like, 'We're gonna have our own *stairs,* and our own *bedrooms!*' So that kind of says to me that, actually, I didn't spend much time in houses. I remember running around the house like, 'Wow! It has stairs and light switches and taps and more...' We went running around, we were so excited, me and my little brother!"

"Can you recall any other times when you lived in a house?"

"I remember we were on a piece of land which was a community in Westmeath. It was a transition phase between being on the road and being in a house, with quite a lot of people, in caravans and stuff, and the guy that owned the land had a house that he built himself—my mum was going out with him for a while. But I don't think I ever lived in the house. I think we lived in our caravan and wagons.

"And that was a good time, as well. I don't know what kind of community it was, but from a child's perspective, it was *fun:* they had parties. I think they probably drank a lot, I don't know, but it was probably that kind of scene. And there was a lot of art as well, because the guy that owned the land was called 'Copper Kettle Kelly.' He used to work with copper, so he did a lot of art and had a big studio. That was in Westmeath, when I was seven or eight. He died recently, actually, he got malaria in Kenya. They did the spreading of his ashes at the Hill of Uisneach, actually—do you know the Hill of Uisneach?"

"It's in Westmeath, but apart from that, no," I said.

"It's just one of those ancient places," Rudi replied.

I smiled at this. Having grown up with an historian for a mother who'd majored in English and History in her degree, I'd spent much of my childhood years visiting many of those "ancient places" that Rudi now referred to, though evidently not the Hill of Uisneach. It was more museums that we frequented, and graveyards, especially the local one. One of my earliest memories is of being in there, scrubbing an old gravestone with grass, so that the engraved writing could be made legible for mum. There were many old gravestones like this one, so old the writing had become very faded with time.

"It's the centre of Ireland, a big historical centre and they had the Festival of the Fires there for two years there," Rudi said. "I don't know the history, but they said it's a meeting place of Kings of Ireland. In the festival, what we did was light a fire and on all the hills around, so that you could see they had fires lit, too."

This had been an ancient form of communication: the lighting of fire was meant to be wary of a certain invasion or enemy approaching, and to fortify all the protection people could.

I asked Rudi about her moving from place to place when she was young. "Do you remember leaving, and arriving, and how it was?"

"I don't have a lot of memories. I remember arriving to a few camps, so maybe that had more of an impact for me. I remember definitely excitement, because there was a new home! I think it's a lot of work, it was a hard life, a really hard life, and there was a lot of work in everything—like you can even see it here, on a smaller scale. We've got it a lot more easily, but we've to turn the generator on to fill the water, to fill another tank, you know. So, it was like that but more extreme. So, to pack up and to move was a big deal. We would have had goats strapped onto carts and children on bikes and dogs running along, and, I suppose, chickens on the back of the wagon—there'd be a little chicken house—and horses tied on along the sides. Actually, one of my brothers fell asleep on his bike one time, cycling, he was that exhausted. But once you go, I mean, what do you do, you can't just stop anywhere, really, can you. You have to get to a safe place."

"Do you know if you generally knew where you were going?"

"Yeah, we knew of camps, because with horses you can't just say, 'Okay, we're going to go for, you know, twelve hours.' I mean, I don't know how long the journeys would be, but it's hard work for a horse, pulling the wagon. So, there's all these different camps and different places all over Ireland that would be known to be good places. And some of them would be big camps and some would be little ones, maybe some would just be short-term and others you could stay for longer. There would be a few of us, there would be a convoy. And sometimes it would just be with family units, or maybe one other person with their own wagon, or whatever, or sometimes two small families."

"Was there a time when you realised that your idea of home was different than people who lived in a house? Can you remember?" I asked.

"I would've been very young. I'm not sure exactly, but I do remember we would live next door to Irish Travellers. We used to play with the Irish Travellers, sometimes, and in this one camp, we were quite close to town for some reason; maybe it was even Ballinasloe—we were talking about the horse fair that's there. I remember there was us, and then there were Irish Travellers, and there were some houses nearby, too. And there was no way I would've gone over and knocked on the doors of the houses, or gone on over and tried to play with those children; but we went over and played with the Irish Traveller children instead.

"Later on, I went to school for a little while, in Westmeath, in a really small school and they were just horrible. They bullied us constantly, I'd come home crying all the time. Saying that we lived in bin bags, and just crazy stuff. They didn't like us. They didn't understand us or whatever and..."

"They already had this image, and that was what they would continue to keep, is that what you mean, or something else?" I asked. "Perhaps it was not down to you to change that?"

"I remember one of the girls who invited me to her birthday," Rudi said. "So I went, and then, a few months later she was like, 'You never invited me to *your* birthday.' And I actually lied to her, saying, 'Oh, I was in England,' because I didn't want to have them over to where we lived because we'd only give them more fuel, really. So, I never invited any of the children from the small town over.

"For a while there, I thought, maybe I am normal, maybe I am actually friends with these children, and then they would just do something really evil, and say mean things and I'd be like, Oh my god, I actually have no friends. Wow. But this is the time where I was living in the community, so I did have my friends outside of school, and, I think I had a *couple* of friends inside the school that were living there, as well."

"Tell me about the places you stayed, where were

they?" I asked.

"The time when I started going to school for a little while in Westmeath and we were living in the kind of community there, all they taught us was prayers. I don't remember learning anything else, and I only realised that when I went to a *proper* school—in my opinion anyway. Before that, I couldn't really tell you where I was at what age, because we were travelling so much; and I guess when you're not in school, as well, you don't think about age the same way, maybe, because you're not separated into ages. We were all just a little gang of different ages running around together."

"And recently, as you travelled, did you consciously try to recreate a sense of home and whatever that is to you, when you were travelling?"

"Well, having my bed is home for me—I think it is for everybody: we all need somewhere comfortable and warm to sleep. So, once I have that, I am quite happy. And after that, having my own car is really good, because it's the same sort of thing, isn't it: a travelling home. I lived in some houses and apartments and hostels and things, as well, but they didn't feel any more homely. I even bought a bed, actually in one house, in New Zealand. And then I left!" Rudi laughed. "Just starting to make it like a set-up

156

bedroom, and then I was like, 'Whoa, wait a minute...' and I left."

"Why? Do you know?"

"Because I was spending too much time in one place, and I wanted to see more of the country. And maybe other things too; maybe a fear of commitment or something, I don't know. I had this fear of one place... Anyway, I bought a car and left."

I decided not to press Rudi about this, but wondered to myself how much of her identity was found in *being* a traveller—in constant movement—and how this affected her life, as I wondered the same about myself travelling also.

"When I think back on my childhood," Rudi continued some moments later, "we went on long adventure walks, probably every day, to discover what nature had to offer. We went eating our way along. We'd run along the bogs, jump over the ditches, have races. We swam in bog holes—something we were definitely *not* supposed to do," she laughed. "But we were so wild and free and happy.

"As a child, living on the road—we call it 'on the road,' but, really, we were living in the countryside—it was the sense of freedom. When I think back and wonder, 'Did

I have a good childhood?' I'm like, 'Yes, I really did!' We were so free and wild and in touch with the earth."

To close, I asked Rudi, "Did elders play a role in your upbringing, can you remember? And did the concept of 'it takes a village to raise a child' hold some truth to it in the travelling community, too? If somebody couldn't raise the child was the child taken into another family?"

"The other people that would come and go, yes, they would play a role, definitely, of an elder. Like, if you were making dinner and there was a stray child, you'd feed them," she said. "And, yes, other mothers would play a role as a surrogate mother. Debbie had taken in two of my brothers: they were the sons of her friend."

"Thank you, Rudi. This is... beautiful," I finished.

Rudi and Deb shared an enormous amount of their personal lives with me, of their lives on the road, and their life now at Glendree. Rudi's wish to let people understand and explore, and perhaps expand their definition of *home* and ways to live, really touched me.

That night, Debbie told us about her Moroccan travels on a donkey. Sitting together in the mobile home, she said she'd first been taught how to say "donkey" in Arabic, to converse with the locals as it was essential to find food for her donkey each time they stopped. "It was most important, like with the horses and the wagons: they came first. Well, no, the kids came first, *then* the horses; that was how it was."

While I stayed at their home, Rudi and I helped make the foundation for the wagon that Deb was building; its wooden skeleton was visible already; later she would paint it.

As Deb and I drove the winding roads of East Clare to do a little shopping, in true, practical Deb style, she spoke of her experience at a festival the year before. "They'd said 'We're human beings; *beings* not doings.' And yes, I get that, you know—but I'm being *while* I'm doing. We've got to *do* stuff! It's urgent, we've got to do something for this little country! And we've got to have the clarity: what tasks and when, who's good at what, and what needs to be done first."

There was depth, and an air of strength and capability to Deb, and it was especially from comments like this and how she said them—so matter of fact, so full of practical wisdom, that made me wonder was this the only way she could have survived on the road as she did: raise her children and do everything else that needed doing; the constant work and moving, the finding safe places to go to; looking after the animals, food for the kids, making a fire, and a sense of community and home wherever they went.

12.

Learning to Love Ireland

After three days at Rudi and Deb's, I visited my sister in Gorey, County Wexford, in the Camphill where she was working. Another reason for my visit was that I'd been invited to a book launch in Gorey: Althea Farren's *Learning to Love Ireland.* I sat in Zozimus Bookshop and Café[6] some hours early as I'd come to write.

Althea spoke about shared history, and mentioned something that stayed with me about recovering her identity and sense of self. After a few years, "Zimbabwe no longer clamoured for my attention," she said, and that, presumably, was when she began *learning to love Ireland,* and it her. In fact, John, the bookshop owner said, laughing, that the locals, with their praise of her book said it ought to be called, 'Discovering our Love of Althea!' I saw so much of myself in Althea's story: of adapting to a new home and finding herself in it, and admired her courage to

---

[6] If you are ever in Gorey, County Wexford, and you are a booklover, and even if you are not, go to the Zozimus Bookshop and Café on the main street: lots of character and unusual or hard to find, books. Everywhere.

embrace a country so unlike the one she had been born in, and so completely.

Leaving the book launch a little early to get the last bus to Waterford, I moved aside the board at the front of the café so I could get my backpack and myself out the door. As I picked up my smaller daypack, a man got up, offering to put back the board when I'd left.

He asked had I been away.

"Not really. I'm not going far—just to Waterford on the bus, where my mum will pick me up."

"But you missed the good weather."

I wasn't sure if this was a question or a statement, either way, the weather is an important topic and mystery every day in Ireland.

"No, I was in *Ireland* with this backpack," I explained then. "I've been travelling around the country for the last three weeks. I got the good weather, don't worry," I smiled.

"Ah. You're going *home*," he said, with almost audible relief in his voice.

I smiled as I thought how used to this I was: a home on my back.

On the bus, I watched the first of Peter Cowman's short films on *Living Architecture* that he'd given me. He said that he first had to admit a lack of knowledge on the subject when he began teaching people to be their own architect. He studied traditional buildings: characterised by simple layouts and forms, use of local materials, and by the fact that they were made *by the people* themselves. "These buildings catered for people's entire lives—their physical and emotional needs, from birth through to death, *and* on a deeper level, a person's belief system, expressed in ritual, in myth, in storytelling, and in the fire: creating a *living* building. Out of these studies, I was able to teach myself the intricacies of house design, to give this information to others." [44]

Peter explained how, in the Industrial Era, shelters and how we built them changed radically. Other people began to build the houses for their owners to live in, and design, therefore, also changed profoundly. One key difference was that none of the design involved or incorporated the traditions that had evolved over time— they were, essentially, containers for people to sleep or rest in. Men could return to work, refreshed, the next day, while women stayed at home. "In the traditional lifestyle," he said, "men and women shared the home territory, shared the survival activity. Essentially the whole male and female territory were split: the women occupied the home territory, the men, basically, fighting for territory in the workplace."

At its basic level, living architecture is a design system for physical and emotional aspects of ourselves to be harmonised, an integration as a reflection of the inner and outer aspects of ourselves: "shaping architecture to reflect the reality of people's lives," which, as Peter said, is in contrast to the norm where people and their lives must conform to architecture.

Peter later realised that the designs people were creating were an essential part of the lives that they tended to live. "The integration of the emotional and physical aspects of ourselves forms the core of a sustainable life." [45]

I loved this as an idea, but even more so knowing that it was *possible.* That a house didn't have to cut one away from the natural world around me, where I feel most at home, most free, most creative. That it was organic, and could blend with the landscape and its contours. If integrity was about making it my own, taking responsibility for it, I began to see the link between my body and living structures which are a part of the land: a choice to respect it, above all else. To live with it, not fight it. In its natural state, in its constant changing and my accepting this, there was in essence a freedom, and my *home* was an extended yet integrated part of this.

13.

Same Love

I returned to Dublin some days later, where my first stop was Lorna's house. She had been on the Earthsong teen team, and was herself becoming a young woman: seventeen years old. At the time we spoke, she was in her last year of secondary school. I wanted to speak to her about something she had once told me about her dancing, and her finding home in an unexpected place: on stage, and in her love of a community she had found which supported her.

"The dance studio and the Earthsong field are the two places I feel the most comfortable," she said, her brown eyes lit up as she spoke. She led a very active lifestyle in suburban Dublin, where she danced many hours of the week, when she wasn't in school.

"I think I am only beginning to realise—or touch the tip of the iceberg of—the power of dance to tell a story," I said. "I was nineteen, I think, when I went to the World Festival of Children's Theatre as a volunteer. I was totally blown away by the whole thing. There were kids, teenagers; the anger, the expression of it. Two of the best performances that stayed with me, the only ones I can really remember now, were where there was lots of anger expressed. They were so present and powerful, from Venezuela and Burkina Faso. The first was a performance by teenagers from the slums, I think, in Venezuela. They quite literally *danced* their anger. They used chairs, it was very powerful because it wasn't 'flowy,' it was fast and direct. And the group from Burkina Faso, they were young girls, their performance was about AIDS. The symbolism with which they did it and how that was chosen, was so effective: the isolation, sadness, despair—the anger, too. What struck me was the poignancy of children so young affected by an adults disease that had been carried down."

"I think it's really cool that people are beginning to find different outlets for anger," Lorna said, "rather than physical because clearly it's a lot better to do something like dance, where it can be an *art* and people appreciate it. But also, it's therapeutic. I feel so blessed to have found it: that I can do something for other people, entertain other people, but also get something out of it. I think that's my ultimate dream, you know."

Lorna mentioned a contemporary show in London she'd seen in which the performance was a woman who peed herself on stage, followed later by another dance.

"But that was a *part* of it!" she said, still incredulous. "She was *in the programme!* My friend didn't believe me, so she went the next day. And there, the same woman in the same costume did the same thing... The whole audience was like, 'Oh, eh... *okay!'* There was shock, but then there was empathy: we weren't sure whether she'd pissed herself because she was so nervous or because she was meant to, so we were saying, 'Oh, poor girl—do we clap? Do we...'" Lorna paused. "And actually, thinking about it now, maybe that was their whole point. To feel, to..."

"To come into her shoes?"

"Yeah. To feel the nervousness."

"Isn't that one of the reasons why we go to these things?" I said. "We're drawn *into* art—that's why we look at visual art and listen to music and go to the theatre—it transports us to someplace else, but it can also transport us into *someone* or *something* else. That way, you can experience things that you couldn't otherwise, and feel things we've forgotten or not allowed ourselves feel.

"Street clowns for example, they have to take everything, because as a clown the whole thing is presence and authenticity, isn't it? From my friend Cian's perspective, he loves that and takes it as a challenge. He'll acknowledge, and decide: I'm gonna make this into a joke now, something funny. That way, we can all relate, and suddenly it's not such a problem anymore."

"It's the whole idea!" Lorna added.

"Yes, exactly. Nothing's avoided. Everything is brought up and played with: everything is a toy. Cian said to me recently, 'An accident is a gift; mistakes and problems are all gifts. The rest, outside of clowning, is quite subtle: play within the limits of what your job allows. But there's always a way.' He said that what he feels is actually what the audience feels, too. 'Feel what you're feeling and trust that it's the thing to do.' I feel that he meant integrity is in the truth of what's happening," I said, smiling. "Though, sometimes I forget of course—it seems like that is the human experience."

Lorna said there was a time when Lisa, her dance partner during a performance on stage, had to pick up and improvise when Lorna did the opposite move than they'd practiced. Lisa then proceeded to do the whole dance backwards.

"We saw each other in the mirror, it worked! I messed up, and Lisa managed to work with it! That's improv—you have to be real quick on your feet to think, how's this going to work? But that's something you can't even think, either, you have to just go, just do it! That's improv in the choreography sense, but I always think of improv as training myself to be freer with my mind.

"I love improv, and I hate it," she said then. "It's scary because you have to break out of what you know, but it's still freeing in the way that you have no rules! In the way that, in ballet, that 'mistake' in my performance with Lisa would be bad technique, but in my dance, that's *good* technique. It's like, you can do whatever you want, and it's still your own dance. It's like my own form of playing. And it's not always good, and I sometimes repeat what I do, but it's just freeing and fun and it makes me happy."

"And you danced to *Same Love,* didn't you?"

I was referring to the song by American hip-hop duo Macklemore and Ryan Lewis; I had seen Macklemoore in concert with Dave, and it had made a huge impression on me, as well the song name and its video, online. This song had, and still continues to, make gay and lesbian equality more understandable to mainstream audiences. In it, Macklemoore defends homosexuality, which was seen as a rarity in hip-hop.

"Yes! Obviously me dancing to *Same Love* was really emotional and amazing," Lorna said. "Because my dance teacher—I didn't think she found it that important to make a dance of it. For me, dancing with a group of people dancing a song that was all about gay people, it felt really amazing because it felt like they were really supporting me, in dancing with me.

"I was so proud to put that on stage, because we performed it in the Olympia Theatre in Dublin. I felt that, Wow, I'm getting to show this amazing song—almost speech—about same sex, love and marriage, and that it's nothing different! And all these kids (there were forty of us, ranging from the age of twelve to eighteen) all care about this. Aoibheann, my dance teacher, thought about it a lot. For her, it was, 'What do I feel right now is important and relevant to them so I can get something personal out of them?'

"She said, 'It's not just about gay people! It's about being an outsider, feeling different.' And she kind of made it relate to everybody, because there were twelve-year-olds there, and not all of us were gay. So she said, 'This is about feeling like you don't belong somewhere, and trying to make it happen—that you *do* belong. Dance for feeling like you belong, dance for belonging somewhere, in something, or to someone. Dance for the feeling that you are just as valuable as everyone else in the room.'

"That was the only dance I've ever done that made a lot of the audience cry," Lorna continued. "After I came off stage, I cried. It wasn't even a dance that everyone could relate to on the lyrics point of view—you had to *find* something to relate to in it—but everyone just seemed to have such a massive reaction to this dance. It made everyone so intrigued about it.

"The audience obviously really saw our emotion that we put out there. Just before we went out, Aoibheann had reiterated what she said in the beginning, 'Remember: you're dancing for belonging somewhere, you're dancing to find yourself.'

"For someone that I look up to, to acknowledge that and acknowledge that it's a thing for me, it meant a lot. I think that was the best dance I've ever danced, because I really felt it. I knew it wasn't just for me, but it *felt* like it was my dance, it felt like I was dancing my life. Well, not *my* life, because I haven't got the same story as the lyrics in *Same Love,* but, someone witnessing that about me: my being gay. People watching it, the response I got; it was really powerful to see people care about it. People *want* to watch it.

"When we ended the dress rehearsal and Aoibheann saw it all properly—with the costumes for the first time—she looked at us and said, 'Wow. You guys have done a really good job! I really see all of you.'

"Even after she finished the choreography, she made us dance it for her before we went on stage. She stood there, and she said that, in our actual performance, we'd each have a moment. We'd be placed so that we'd all be able to see when each of us stood up; the back-line would stand up last." She said, 'When you see one of the other dancers stand up, wait at least three seconds. And *give* them the three seconds. It's their time to say, 'I'm here.'

"And that was when I started kinda welling up on stage, because it *was* like: I'm here, I'm present, this is my dance; and to have someone witness that! For Aoibheann, we all stood up, the music faded and we stayed for more than three seconds: we wanted to leave the audience with a *feeling*."

Lorna finished, and I laid down my pen, glancing at the growing number of pages I'd filled as Lorna had spoke and my gratitude which had grown alongside, for her and her courage. I was immensely grateful for her reflections, and her excitement that shone through her in her dancing.

14.

"Die fremden, die fremden!"

From Lorna's, I went to the airport to catch a plane to Düsseldorf in western Germany where my grandparents on my father's side (Oma and Opa) and step-grandfather *Robbi live nearby, in Krefeld. The centre of the city lies just a few kilometres to the west of the River Rhine—in fact the suburb Uerdingen, where my grandmother lives, is directly on the Rhine.

Oma (my grandmother), Robbi and I were sitting in armchairs in their immaculate apartment in Uerdingen. My grandmother married again after her divorce from my grandfather, Paul, when I was three. Once a year since I was seven months old, I visited her and Opa with my parents; later, when I was twelve, I began travelling there alone or with my sister. Oma is a tall, blonde lady, tidy and beautifully turned out in her appearance, and large in her views—I've never seen my grandmother afraid of voicing her opinion. I love my grandmother, and this is something I admire about her, though this means we don't always agree with one another. Our conversation, in German, has been translated.

"Refugees, so many refugees. Germany is the first choice. Top of the list," Oma said. (Oma was referring to the fact that, in 2014, Germany received the highest number of refugees in Europe.)[46]

"But Europe says no!" Robbi said next.

"They think it will be paradise," Oma added, "and then they get here, they realise, Oh, I need a house, and so on. And they have to live with so many of those people, all together. So much war; so much poverty. They need to go *somewhere*, but *we* can't take them all! And they're not individuals, or workers—all these women, they have four, five kids, and then another in their belly. These are our new neighbours!"

I managed to change tactics and steer away from migration and on to something very different and less political, as I didn't want to argue with her and Robbi. It was a topic too close to me personally now, and it seemed I couldn't talk about it objectively or calmly, even though I recognised her point of view: there *were* a lot of refugees in Germany, and there would be more, that was true. And certainly, all of Europe was different than it had been thirty, forty, fifty years before.

I knew that what was now "normal" had changed immensely in Oma's eighty-seven years. The Germany and

Europe that I knew were very different to the one she did. And then there was the rest of the world: the massive societal, economic and technological changes, the wealth and quality of life in Western Europe compared to fifty years before, the World Wars that I had no direct experience of. Oma had been eleven when World War II broke out, and had been born in the decade of the aftermath of World War I—also the time of the beginning of the Great Depression (1929), which seriously undermined the stability of the German economy and wiped out the personal savings of the middle class, bringing massive unemployment.

It was my first morning after having landed in Germany, and the news they'd put on had reminded her of a changing Germany. Ever since I could remember, there had been people in Ireland, even rural Ireland where I'd grown up, who were from another country or whose parents were. And, though few in the beginning, there were more each year, and in Germany, where I'd visited at least once a year, also. In my very early childhood things were more traditional and "close knit" in rural Ireland certainly, but the circles I'd been brought up in were where I met and made most of my friends and came to know people from countries all around the world. For this reason, I found it difficult to engage in conversation about saying no to "foreigners." There are cultural differences and subtleties across different ethnicities, but that does not make another person different on a fundamental level.

I asked my grandmother whether she had any photos of Kurt, the uncle I had never met, my dad's only brother. I had never tried to speak about him this directly before, but I was as curious as ever, given what I thought were similar interests of ours, and nobody had ever told me much about him.

In 1985, Kurt was killed in a truck-car collision about 300km north of Bangui, the capital of Cental African Republic. He had been en-route to establish a refugee camp at the border with Chad, for refugees fleeing civil war and had been stationed in Kinshasa, Zaire (now The Democratic Republic of the Congo, or DRC) with the UN High Commissioner for Refugees (UNHCR). Even my mother never met him, meeting my father shortly after Kurt's death. I was curious about this uncle, his studies in Winnipeg, Canada, and his work in Zaire. I understood it was difficult, still, for Oma to revisit her memories, but I knew I hadn't many years left to ask her either and felt I had a right to ask, to know something about him. If the conversation wasn't happening, I would not press it—but at least I would have tried. I knew dad and Kurt had been very different; though both had been active politically and socially, beyond this, Kurt was an academic genius, dedicated and professional, and dad more practical: a social worker, entrepreneur, mechanic, and gardener.

"No, Ciara, I haven't," Oma said. "A piece of my heart has been broken. It's been thirty years since the accident, his death, and it's like yesterday."

She couldn't look at photos, she said.

"War everywhere. The world, the environment is *kaputt*. Why can't we live with understanding, in harmony with each other? With the environment, to nature, we've done badly, I think. They say we need to clean it up. They talk about doing this or doing that, but we're not doing it! One day it's just all going to be gone because we're using it all up! *Die Flüchtlinge*, they pay their way, get shoved on the boats, get shoved *off* the boats then, too, if it's overcrowded, and into the water."

Though I knew what Oma said was true, I was angry and didn't want to talk about migration in an impersonal and general way, anymore. I prepared to leave as I said, "But what about the opposite, as well, because that's true, too. What about the good things that are happening all around the world? Because there are plenty of them, we just don't always hear about them on the TV."

I left to walk in the park and do some writing. It was beautiful that evening—the night sky, the light rain, the streetlights in the park shining through the wet leaves with an orange glow. When I returned, Oma opened up a little about her family: her two sons, Kurt and Dieter, were born in Krefeld, Germany, in 1953 and 1957 respectively.

"They were like chalk and cheese," she said. My father, Dieter, from a very young age had given all his money away. "He was about six, I remember," Oma said laughing, "and we were at the swimming pool. There was a poor family there, and so he paid for them to come in. Later, he couldn't find his purse—they had taken it. Kurt, now he was the opposite, always counting, taking note of his money, in and out. Grass-cutting and whatever way he was earning money, he wrote it all down. And about homework and thinking, when Dieter came home from school, he ate and was gone. *Freiheit!* (freedom!) that's what he was always after. And play. And then, when he came back in the evening, he might do a little homework. If he didn't know something, he'd knock on Kurt's door; Kurt always knew the answers, or knew who did if he didn't.

"When *he* got home from school, it was the opposite—straight into the books! I remember the teacher once, saying, 'Your son, Dieter, he's got to do more work.' But that just wasn't him: he wasn't into it, he didn't want to study. He wanted to *do* things—and start young!"

"And Oma, you danced, right?"

"I danced, yes. All my life, I danced. I danced everywhere, and wherever there was dancing, I went. And the parties, oh! We were up so late; we'd walk home, ten kilometres maybe, and then up two hours later and off to work," she said, laughing so hard she almost had tears in her eyes.

We looked at photos. She was beautiful, very well dressed: simple, yet elegant and classy. The youngest she was in any photo was of when she was perhaps forty years old: a small, square shot of her in the *Schwarzwald* (the Black Forest) walking in a long, red coat, in the snow. There was another of her dancing in the cellar of her neighbour's home when she had lived where my grandfather still lives. It was one of the many parties on their street, most of which were her own making, in the cellar of what had been her and my grandfather's home. In this photo, she was wearing a sleek white shirt, black skirt and high-heeled dancing shoes.

"At twenty-three I got married—like you now," she said, laughing. "But you have plenty of time yet. *Plenty.* Make money, earn money, and see if you can do it alone, be independent."

We spent the rest of the evening reading, catching up on news and cooking.

That night I thought to myself about independence and what Oma had said. I thought of myself as independent in spirit and mind, and though I had been single much of my adult years, I didn't think that being in a relationship had to take *away* from independence of will or work: doing what one loves. Though I saw Oma's point and agreed with it in one way (knowing one could achieve something alone, and the sense of satisfaction derived from that), I didn't think that was the only way to be independent. Oma had had two more marriages than I and sixty-five more years of life experience—of a very different life than mine. The expectations of marriage and specific gender roles of work and family have changed and relaxed significantly since Oma's youth; her perspective was therefore one I couldn't fully understand. I wondered what it must feel like to have grown up throughout such changes, to have witnessed Germany's technological advancement and the many material, economic and medical changes, let alone the more subtle and social ones.

Out running in Uerdingen the next day, I came across a billboard: *Nine million people from Syria are on the move. They need our support. The greatest catastrophe would be to forget.*

I kneeled to sketch the image from across the road. It was striking: a couple of children letting water into canisters from a large tank, with flapping canvas homes—a whole village of them—behind the children, in the distant background.

For forty years, Syria was ruled by one family, the Al Assads, who exercised tight control, and profited hugely. Marese Hegarty, Irish Syria Solidarity Movement member and friend of mine, wrote by email: "Four years ago, inspired by the neighbouring Arab Spring uprisings, Syrians came onto the street asking for reforms. Very swiftly, their peaceful mass protests were fired on with live ammunition. Some armed themselves to defend their families and communities, forming the Free Syrian Army. Assad's regime response was to brand them all as extremists—which they weren't—and allow an extremist group, ISIS, to expand. This was both because they had killed off the moderate opposition, and because they legitimised the role he had chosen to project to the world: of protector of minorities against Islamic extremism. That strategy has not worked, but despite his manipulations—mass-murder by siege, starvation or bombing of citizens and destruction of vast parts of the country—the world has not seen fit to stop him. This failure has led to the radicalisation of impoverished and abandoned Syrians who see no point in trusting a world that preaches democratic rights and permits tyranny. Over 200,000 have died (possibly far more but records are not accurate); at least two thirds of those were killed by the regime, many under torture and barrel bombing. Four million have fled, a further 5 million are internally displaced.

"Just over 50,000 Syrian refugees have been taken by the rest of the world, while Turkey, Lebanon and Jordan have taken millions between them. Multiple other countries have played a role in this war, a great geo-political drama played out in a country with an ancient civilisation. Atrocities and war-crimes, committed by the regime, but also by ISIS and by some rebel groups, continue on a daily basis. Assad bombs schools, hospitals and public markets. More journalists have been murdered in Syria than in any other conflict.

"If you cannot understand the politics, you can grasp the humanitarian needs of children who are bombed, starved, orphaned, unhomed and unschooled," she said, to close.[47]

According to the UNHCR, by mid-2014, Syria had overtaken Afghanistan as the largest refugee population, accounting for almost a quarter of all refugees.[48] Building on its long-term presence there, the field-based offices were expanded in 2014 to improve access to refugees, across conflict lines and borders.[49]

As I was kneeling and sketching, a man walking by on the street in Krefeld suddenly stopped and looked at me, drawing the billboard.

"What do you think is the solution? Is there a solution? About the *Flüchtlingen?*"

It was a rare occasion for strangers to speak on the street in Krefeld; it's conservative, and generally people keep to themselves if they don't know someone.

He seemed serious. I thought for a moment about saying that I was writing a book that included refugees in the dialogue and decisions that ultimately concern and affect their lives. A book that includes refugees—*people*—when we all seek refuge in our own country or another, and by law should be allowed to seek it in another country.

The man still stood beside me. I tried to answer, though it was difficult, especially in German. I said I didn't think there was a simple solution, but that there was one. I wanted to say that I thought we needed to find or redefine a sense of shared humanity, and start from there.

He asked me what language I spoke, and started to rummage in his briefcase and folders. Eventually he produced a leaflet, along with an apology: "*Ich habe das Englisches vergessen.*" (I forgot the English version). "Here. All the words are here. All the answers, the solutions. In the Bible."

We went our separate ways after that. I wondered what a book written 2,000 years ago had to say about EU borders, politics and migration, and how it could have "all the answers."

I continued my run before returning to Oma's flat and preparing to meet Agi, Kurt's ex-partner, for the first time in my life, the following morning. She'd been obliging and friendly when I'd called her three weeks before, yet I was excited and a little nervous. Kurt's early death, just three days before his 30th birthday, was premature—no parent should see their child to the grave, and it had taken its toll on Oma. Her telling me stories about his childhood was rare, and I appreciated it, but I wanted to know more.

For years, I'd been curious about Kurt and his work in Kinshasa with the UNHCR during the time of the Chad-Sudan conflict and the many, resulting displaced peoples coming into then Zaire, in the 80s. There had also been refugees internally displaced (people "living like refugees within their own borders.")[50] He had, like the billboard image I'd been sketching, tried to create and manage temporary dwellings for those in conflict zones: people in need of homes. Tents and refugee camps are not homes and never will be, nor are they a solution because they do not address the cause of the problem of forced migration; and, unfortunately, since Kurt's role with UNHCR thirty years before, the numbers of refugees and camps have increased since. However, in the immediate circumstances of need, they serve a purpose: a temporary place of shelter and aid.

I knew that Kurt not been in Krefeld for most of his adult life, as he had studied in Canada and had travelled, having left Krefeld after his undergraduate degree. He had been studious, but also revolutionary in his own way—perhaps less visibly so than my father, in his youth—through his mind, his ideals and his work. It felt important to know more; I'd always felt a connection to this uncle I'd only seen photos of, heard a few stories about. I felt I had to see Agi.

Neither Oma, Opa nor dad had seen as much of Kurt in his last years as Agi had: she had been in Africa with him and was the only person that I knew of whom I could speak to, and who had seen him in his last year of life. Dad had visited him the year before he had been killed; they had travelled in Kenya together when Kurt had taken some leave from his work.

During Kurt's time in Zaire, it had been a one-party state led by dictator Joseph-Désiré Mobutu, rife with corruption and violence, and weakened by five years of political upheaval following independence from Belgium. There were also high numbers of people left displaced by the Chadian–Libyan conflict, between 1978 and 1987. As President, Mobutu restructured the state on more than one occasion; however, he is quoted as having said the First Republic was one of "chaos, disorder, negligence, and incompetence."[51] There was growing conflict because of his one-party state rule. To successfully maintain his control during this period, there was much bloodshed which led to international criticism of Mobutu's ethnic cleansing of Congolese ethnic Tutsis in eastern Zaire. The

Tutsi have lived in the areas where they are for thousands of years, and when the Zairian government began to escalate its massacres in November 1996, the Tutsi militias erupted in rebellion against Mobutu, starting what would become known as the First Congo War, alongside Rwandan forces. Massive numbers of people were left bereft, and, as a wave of democratisation swept across Africa during the 1990s, Mobuto promised something better.

In June 1989, Mobutu visited Washington DC, where he was the first African head of state to be invited for a state meeting with newly elected President George W Bush. By early 1990, Mobutu's power was weakened however, by heightened international criticism of his regime's human rights practices, a faltering economy, and government corruption (most notably his massive embezzlement of government funds for personal use). He had enjoyed support from the US government because of his anti-communist stance while in office, but following the end of the Cold War, the US stopped supporting Mobutu in favour of what it had called a "new generation of African leaders," and Mobutu was forced to declare a new republic in 1990 to cope with the demands for change from his country. Tensions had also been rising from the neighbouring Rwandan Civil War and genocide had spilled over into Zaire.

Mobuto remained President until 1997, when he was ousted by the Tutsi militia and various opposition groups led by Laurent-Désiré Kabila. Following failed peace talks between Mobutu and Kabila in May 1997, Mobutu fled the country, Kabila named himself president, consolidated power around himself and his followers and changed the name of the country from Zaire to The Democratic Republic of the Congo.

It was a harrowing history, and only one small part of it, which left many lives, homes and an economy destroyed.

I'd recently been drawn into the spellbinding book, *Congo: Epic History of a People,* by David Van Reybrouck. I'd bought it knowing I wanted to study the geography of the DRC before I spoke to Agi. On the train I'd read about the equatorial forest in Central Africa, Congo interior, the Berlin Conference in 1884, and King Leopold II of Belgium. What King Leopold really wanted was a slice of *"ce magnifique gâteau africain"* [52] and the acquisition of land at the expense of many people's home and their freedoms. The European superpower disputes over colonial territory, and their motivations, had come together not only as many thought, to "own and lord over" Africa after they had divided it up like a piece of cake, but to open it up to free trade and civilisation, and to spread Christianity.

Van Reybrouck is a poet, journalist, and author (of historical fiction, literary non-fiction and novels) and I resonated strongly with his writing and style. The Congolese, he believes, have been written out of their own history; he means to write them back in. In the prologue, he said the reason he'd written such a long (and undeniably difficult) book is that the Congo's history is a long and often arduous journey. It is a huge country with a myriad of different cultures, from coastal to interior forest tribes. The book itself took no less than seven years to complete, with over 650 pages, because he believed that the Congo's history *could only be written by the Congolese*. To him, it was vital that it wasn't a book pivoting on a Eurocentric compass.

It seems obvious that a people's history be written by those people who lived it, yet too often we do not allow it: the present *and* the future of the DRC, and of many other countries and people, is written and rewritten and decided upon by a Western hand. We might think we are "expert," but we are not local, and globalisation, by definition, cannot be sensitive to local needs. And this is why we don't know what local solutions there are: we have not asked, we have not listened. And, meanwhile, shackled by trillion-dollar debt, it is no wonder there isn't time for local, long-term thinking. [53] This is (neo-)colonialism, no less dangerous than what we had before, only more subtle.

In the West, we are so sure of our "solutions" we don't question their foundations to uncover the basic prejudice that lie underneath them, and consider the possibility that "other cultures may have chosen other approaches to life," as Patricia Fara says in her book, *Science: A Four Thousand Year History.* It is "not because their finest scholars were stupid but because they had different opinions about what is important."[54] People are experts on their own lives; though sustainability requires concerted, international agreement and commitment, it is about localising, it can only ever be if we wish to become carbon-neutral. We should never replace the expertise that a person holds on local solutions to local problems with something far-flung and generic. Immediate aid has its place and is needed, certainly, if our current capitalist economy continues, but in the longer-term, we are kidding ourselves and disrespecting those we so wholeheartedly want to "help" if we only give handouts and charity, and think we have the answers. As almost everything we own (particularly technology) is made from minerals that are mined in Africa, we might consider alternative ways to meet our needs that are less harmful to the earth and people. We would also do well to think about issues closer to home: our own lives and homes and how we make them, our food and energy and how we can provide for ourselves.

15.

From Manitoba to Berlin,
Kinshasa to Kevelar

Next morning, I left my Oma's apartment and took a train a half-hour north-west of Krefeld. Agi Tebarts, my uncle Kurt's ex-fiancée, showed me around the square of the quaint little town, Kevelar, a well-visited Catholic pilgrimage location, where she lives. We stood in the main square, where a light breeze ruffled the big tree above our heads. Agi told me before we drove the few minutes to her home, that Mary is said to have appeared here to a woman (a Christian believer) some few centuries before.

I had not known what Agi looked like, but she was still recognisable from the few photos I'd seen of her in the 80s, with her red-brown hair and comfortable smile and we found each other easily. It was perhaps also because of my resemblance to my father, as dad and Agi had kept in occasional contact over the years since Kurt's death. She introduced me to her husband, working outside. In her kitchen, she got me a drink and we sat down, a view of her garden out the window to our right.

"Thank you for this," I said. "I'd been wanting to meet you for years, and now I'd a reason to contact you." I smiled, a little unsure how to begin—I had notes, but this was a different kind of unprepared. It was hard to believe I was actually there, in her house, and so soon after I'd made contact. But Agi was a grounded, practical woman who made me feel instantly at home with my questions, my curiosity.

"I'd love to hear about when you and Kurt first met," I said.

"It was in 1978 or '79. Kurt had just arrived a couple of weeks before to Krefeld. He had problems then with the army, same as Dieter."

(I recalled my father telling me how it was mandatory to join the German army at that time. Neither my father nor my uncle were willing to, and so escaped it by various means: not giving away their addresses to people they knew would be approached for information on their whereabouts, for example.)

"Dieter went to Ireland and Kurt was finished studying in Canada and was back here looking for a job. I was looking for a job too, or a training. I wanted to study midwifery. I tried in Berlin, but it was impossible, and finally I got a place in Paderborn, in the centre of Germany.

Kurt lived in Berlin, before he got his job with the UN and went to Africa. We visited each other, though there was the Wall then; we flew or drove. I remember going there as a woman on my own, looking at the frosty glares of the security officials, and paying the fee to get through.

"Then Kurt got the job, after his interview in the UN office in Geneva. I took my examination in 1983. After the exam, I went to Kinshasa—where he had been stationed—for three months. Finally, I got a job in Kenya, as a midwife. I took the train to Nairobi. He went with me, and then we said goodbye. I worked for a year in Kenya, and he changed to the Central African Republic, to Bangui.

"Kurt was very... *rational*," Agi said. "He had a good job and looked out for that. He was quite... structured. He'd gone for his Masters in Sociology in Winnipeg. He left his wildness in Canada; he came back serious."

She paused for a moment.

"After Kenya I went back to Germany, I took a job here in this area. But I had a return ticket to Bangui, I think. And then one day we got the message that he had had an accident, so I didn't see him again, after Kenya... where we were before we parted.

"There was a big funeral back here. We played a lot of Cat Stevens at it: *Tea for Tillerman*, I remember."

Agi did not speak more of the accident or Kurt's death, and I did not press this for obvious reasons.

"I was trained here in Germany in my midwifery," she continued. "It was a horrible training, our teachers had no respect for women. So, I decided I can't work here in Germany, I have to go for a while—Kurt had already gone to Africa. I travelled around and asked, 'Do you have a place to work in Africa somewhere?' I got an offer for the centre of Zaire, but I couldn't speak French at that time so I went to Kenya, close to Nairobi. I lived upstairs; it was a birth house. We worked without doctors, only midwives, mostly from Uganda, and me, German. The woman in charge was an Austrian nun, trained in England."

Agi said that she worked in this birth house for a year before returning to Germany from Kenya, when her placement finished.

"I went back to a small hospital in Emmerich. I was—I would not say young, but I was *inexperienced*. I had just one year of professional experience, that's not much—and, in Africa, I had very *different* experiences. In Germany, the doctor would give the instructions. In Africa, I learnt to *work*, to be independent, and the doctors, the medics, could not stand that. But, in Germany, I was not confident or self-aware. I didn't have the experience to carry through and assert myself with my colleagues: there was confusion about who was actually in charge.

"In other words, in Germany, I was told what to do; in Africa I had to take charge. Being a midwife is a profession. It takes study and time, experience to be trusted and listened to. Today it might be different because they're differently trained. But, at that time, in Germany, we were treated like *dumekuhe*—dumb cows—during our training *and* when we were already practicing. It was horrible—I have never been back there, working in a hospital. Never. 'Things are not done here as they are in *Africa,* you know,'" Agi imitated the doctors' voices, the derogatory nature of their tone still present in the stressing of certain syllables.

We sat, silent for a moment.

"During our training in the Ivory Coast," Agi continued, "we were in a clinic with young women, pregnant, from the villages. Because it was very Catholic they weren't allowed to be pregnant, so they came into our clinic.

"There was discrimination. They lived in the hospital, they didn't live at home because it was forbidden to be pregnant without being married.

"My husband Willi lived for about sixteen years in the Ivory Coast, and I went there in 1985. I had my two children there, and after the first baby—Lea— I tried to find a job in a hospital. But in town, there, everything is private, so all deliveries are done by doctors, and midwives are only, well, *'hebees'*—assistants, as we were called. We just helped. So, finally I found work in paediatrics, and it was very interesting because there I saw sicknesses I never saw before—worms under the skin and things like that. Willi was running a plantation, and in the villages nearby there were maternities, but they were dirty, and they had to deliver on a table—a *naked table!* No, I couldn't work like that.

"I saw different work in Kenya," Agi said suddenly. "It was work *without* doctors. We prepared the woman, we examined her months before. They got a card and they chose whether to give birth there or not. Premature births were not allowed, those having their first baby, and I think, after the fifth child were not allowed. So, it was only the second, third, fourth or fifth delivery. It was around Nairobi—in French they call it *dome-ville*—a slum. There were women of three tribes: Kikuiis, Luo, and the Masaii, and all these women were so different. Everything depends on the tribe, there. So, it was sort of, 'We are the leaders, the Kikuii women.' Then we had the Luo: large, very, very black people, strong—and you couldn't even see that she was delivering. Then, the Masaii: those tribes, they have been cut... everything..." Agi sighed, "How do you call it?"

"Female genital mutilation," I said.

"Yes. So the birth was very difficult. We had to cut *open* the vagina, again, you know."

We sat in silence for a moment.

"Did they have issues with you, a white woman, delivering their babies?"

"Not so much, but the problem was I thought I'd speak English there, but everyone spoke Kiswahili, so I had to be trained first of all just to get into the language. I did it with a nun. And after six weeks, you talk every day, it's an easy language, *then* I really started working!

"What I have really tried to do with our limited means was promote hygiene—so that the mothers or mothers-to-be were clean, they had a house they could come to. They came from the slum. Friendly, but it was dirty; walking barefoot in the mud, that was normal.

"When the women came to give birth, they had to hand in their things which went into a wardrobe; they were given the key. They would bathe, and they got clothes: the Maternity House clothes were colour-coded whether she had given birth or not given birth yet. Green-red if they hadn't delivered yet, and white-green after they delivered—because, sometimes, the Luo, they went to the toilet and they came back with a baby! They were very strong.

"They stayed three days after delivery, and they had to pay, let's say, twenty-five Kenya shillings. They got food—breakfast, lunch and dinner—and after three days they had to pay, and go home," Agi said coming to a close about her time working in the birth-houses of west Africa.

"In those times in Germany," she continued, later, "those with a little courage *flew* from the little villages—Krefeld and others—because they were just too small. Our parents were conservative; we wanted liberation. We couldn't find that in the smaller towns. I remember the army coming to look for Kurt and Dieter, at your Opa's house, their family home; so Kurt left to Berlin and Dieter to Ireland.[7]

"Our parents, after World War II were concerned with rebuilding houses and towns and the economy; Kurt,

---

[7] Having a West-Berlin address meant that the army could not reach Kurt because, at that time, the Allies of World War II ruled Berlin. The German military had no authority there, until re-unification in 1989.

Dieter and I were *travellers*—there were things we were curious about. In a world of poverty, our parents didn't have that. Money, we hadn't much, but we had more than they had at our age, and we had more *time*. We worked, yes, but not to *live,* not for survival.

"As children, Kurt and Dieter had each other; I had my sister. We were part of a revolutionary generation. There was a spirit of freedom, and peace. We all lived together and moved out young, as our houses were too 'small' for us. Every night, we would go partying. These were two completely different lifestyles: our parents' and our own. They feared a lot for us. My mother suffered because of my trips as a school-girl. When I was sixteen, I went to Morocco! I *hitch-hiked*! We did things that my own mother never could've done. She nearly died of fear several times!

"It might have been because of my childhood, why I travelled so much and wanted to meet people from around the world. Growing up in small flats, our games as children, my sister and I—*we lived in another world.* There was an empty attic: a playground for our fantasies. There, we travelled all around the world," she smiled.

Agi and I continued sitting around the table, and later, she showed me round her garden. It had a sense of wilderness, and yet one could see the amount of time and love spent on it too. It was beautiful, and so colourful. "It's my yoga," she said laughing, "but I don't want to make it perfect—that's not how I want a garden to be."

Later, as she drove me to my Opa's house, we chatted about the video of Kurt's travels on the Yukon River in 1978. A German film company had recently digitised it from the slides that he'd taken, combined with his audio recordings, crossing the 3,100 kilometres by canoe, across Canada and Alaska. He and five friends had begun in Whitehorse in the Yukon territory, and planned to end their journey at Alakanuk by the Bering Sea. They hoped to travel an average of fifty miles per day, and managed to live up to this plan, while the river became their temporary home. Depending on the time spent on shorter stops and a lunch break on the river, this was an exhausting nine- to twelve-hour day paddling from camp to camp. I enjoyed watching this and did so a number of times, as, until that day with Agi, it was the clearest place I could learn something of Kurt's life—occasionally a slightly blurry picture that, nonetheless, had *motion*, and his audio recordings. It spoke to me of his curiosity and willpower, his wish to travel and take to the road (which he had done previously, overland to Asia, when he had finished school), and this time, to the water.

They were amateurs on the river, and had read a guidebook on canoeing, Kurt said. There were early accounts of their loading and unloading the canoes, trying to balance their loads, aching muscles and attacks by swarms of mosquitos. I laughed, thinking of the times I'd been unprepared when I was travelling, too, though I'd never had any great emergencies. In Kurt's film, from the footage I could make out, they seemed well-prepared in terms of provisions and had thought of all kinds of potential hazards; of course, there are bears in this territory that they might have had to contend with.

On June 1st 1978, four Canadians and my uncle Kurt set out on the Yukon. Their route ahead was long, very long—although nobody knew exactly how long it would be. "The last survey of the river had been done in 1955 and the maps were too inaccurate for our purposes," he said, though he admitted later that "nevertheless, a morning debate with all of us bending over the charts became standard procedure." Although it was too difficult to identify the numerous islands along the route, which made precise navigation impossible, they were at least able to estimate distances and predict where to watch out for landmarks. Kurt seemed a calm and organised man, good at planning and navigating; more contained than my father. Less spontaneous, he had a more reserved sense of humour; though I could hear it, it was more subtle from what I saw in the film.

Hootalinqua, at the mouth of the Teslin River (the Indian name for "where two big waters meet") was the first settlement the canoers found. It was the site of a mountain police road house for the winter hiking trail between Whitehorse and Dawson, but, at that time, Kurt said, the house was a shelter for travellers and people travelling on the river.

After only one week on the river, it had taken its toll and two of their party quit: "Two months in the bush wasn't their idea of how to spend a good summer, after all." However, they found fine replacements, because like everyone you meet in a canoe on the river, the two new men they met were heading downstream too.

They soon reached Dawson, the city of the great gold rush. In 1898, 40,000 adventurous men had struggled across the snowy Chilkoot and White Pass, then down the Yukon River in a hurry, hoping to strike gold. They made Dawson the biggest city west of Winnipeg and north of San Francisco. Two years prior to that, the site of the juncture of the Klondike and the Yukon River had been untouched wilderness—until the prospector George Carmack discovered glittering nuggets at a nearby creek.

I wondered what this must have meant to locals and their lives and homes because news spread fast of that brief luck. "It's easy today to look at the skeleton of Dawson city and imagine a long, glorious past, filled with revelry and hail-thee-well times," Kurt said. "The truth of the matter is, Dawson's heyday was but a flash in the pan. At best, it lasted two years. The prospectors left almost as fast as they had arrived." When new gold was found in Nome, Alaska, people abandoned the city by the thousands. Kurt recounts how the Carnegie Library was founded by several women, but on its completion "there was nobody left to read the books."

I found this stark imagery of abandoned hope and loss; there are similar tales of projects that were begun (and later left unfinished) in the Celtic Tiger years in Ireland—our own brief, glorious past. There are also many commuter towns without a central piece, a sense of community that binds the town into any long-term creation or connections which binds a people and place when the gold has left town, so to speak.

The canoers next destination, heading north-west, was Forty Mile. This settlement, the first in the whole

Yukon territory, was built in 1887. Similar to Dawson, nine years after its foundation people completely abandoned it—ironically for the "more promising" Dawson gold fields which had been discovered in quick succession. "Not a soul inhabits the place," Kurt said, when they arrived. The next day, they crossed the international boundary between Canada and Alaska. "Instead of flagpoles and custom houses, they found a straight sixty-foot wide clearing, cutting across the hilly landscape. Thirty feet on either side of the border have to be maintained by the US and Canada respectively."

He recounted how Alaska is stereotypically associated with snow, ice and eskimos. "For us, too, it was quite a surprise to be able to enjoy a tanning July sun in the vicinity of the Arctic circle." The water temperature became warmer, and they were able to bathe in the Yukon.

Kurt was the one who liked photos and documenting, dad said, and documented his travels in great detail. I was glad the slides had been turned into a film, it was very well done.

It was interesting that Kurt's sense of home with his companions, revolved around developing rituals and habits to cope better with the unfamiliarity and sense of the unknown that lay around every bend in the river. "The day's activities became centered around our eating schedule; but also psychologically, whenever I felt my muscles aching and my body drained of all energy, my thoughts turned to food," he said. He spoke also of the salmon run that had not yet begun, and therefore any change in their dry, basic staple diet was highly appreciated. Because they hadn't known what was ahead of them when they'd started out, they'd had to carry enough food for the entire two-month trip (their canoes were eighteen feet long; doubles).

Stars and stripes and Alaska's flag of the Little Dipper were fluttering over Fort Yukon, where they arrived next. Eight miles above the Arctic circle, this community is at the most northern tip of the Yukon river, and was established by the Hudson's Bay company. (As the first English-speaking settlement in Alaska, it was in violation of Russian sovereignty. In 1867, the US, in history's most famous land purchase, bought Alaska from the Russian Tsar for seven million dollars.)

Kurt related what he referred to as the "social climate" of Fort Yukon, which he said was "a blend of a small integrated northern community and an agglomeration of socially uprooted people who do not have anything to identify themselves with." I wondered about this: how the local history and traditions had perhaps been eroded as was their landscape, with the gold-rush; and something else: a promise, an idea, put in its place, as seemed often the case with mining and gold-rush towns, indeed with colonialism.

One evening, Kurt got a bird's-eye view of the jungle of water channels which had become the home for him and his friends as they had attempted to traverse it in their canoes. A school teacher in Fort Yukon had offered him a flight across the river flats. While in the air, the pilot confessed his history of crash landings. "He assured me that all were successful so far, so for me, I needn't have to worry," Kurt said with a measured dose of humour. And sure enough, half an hour later, they were back at Fort Yukon, the helicopter and both men still fine.

Their trip would reach the halfway point at "the nine billion dollar symbol of what some people call progressive development in modern engineering," he said. Built only several years before Kurt would have passed it in his canoe, this is the controversial Alaska oil pipeline which crosses the Yukon River. Along this route, Holy Cross is the ethnic borderline between the Athabascan Indians and the coastal Yupik Inuits. The pipeline became the subject of heated debate and protest, with five Native

Alaskan villages, alongside environmental NGOs, fighting against its construction. It caused massive displacement and danger to the Alaskan environment and associated fish and wildlife, disrupting migratory routes for caribou, and all the while ignoring the needs of Native Alaskan tribes who controlled lands along the route and whose home it had been. The other problem was that, in addition to crossing the Yukon River, about seventy-five percent of the terrain along the pipeline is what's known as permafrost, which never thaws. This meant that the pipeline would be built above ground or heavily insulated and/or buried in refrigerated ditches. Oil passing through the pipeline is hot and can potentially melt the unstable permafrost, as well as cause actual movement of the pipeline.

A long and arduous legal battle continued, and though environmental groups and Alaska Natives were unable to stop the pipeline, they were able to influence how it was built, and along the way they created a template for fighting other similar projects, including the more recent Keystone XL pipeline.[55] However, "the North American press hailed the project as a masterpiece of technology and a major achievement for Alaska," as Kurt said. The native people and the "sourdoughs" (experienced gold prospectors) Kurt spoke to were not so sure. As Kurt spoke, the flickering picture showed a lone caribou ambling across a desolate landscape, with the pipeline clearly visible, jarring and out of place. For, with its introduction, came the devastation of the natural landscape the caribou had known.

"The ecological damage caused by the pipeline and the service road running parallel to the construction would remain to upset the east-west migration of the northern caribou," he continued. "Many native people subsist on these huge herds: their lives are centered around the migration pattern of these animals. Hence, the pipeline would not only cause ecological damage, but also socially uproot many true Northerners. Whether a gold rush or an oil rush, any uncontrolled development inspired by a quick profit motive is likely to cause damage to the delicate ecological and social balance of the North," Kurt spoke into the rolling audio recording.

On their way downriver in Nulato, Kurt recounts how they met "Jesus on the raft." An old Inuit woman had given the man that name after having seen him drifting by on his oil drum raft, clothed in a long robe, a plastic bag over his head as protection against the mosquitoes, and all the while, reportedly playing the strangest melodies on his silver flute.

Reportedly, in Circle, Alaska, 950 miles upstream, Jesus, completely broke, had made up his mind to raft down the Yukon. Everything—the material for the raft, his food, and a revolver—was donated by the people of Circle, who were glad to be rid of their "strange guest." A few miles downstream from Holy Cross, "Jesus on the raft found new friends among the Inuits," Kurt said, a splash of humour evident in his voice at this strange coming together of words and clichés.

Eventually, the crew reached Alakanuk at the mouth of the Yukon River, where everything is flat, swampy, and in danger of erosion. Here, the river culture ends and a new coastal culture begins. The Inuits don't have any fish wheels or traplines—they go out on the Bering Sea to scan the horizon for whales and seals. Out here, was a whole new world "awaiting discovery," but, for the time being it was inaccessible to the four river canoeists who had to rely on the downstream current to take them only as fast as it ever goes. They reached Alakanuk, after their start at Whitehorse eight weeks before, exhausted but happy. They had had the motivation and willpower to make it; the relief in Kurt's voice and in their achievement was audible after the gruelling workout of their muscles.

And then?

"It was time to celebrate with the Yukon River's very own gourmet delight: salmon steaks." After that, they would sell their boats to the Inuits and fly back to Anchorage by bush plane—the only link to the outside in northern and western Alaska, other than the Yukon river which had become their home, for a total of eight weeks.

16.

Ní bhíonn in aon rud ach seal

I had no idea my making contact with Agi and my landing her on Opa's doorstep would bring me where it did. He had, in fact, not recognised me at first, when I stood in the doorway beside Agi. He'd suddenly laughed then, stepping back, "Ah, *Agi!* And... *Ciara!*" Later, he told me that it was because he had never thought he would see us two women standing beside each other on his doorstep. He hadn't thought we would ever make contact with each other, and thought his eyes were playing tricks on him. The next day he said he had things he wanted to tell me. "Maybe we can sit down and do that, while you're here?"

That same afternoon, Opa placed a large, black, leatherbound book—or what I thought was a book—on the table.

It turned out to be Kurt's 250 page MA thesis, dated 1980, from the University of Manitoba in Canada: "Problems and contradictions of the transition to socialism in post-colonial, peasant-based societies and the case of Ujamaa-socialism in Tanzania."[56]

I rifled through it, feeling excited to finally have something he had written—and about Tanzania! I'd wanted to read this since Opa had mentioned it a year before.

Next morning, Opa came out of his room—"*Ciara, Ich bin verschlafen,*" he said. (I slept in.) I laughed—it wasn't even eight am, and Opa is ninety-one years old! Nevertheless, a half hour later, he was on his way downstairs (having had his breakfast and watched the morning news, as he does every morning) for his *Runde,* his daily four kilometre walk. Apparently, that walk takes him around the world every seventeen years, give or take a few days if you take into account the earth's circumference, he said, smiling.

Opa had said that there were letters and things belonging to Kurt that he wanted to go through, and that he wanted to get rid of some of them, but "Not just in a landfill, and I think you are the right person for that. You're not so close like Dieter, like your father is, to all this. It's easier for you, I think." I understood what Opa meant and agreed that I would help, if I could. We suddenly laughed then because he said, "*Dein Vater, er will die Welt verändern die ganze Zeit.*" (Your father, he wants to change the world all the time.)

It wasn't clear whether he thought that a good or bad thing, or didn't mind either way. "He has too much energy," Opa said. "He wants to go out and about all the time."

And then I laughed, because, of course, I saw myself in that too, though perhaps in a different way, growing up in another time and country to my father. There are varied forms of activism, and I think each have their place and are as powerful as the next, regardless whether that's poetry or direct action, growing food or spraying graffiti. I thought about Kurt and my father in this, too. I knew that they had both been radical in their time: they had independently refused to join the army at conscription time, Kurt had received a scholarship to study an MA in the Department of Sociology in the University of Manitoba, in Winnipeg, and that my father, with some friends in his late teens, had taken in young people in need of foster-care into their house. He'd also started a car-mechanics business with another friend, where they had fixed and re-used old car parts.

Opa brought various letters, envelopes and documents to the table, explaining what he could of each. There was one note in particular that he thought Kurt had had with him on that last journey out of Kinshasa. He thought Kurt had written it hastily, after the crash, but before he died: his death hadn't been instant.

"There were things that needed to be done, that perhaps we were to take care of," Opa said. "Perhaps he'd had the time to do that. Like Agi, here, that is her number. The words and telephone numbers were written here because he knew somehow that we—his mum and I—would later have them, would hold that piece of paper, and it would be important."

There was silence for a moment. Opa sat watching me surrounded by notes, papers and books spread about the table. I dug out the dictionary and German *Worterbuch* (thesaurus) and started jotting down words which I didn't understand in the official letters I was reading.

"You… you have the makings of a journalist."

I looked up, "I suppose I am one, at the moment." I began to realise that it was important to me, too, for my understanding of my own roots and what came before me.

While Opa cooked us a lunch of cauliflower, potatoes, carrots and onions, I pored over maps and letters, official documents and postcards that Kurt had written or which had been sent to him. Most were of his last months or weeks, though others were dated 1980, and many of the postcards had been sent from Canada. There was a report from his primary school, with teacher's comments each school-year semester, all saying, like Oma had, that he was studious and dedicated. I'd always known that dad and his brother were different, but I was only beginning to understand how much, and in as first-hand a way as would ever be possible.

There were Kurt's UNHCR documents and identity cards, travel passes and visas—many of those. I noticed the irony in his UN identity card being "the property of the United Nations" and not his own—like a passport, which is the property of the state. There were postcards, letters, a photo. There were legal items, too, following his death, much of which I knew had not provided many answers to my family's distressing situation after the accident. There was an account by the truck driver Kurt had got a lift with, who had survived—the driver had leaned down to pick up a music tape and had lost control of the vehicle; there had been no seatbelts, or Kurt's hadn't been fastened. My family had been left with little information; and as Kurt died while travelling near Bangui, the capital of the Central African Republic, and had only been in his role with UNHCR in Kinshasa for two years, it was very difficult to form a picture of what had happened. The documents indicating his death were rudimentary; there was no internet or direct access to speak to officials or Kurt's colleagues. I knew that Kurt had communicated normally with his parents by way of postcards and letters. Many items were either in English or another foreign language to my grandparents, and in true *Amtssprache* style: bureaucratic and impersonal—the time, the date, the name of the truck driver, the location of the accident.

Apart from my father's visit and travels with him in early 1985 in Kenya, nobody had visited Kurt's work place, and Agi had spent the most time with him in years previous, though only when travelling. I wasn't sure my grandparents had wanted to visit him in Zaire, or whether it'd been possible at that time, given the level of conflict there: they were not seasoned travellers.

It felt very sad to be leafing through the few remains of Kurt's personal items and belongings; I had never met Kurt and knew him only from our family's memories and anecdotes, photos and a CD of his slides in his student years. Were these the last remaining clues to his life and what happened in Zaire?

I'd asked Opa if we could go to Kurt's grave. It'd been a few years since I'd gone there, and it hadn't meant anything like I thought it might now.

We took the flowers Agi had given us from her garden and drove the short distance. It was a sunny and peaceful day at the cemetery.

I stood at his grave, and looked at what seemed like a little equatorial forest: ants nestled into the little twigs and leaves, who soldiered on and around the bumps and crevices in the soil, a creeper plant that had grown over most of the grave, ferns poking out of the middle of that, and the yellow dahlias and a sunflower we'd brought from Agi's garden.

I looked at the silvery web in front of me, the spider upside down inside it, a red squirrel that hopped across the grass between the graves and little trees that had been planted by families and friends of loved ones. Some trees had grown quite tall, depending on how long ago the grave had been dug. There was a big one just to the left of Kurt's grave, and the one by his was much taller than me: Oma had planted it long ago.

I put an acorn in the ground near the deep pink flowers that grew at the head of the gravestone and noticed the words, *Des Bleibens ist eine kleine Zeit…* etched onto a gravestone nearby. *To be is but a short time.* Words I'd heard my Irish grandfather say, too: *Ní bhíonn in aon rud ach seal.*

I stayed a little longer, on my own before turning round and walking back.

"Did you pray there?" Opa asked, when I found him on the path.

I nodded and shook my head at the same time. I didn't say anything aloud. What had I done there? It wasn't an easy question to answer to anyone, even myself. I'd spoken to Kurt, and had felt something or someone speak to me in response. In many meditations, and in shamanic work, I had often sensed someone's presence or their spirit and been able to communicate. Words *arose* in my mind, and suddenly they were there as though they had always been, like how poetry comes when I walk outside or when meditating. Distinctly different than my own thoughts, it was not a voice, either, but simply, *words.*

"That's good," Opa said. "Because I don't pray."

Some days before (at 10pm, an unfortunate time for me) Opa had asked me did I follow any religion, and did I believe in God. I knew from the way the question was phrased, that this was a god with a capital letter. I knew him well enough to know I wouldn't upset him with my views whichever answer I gave. I had never felt a need to be part of any religion, and was atheist for many years. Perhaps, if asked to choose, I would say I'm pagan and have often felt drawn to Zen Buddhism—but, really, do not follow any religion at all.

"Well, do you believe in the afterlife? Do you believe in God?"

I thought for a moment about how, in national school we'd been asked to "draw God." We were about eleven at the time, and my classmates were making their Confirmation; my friends and I, who had recently moved from Steiner school to national school, were not, as we were either not religious or not Catholic, and didn't have to draw anything.

This in itself was very interesting—that we didn't need to draw—but I'd thought the whole situation in general, fascinating: most people drew an almost identical man in white robes, with sandals and a beard. I didn't care much for religion, though it wasn't that the image was right or wrong to me, but rather that I recognised that it was an *idea*, a replicated one—it hadn't been made personal, it hadn't been questioned by those young minds. Had god an image? What *was* god, anyway? If He, She or It (if we want to think of it in this way) had an image or a form to one person, why should this image be imposed on other people? Why would anyone accept someone else's image? Wasn't everyone's image or imagination and spiritual experience their *own,* a direct experience, and therefore "purer" (a favourite word in Catholicism) anyway?

And how could something so personal and transcendental as spiritual experiences be subjected to our mundane, analytical and confused minds, which thought only in terms of what's possible and what's known, rational and explainable? Perhaps, through organised religion, our allowing this—the mind to rule and win—over time had permitted one image or experience to be dismissed in favour of another?

I understood that religion or faith provides a kind of home, a way to live and be and understand ourselves in the world. But to me it wasn't fully realised if it went unquestioned and had already answered all the "big questions" when it arrived in our lives: organised, intellectual and abstract. Wasn't it about experiences, our relationship with the world? Wasn't it about wonder and humility, and asking why, how?

Finally, I began to come out of my reverie, and to answer Opa.

"I know we are not alone," I said. "Ever. The world to me is sentient and interacts with us, and it is so synchronous there is *something*—some consciousness, or energy—beneath it, taking part in our lives and our joy. But I don't think of this as being a "God" and certainly not in the Christian sense of the word—someone who sits above and watches us—but simply as a Universe that is mystical or sacred, and not wholly random."

Opa agreed that there seemed to be something at work in the world, that appeared to us as synchronicity. He had not taken any great interest in organised religion, and our views seemed to be quite in agreement, though approached and reached from different places. Though Opa and I had never felt a need to discuss religion or theology before, some of Opa's family members (my father's cousins) were missionary workers who had lived in Pakistan for over twenty years, doing community development work and aid, building houses and shelters.

I discovered that Opa had begun reading theology books as well as those that exposed some of the scandals of the Catholic church. He had been born into a Protestant family in a conservative area of south-west Germany, and though many of his family are deeply religious, he lost interest in it very young and was atheist. His mind had opened in regard to many things and this was why he wanted to talk to me about faith and religion. He said that there were things he'd never considered before.

It was interesting having these conversations, particularly as it challenged my German, but also because I had never had such deep conversation with my grandfather before. It made me wonder about my place in the world in a spiritual sense. For Opa, though still very active and healthy for his age, he was ninety-two, and had begun to look back, over the years. He wanted to reflect on some of the bigger questions about life and what it had taught him. Religion, faith and theology hadn't featured much in his life since he had left home at a young age. Now, he had time and was interested in finding ways to expand his way of living and being in the world. It was not going to be radical; these were gentle, last changes and reflections to his thoughts and his choice of reading.

17.

"A piece of my story"

From Germany, I flew to Malta, where I had to do my last exams at University.

It was now September. It was funny to think it was just four months since I'd lived there and called it home. It was different now, with sweltering heat and humidity.

I met Amanuel for some last clarification on everything he had told me. I was at Portomaso complex, in Paceville, a place I used to frequent at the back of the Hilton Hotel, where the fish swam round in circles, and the sun, if you were there early enough, sparkled on the water as it shone through the pillars and lit parts of the water not in the shade. I'd always found it a peaceful and meditative place. When Amanuel arrived, I was standing by the edge watching the fish swim and glide through the water so gracefully, their tails swaying from side to side.

"Sometimes I wonder what I'm doing telling you all this, you know?" he said. "My story, well, who's going to relate to it, who *can* relate to it? People from Ireland, have they had the same experiences? Probably not. So, it's

Eritreans! Others will *relate,* maybe, but they cannot *know* and that's the difference: I lived it."

"Yes, and we cannot take that away from you. Your story is still just that: *yours*; your story. We have only a little of it, a window into it."

"I am a refugee. I live the *life* of a refugee—and that's not easy."

"No, it's not," I said quietly.

"But, somehow, you are kind of a refugee too," he said suddenly laughing.

I waited for him to go on, but he didn't.

"Well," I joked, "I've lived in a tent, but, no, that would be disrespectful. I've always had *choices,* privileges, though I've often had little money. It's different—I've always been able to move freely." And then, more seriously, "I want to thank you for telling me your story."

We were quiet as we walked, until Amanuel said, "I don't want people to think of me as a refugee, I want them to think of me as a human—just like anyone else, just like them. I have dreams, wishes, and hopes—just like you. Only thing is that I do it another way: I had to leave my country first. My country, my government, did not show me respect. I respect myself, so I left."

We walked farther into Portomaso harbour, and out on to the rocks by the sea, and watched the clouds. It was overcast, unusual for Malta, and rain was on the way.

"You have a piece of it, a piece of my story. You have started, and now I will have to do the rest sometime: *Life of Amanuel*," he said, trailing his hand across the sky in front of him, mimicking the *Life of Pi,* a book he liked.

"Yeah," I said joking, "and then your life will be finished. You can put it away in a box, and you'll be able to tell your grandchildren—"

"Just look in that box, *that's my life!*" we both said, laughing.

Amanuel was becoming interested in writing and art since he'd got to know me. He had painted and sketched as a child, and he wanted to start creating things again, he said. I told him to start with *The Artist's Way* and *Morning Pages*— three pages free-hand, free-flow, when he woke up: no editing, no thinking.

I asked Amanuel about the positive aspects of his country, about what made Eritreans feel Eritrean, and *proud*.

He thought for a moment, then said, "Community. We want to help each other out. You know, if I told my family back at home, 'Oh I have this friend Ciara,' they would be hospitable, they'd really take care of you. We are very quick like that, we don't need time. There isn't this, 'Oh, she's different than us,' there is this *curiosity*. Between *us* we might arrive at a point of discrimination between our tribes, but not to foreigners. Foreigners are safe in our country. We might think, 'Oh, you are a tourist, and have a lot of money because you are in our country,' but that is normal, I think.

"There are nine different tribes, nine different cultures and nine languages in Eritrea," Amanuel added. "I cannot relate myself to some of these tribes. Me, I am Tigrania tribe. We are hard-workers, and quick learners. We want to *make it*. When there are hard moments, we will deal with it. It's part of our history: the war, the hard times...

"My father, my family, lived through this. I remember what they had to endure: I was born in 1986 — we still hadn't got our independence; that was in 1991. We deal with hard times in a very unique way. 1961 to 1991, we proved it to the world—we can do it! Those were the years of the ethnic regime: the Soviet Union *and* the US were supporting Ethiopia to fight against us. It was a struggle. Ethiopia was backed by the Soviet Union with all their tanks, and financially, too. So, I think that makes us proud—we did it on our own."[8]

Later, I thought about what Amanuel had said. He was right of course. It was true—I couldn't know, I could scarcely even imagine what his life had been like at the Unit, what he'd endured. I'd said that from my perspective there are many of us in the West who *want* to know and change the dialogue and injustices. He told me a little of his life in the Unit.

"When I think of it, the heat—much more than here," he gestured. "The desert, and the uniform from top to toe: long and heavy, and a backpack, maybe ten kilos. Sometimes we got no water, when we were training. You know, we had two litres for *fifteen* of us. Every three hours we got a sip and that was it. We were up at 4am, and outside, ready to go at 5:30. And all the time, of course, they counted us—three times a day because there were many who fled, who ran away. So, we had to stand, like a battalion, you know, and they'd count us.

"We had to build shelter for the new ones being recruited, so we carried rocks. I remember one day we'd to carry wood and it dropped right on my foot," he pointed

---

[8] Eritrea officially celebrated its Independence on May 24, 1991, when the Eritrean People's Liberation Front defeated the Ethiopian government.

at a tiny white scar. "It got swollen right away, because the blood didn't escape, it couldn't burst out," he said indicating a vein near the top. "But, still, it *looked* ugly, so I..." Amanuel mimicked falling backwards, fainting. "One of my colleagues, they rubbed it, and it was okay then, the swelling went down. I am lucky to still have my two feet, that I'm not blind or something worse. There are so many in the military who never get out, so many veterans without limbs, without..." he trailed off and was quiet for a moment.

I asked about men who had family.

"Oh, you got to go twice a year. Imagine! It's so much worse if you have a child or a wife. It's a mess, it's really a mess."

At Portomaso, the sea got wilder and rain clouds were coming in quicker now. I asked Amanuel about the faith or religious groups he'd mentioned in Malta, and whether he had joined any. I knew that spirituality was important to him.

"I don't trust them, don't want to join religious groups," he said. "I want to use my *own* mind, you know. I'm afraid I would end up closed-minded. But trust me, this spiritual thing is important for me, in my life. Following this path, it makes life easier: you become a good person because if not you do the things that destroy your life—like drugs. It gives me the strength and the will to hold my heart. It is something I can shape my life with, guard my heart with this kind of knowledge.

"Spirituality is an *experience*—*your* experience," he added. "I cannot explain, or make you believe something unless you experience it. There are things you will not understand that I'm trying to tell you. I think about this a lot, read about it a lot, but people are like, 'What's *that*?!' They want to talk about science and the economy..."

I smiled then, agreeing, "That's an exceptional thing you've realised: *I cannot make you believe something unless you experience it. There are things you will not understand.*"

Later that week, I went with Amanuel to a faith meeting he'd invited me to, as I thought it important to give representation to this side of his story, though it was new to him. Every Friday, this group gathered for more sociable events, like films or going to the beach. This was the first time Amanuel had gone; there was a BBQ and songs, and people shared their stories of how they had each come to believe in Jesus Christ, or God. They'd also played ball games, and sat around in the warm evening sun and sand.

Afterward, Amanuel and I sat outside his house in Sliema. Both of us are blessed—or cursed, it depends on the perspective—with analytical minds that are forever questioning, asking why and how. I was interested in what Amanuel had thought of it. As I sat looking up at the night sky above me, the fig tree branches poking out over the concrete wall, its roots growing in and around the cracks, he asked me what I thought of the faith evening.

"It's not something I actually *need*," I said quietly.

"Why though?" he asked. "Don't you think you've got to have faith, got to believe in something?"

"There are parts of it that are beautiful," I replied. "But apart from all the atrocities and wars, the ways that religion is used to justify certain actions with half-truths and manipulation, I still don't need it. I'm happy that they have found something they love and that brings them happiness—something to believe in, I suppose. But that's different, I think, than spirituality and direct experiences that we can have without anyone organising it, for me, for anyone. I pray already—I mean, I have my own prayers. And to me, it's not something I *believe*: I know, or I see, or I sense it. I think that's different than faith. Like you said— it's an experience. And, it's nature for me, too."

I looked at Amanuel as I finished speaking.

He nodded, "It is nice for people, but there was too much left unanswered for me, too much I can't accept, taking another's person's word if I have not experienced it myself."

I knew from what Amanuel read, and our conversations (for we had had many) that he often thought about how he lives in the world, how his mind works; how to cultivate hope in the face of everything that sometimes held him back. I enjoyed our conversations and felt that he did too.

I thought that oftentimes faith, and hopefully religion, was a place that the soul and spirit reside and shine and call to us from. And yet as soon as it's "finished" or "complete," when we have stopped questioning and seeking, it's done, it's no longer *alive*. As the poet David Whyte says, "The world is too compassionate for that"—to be finished, immovable. It is always changing. In other words, in a way, it is always incomplete. We can be comfortable in our own skin, at home in ourselves, but if we've lost our curiosity in the world and our deeper place in it, then we have lost everything.

There was something far more important to me than following an organised religion: making my own way, and discovering my own prayers along the way. And, for Amanuel, it was using and understanding his own mind.

18.

"Poetry is dangerous"

Later that week, after the late-night discussion on faith and prayers with Amanuel, the following evening I went to the annual Malta Mediterranean Literature Festival, as I wanted to break my studying for exams. Within a few moments of arriving, I was buzzing with excitement: there were little children dancing and there was music, but most exciting to me was the poetry, in particular, a cardboard stand bearing small blue, black and maroon-red booklets: *Passaports*, by Antoine Cassar.

I asked for Antoine at the bookstall and sat down to wait, listening to a woman on stage. Suddenly, Antoine was beside me—I recognised him (his dark brown eyes and Mediterranean complexion) from the photos I'd seen months before on his website, after my performance at *f'Darhom* in Valletta. When I'd read the *Times of Malta* articles by Frontex (EU border agency) about migration, I'd begun researching online to find activists and artists who were also engaged in awareness-raising and creating solutions. I was delighted and amazed that, with no effort of mine, we had unexpectedly managed to meet.

We introduced ourselves, walking away from the crowd so that we could hear each other, where we sat down beside a palm tree. I told him about *Integra* and the works I'd written and performed in May, and we arranged to meet in Valletta in a week.

Talking with Antoine made my memories of *f'Darhom*, four months before, come streaming back: the music, lights and decks spinning, my nervous heartbeat when I'd rapped and performed. I'd had certain thoughts, poems and memoirs as my starting point, though I didn't know to what until *Integra* had emerged. Things were different now and had become... bigger. That was why I'd forgotten about the poems and their being a pivotal point, the centre from which everything else had come.

Antoine was next to go on stage. We shook hands, and I sat down on the warm ground by a large stone at the front of the audience.

The *Passaport*, alongside Antoine's other work[57] had fascinated me ever since I'd found it online: *Passaport* is a poem published in the form of an "anti-passport," dedicated to those whose lives are or have been affected by border regimes and migration law. Translated into nine languages since its birth in 2009, it has also been made into a theatre production, often accompanied by local performers or artists around the world. *Merħba,* ("Welcome") another of Antoine's works, had been awarded the United Planet Writing Prize contest, and more recently *Mappa tal-Meditteran,* a Maltese poem in sixteen stanzas describing the shapes of the Mediterranean Sea, its coastlines and some of its major and minor islands, in relation to the early and modern histories and migrations of the Mediterranean peoples.

On stage, Antoine was speaking: "A Syrian boy paints houses on his tent—And people cross borders since borders crossed people!"

There was a spattering of laughter at this, as the absurdity rang true and was touched on in us with his words. Everybody had a story of not being accepted, of moving, and everyone could relate. If we consider our evolution, we have all moved, forever, since the beginning: humanity *is* migration, is movement.

The emotion in his twelve-page poem *Passaport* was tremendous, and there were spurts of both laughter and outrage throughout the piece. He was joined by a number of other writers who had translated *Passaport* into their own language and spoke extracts in their native tongue. A French man, Karl, read; his voice rang gently in the air, like it would've carried over and calmed the sea, rolling in with the waves, carrying precariously small boats with hopes of reaching shore not far from here.

In solidarity with fellow citizens and villagers of the world who, with or without a passport, do not enjoy the fundamental right to leave their country or to return home (Article 13 of *The Universal Declaration of Human Rights*), nor the fundamental right to request asylum from persecution (Article 14), the *Passaport Project* represents a call for action and participation, and an important space for dialogue.

> *"Valid for all peoples, and for all landscapes. For all citizens and villagers of flesh and blood, wherever they were born. Your worth is not proportional to the population of your country. Entry free of duty, no need for a stamp or visa, the doors are unscrewed from the jambs."* [58]

At each presentation of *Passaport*, audience members are invited to bring along their passports or any other form of ID, to symbolically "renounce" their nationalities during the recital. All documents are hung from a migrants' "tightrope" on stage, and returned by hand at the end of the performance. (Antoine prefers the word *voyager*, as unfortunately "migrant" has taken on a dirty connotation in many people's mind.) This tightrope can be imagined as the space through which a voyager will travel from one side to the other: from danger to safety. What we do—or don't do—in Europe, determines the safety of those concerned or whether they reach any safety at all. Amanuel's voice rang in my mind: "*I have dreams, wishes, and hopes—just like you. The only thing is that I do it another way. I had to leave my country first.*"

It was here, at the Malta Mediterranean Literature Festival, that I met Anna Szabo, poet, writer, essayist and translator.

"Poetry is dangerous, see!" she said laughing when she'd almost tripped over the wires on stage.

"I was raised to be afraid of borders," she continued. "I grew up in a dictatorship in Romania. My young son, recently he was in transit through customs—and he was eating a croissant, as he got searched. He stood there, and he was happy! *We raised a son who is not afraid of borders!*"

The weight of her words felt monumental in the warm Mediterranean air.

I introduced myself to Anna during the break, while the band, *KantiLene,* played on stage. "He is twelve years old, this son," she said, and the incident with the croissant had been in an American airport.

"Many people—displaced people—are coming to Romania, but they are not staying there; they pass through. We are in..." she trailed off, not finding the word she sought.

"In transit?" I suggested.

"Yes. To somewhere else. *Absurdistan,* we call it. Eastern Europe.

"Let me tell you a story, a story about migration. I don't know if it's true or not, but it's something I've heard, and I think, more and more, that it's possible it is true. There was an old lady who used to watch and wait at the border. Watching voluntarily I mean. And then she'd catch them, the people who were crossing, and give them to the police, to the authorities. And she was *proud,* like they were animals or something. Proud, for this...

"And let me tell you something else: I was at the Berlin Wall, I went with my husband and his mother. And my mother-in-law, when she stepped over it, she stood there, looking at it—this line of rubble and bricks—and she said, 'It is this thing, this *thing* which made our life *hell!*'" Anna said, angry.

We sat for a few moments in silence.

"What Antoine is saying is really important, very…"

"Poignant?"

"Yes. Because sometimes borders cross people, but people don't cross borders."

Speaking to Antoine had reminded me of my performance pieces in Valletta which had led to my writing *Integra*, but something else had brought me back to the core or origin of *Integra* the day before too: my father had sent an email with a link to *Solo Andata* (*Going Alone*) and their song, "The Uncountable"[59] dedicated to the many thousands of people who were trying to reach Europe, fleeing his or her country. It was made in collaboration with Amnesty International in 2014, and had been sung by an Italian band who had recently played at the Kilkenny Arts Festival, where my father had heard them. The song opens with the words *the uncountable(s)* and the video's imagery was both stunning and heartbreaking at once. Its message, and opening line, resonated with how I'd felt when I'd written *Migration Pressure Ballistics*, the main piece I had brought to the performance at *f'Darhom*. It was a direct response to the article that fuelled my research in anger at its impersonal and statistical nature.

The song and video displayed the horrific violence

created by our system of border control and defence. As South-American activist and educator Harsha Walia states in her book *Undoing Border Imperialism,* "Border controls are most severely deployed *by* those Western regimes that create mass displacement, and are most severely deployed *against* those whose very recourse to migration results from the ravages of capital and military occupations."[60]

My father had sent another link: refugees who had been detained for *fourteen* years in a detention centre in Limerick, Ireland. *Fourteen years—more than half my life!* This seemed as unacceptable as what Amanuel had told me about fishermen in Italy who were being penalised for saving drowning refugees. "There are so many," he said, "that they are being told they cannot, or must not, save them." I thought at first that I had misheard him—this seemed absurd and absolutely inhumane. I'd thought, somewhat naively perhaps, that we—law or refugee policy, *someone, something*—wouldn't allow people be penalised for saving refugees in danger of losing their lives, and make precisely that level of persecution illegal, not the *saving* of people illegal. What had happened to the *Universal Declaration of Human Rights*? What had happened to our humanity?

No matter how many people, and no matter how

long it takes, it was never acceptable, or even (to my mind) possible, to let someone drown if their life could be saved. It seemed to me that there was an idea about who was worthy of being saved and who was not. Perhaps because of refugees' "precarious legal status" and lack thereof in the labour force, as Harsha Walia states they are cast as "eternal outsiders: *in* the nation-state but not *of* the nation-state."[61]

As the last scene of *Solo Andata* played, wrenching and heartbreaking, Amanuel said, "But it is just what one does, isn't it? We are human, and that's what human beings do: help each other out."

"Yes, that's what I hope," I said quietly, willing myself to believe our words.

19.

Passaports "in ocean blue, or dried blood red, or coal black ready for burning"

Antoine and I were at the harbour in Valletta, the wind whipping at our faces and napkins on the table. I asked him to tell me how the *Passaport Project* had come about.

"It's a very long story... Where do I begin?" he said, smiling. "For a long time, I had a half-idea to publish a poem in the form of a passport—whether it was going to be travel poetry or something similar.

"Then in November 2009, I was travelling with a backpack in South America. On the border between Peru and Bolivia, in a small village called Cassani (a quaint little village on Lake Titicaca) I had my Maltese passport in hand and I was waiting to leave Peru and enter Bolivia. When it was finally my turn, I handed my Maltese passport to the soldier. He studied it, his eyes bulging out. He said, 'Malta?!' looking around at his colleagues.

Antoine continued to proclaim "Malta! Malta! MALTA!" each time his voice rising, and each time my respect rising in turn. He was expressive, and I admired this.

"So, I got a bit nervous," he said. "There was another soldier by a desk in the corner, he got excited all of a sudden. He banged his hand on the table, and said '*Malta!*'"—Antoine's voice rose dramatically in pitch.

"He was excited. The reason why he was so happy, I realised, was that next to him, sellotaped to the table, there was a list of countries, and next to each country the price of the visa. Until a couple of weeks before, what I had seen on the internet was that Maltese citizens didn't have to pay to enter Bolivia at the time. But, a new bilateral agreement or disagreement came into force, and so, as a Maltese citizen, I had to pay fifty-five US dollars. I was almost certain that he was trying to bribe me, but later on I realised that it was true.

"He said a number with all these syllables, '*Quatro ciento noventa y ocho bolivianos.*' 'How much money is that?' I wondered! He said, 'You can pay in US dollars, it's fifty-five US dollars, but you have to give me the exact amount, because we give no change.'

"So, fifty-five US dollars. I had a $100 dollar bill! So, twenty minutes negotiating with other people in the queue—most of them from the US—and explaining each time, 'I'm from Malta. It's a small island in the Mediterranean. No, it's not South America; it's not Greece;

245

no, it's not part of the UK.' I don't think I ever gave so many geography lessons in such a short time. But, they helped me. I got the change, and so I managed to get in.

"My travelling companion at the time (she was from the Czech Republic) got in free with a visa for ninety days. My visa was only thirty days. But the worst part was the humiliation—being put in the spotlight because my passport was strange. There was a cute little lady married to a US citizen, she wasn't even allowed in, for some reason. Some people had it worse, and this is not even the tip of the iceberg.

"This kind of rekindled my resentment for passports in general. I mean, when you're small, when you're in school, or maybe in films, in poetry, in stories, there's this romantic idea of the passport. We think, today, that the passport gives you freedom: to travel, and discover, and broaden your horizons. But just scratch under the surface and you realise that the whole system of global passports is there *not* to give freedom, but to take it away from people who are not wanted. Because they don't have enough money in their wallet or bank account. Or, as our Prime Minister would say, people who don't have enough talent! He was saying in New York last week— giving a conference about the IAP, the sale of Maltese passports to rich people from Russia and Saudi Arabia and China—'We don't want your money, we want your *talent*.'"

Antoine and I laughed at the absurdity of the minister's claim, before he continued.

"So that was kind of the thorn that spurred me to write a passport not only of travel poetry, and not only about myself and my own fears and desires. A utopian passport, yes. It's a dream: poetry allows you to dream. But poetry also allows you to work towards your dream.

"I spent about a month-and-a-half researching different global passports and the politics of immigration in different countries, and all the absurdities and atrocities I could find. One very useful book was published by Peter Stalker: *The No-Nonsense Guide to Global Migration*. It's a small green book that came out about six or seven years ago. When I wrote the poem, it took me about two weeks. I practically didn't sleep. I was going to work like a zombie. Going to work, writing, postponing the work I was supposed to do.

"Obviously it's a very political poem, but it's also a love poem; a love poem to humanity, but also to one specific cause that at the time was inspiring me.

"Then, in December 2009, I presented it in Mdina in Malta. I found a lot of support from different people, many people I didn't know, like actors, musicians. Since then, the project has been growing slowly but steadily, with new translations. There's also a theatre adaptation in France, which is going to be touring France from November onwards.

"There was a theatre adaptation here in Malta, as well. Erin Tanti, half-Maltese half-Irish, who made the Maltese theatrical production of *Passaport*, adapted the poem for a festival in Santa Venera, where it was awarded Best Production and Best Actress. It happened to be the first production in Maltese that had ever taken part in that festival. Linguistically it also had an effect, an impact.

"One of the most important developments has been a collaboration with associations, NGOs, and collectives in different countries. Here, it's the *Integra Foundation*, *Konnect Kulturi*, and in nine other countries there were local associations that I collaborated with by organising readings, or they sell the *Passaport* themselves and keep half of the profits, or I send them donations from the online sales."

I asked Antoine did he have any idea when he produced *Passaport*, that this was the direction it would take, what it would become?

"No," he said, "I didn't imagine that, five years later

I would still be travelling, now and again, with *Passaport*. This summer, I was in Sarajevo, at a conference on refugee law, where they had invited me to perform the poem in the closing ceremony. That was a great experience, I met a lot of experts in migration.

"These collaborations are beautiful. I make such good friends. For me, *Passaport* is not *my* project. It's like a loose collective. The danger is that the project becomes so aware of itself that I distance myself from the poem. That is something that I hope won't happen. Before each performance I have to re-read the poem a couple of times to remind myself of the emotion that I felt at the time when I was writing it, but also the emotion that I feel when I'm reading the newspapers or hearing racist comments here in Malta."

"In relation to that," I said, "there were many parts of the poem that contain lots of double meanings, like 'dried blood red,' 'black coal ready for burning,' and 'ocean blue.' Of course, those words are what brings me into the text, because I can see it, and I can feel it or hear it or smell it, because it's so related to the subject of the poem."

"Yes," he said, "and I wanted it to be a physical poem. I like poetry to be touchable, to feel it on your skin... The first stanza, which is probably the most metaphorical and lyrical part, describes the human face via landscape. I wrote that part while I was walking in Patagonia, in Chile. So, I was completely immersed in nature at the time. Then that tedious list that you have in the fifth and longest stanza—you know the list of absurdities, that crescendo of absurd things that shouldn't be necessary in order to travel—was patchwork, different elements that I took from here and there. The metaphors would come on their own. And then there's the sensual part, especially in the end, that came from the heart."

I asked Antoine about the symbol on the front of the passport: the goose.

"The migratory goose is simply a symbol of migration. It's not the most migratory bird in terms of kilometres that it travels, but in fairytales for example, the goose is the symbol of freedom.

"I've always been interested in migration and borders, ever since I was small," Antoine continued. "I was born in one country, with parents from another, and I've lived in four other countries apart from Malta. Ever since I got my Maltese passport at the age of twenty-four and decided to use my Maltese passport instead of my British one, I started to have more, not problems, really, but uncomfortable situations in airports.

"Once, I was in Istanbul at the airport. This was 2007. When you arrive at immigration in the arrivals area, there's a noticeboard with a list of the flags and the cost of the visa. And next to Malta, there was no number. I found out that Maltese citizens don't have to pay a visa to enter Turkey. I thought, Wow, if I had come here with my UK passport it would have cost me *more!* What happened was, when I was passing through the checkpoint, they took me to one side and left me to wait in an office for one hour, for no reason—they didn't tell me why. I could see that there were government workers there playing cards, another one was reading news on the computer. I was just sitting there. On that day I counted... Have you ever seen a real Maltese passport?" he asked suddenly.

I hadn't, so Antoine took out his passport to show me. He rifled through the visa pages, "Look how many crosses there are!" he said. It was covered, back to front with the Maltese cross symbol.

"Including the photo page and the inside cover, guess how many crosses there are?"

I guessed wrong, twice, though the second time I was only 137 off.

"There are 703! That's a lot of religious and patriotic and colonial fervour to carry in your jeans, you know! But no one talks about this. It's like people accept it: 'Yeah, that's the Maltese symbol; this is my identity—*a cross.' 703* of them!" he said, incredulous.

"The *Passaport* has some multilingual elements, but for me it's a Maltese poem," he added. "I also wrote *Merħba, a poem of hospitality*. It's a long poem, for performance. It's also kind of a graphic dance on the page. It's half monolingual in Maltese, with adaptations into English and French, and the other half is a mix of about seventy languages, with phrases taken from phrasebooks and dictionaries. Phrases like, 'Please sit down,' or 'What would you like to drink?'—all about hospitality. It's a poem that tells... not really a story, although there is a narrative element. It imagines a traveller who is being welcomed by different families in different countries, different cultures. As he goes through the poem, the hosts tell a little bit more about their dreams and despairs. One family, for example, their boy has only one leg because he stepped on a mine."

I asked Antoine some moments later, "And has the *Passaport* gone to places outside of Europe?"

"Yes—the San Francisco Poetry Festival two years ago, Panama, Nicaragua, South Korea. That was a great experience in Seoul, because it was completely spontaneous. I went to Seoul for a conference on multilingual literature, to present a paper. I thought, Okay, as I'm going to be there, let's see if I can organise a reading. I didn't know anyone there and I had five days!" he said, laughing.

"Through a website, I managed to get in contact with someone from Austria who was part of a theatre group. He got me in contact with an art gallery, and within a few days we had got together seven or eight performers: musicians, a comedian from Canada, and other poets. They also got me in contact with a local NGO in Seoul that supports refugees from North Korea. They came and gave a speech about the situation in North Korea, and how difficult it is for refugees to get out. There was one refugee who spoke for about twenty minutes about how he escaped. It took him one year. First he crossed the river into China, swimming. They were shouting at him but he got to the other side, with nothing, only his clothes. Then he managed to cross into Russia, and from Vladivostok he sailed to Japan. From Japan he travelled to Cambodia and then into Thailand. In Thailand he managed to get to the South Korean embassy, and they gave him refugee status. Since then he's been working to try and help other North Korean people get out of the country."

Antoine and I had been in Seoul around the same time, in 2010, I realised. I'd thought, and had been told while I was there, about the hostility toward South Koreans from the North, and had naïvely assumed the same could be said for North Koreans by those from the South. I was surprised and happy at the fact that there was some support being provided for North Koreans. I asked Antoine about this.

"There *is* hostility towards people who come from North Korea, in South Korea," he explained. "This NGO tries to work against it, by organising activities among young people especially.

"In the same year, I presented the *Passaport* in Hong Kong in a bookshop. That was completely spontaneous as well, organised by someone I met at the conference in Seoul. Then, I had a small tour of India, in different venues. So, it's travelling, the *Passaport*. That could help take it to North Africa. To have it translated to Tigrinya or Somalian, would be fantastic."

"I'll look into the Irish version," I smiled. "My mum has the Irish, I have the poetry. I used to speak well, though I don't now, but I must relearn it. We've adapted our own language to suit a culture that's not ours. It would actually be something interesting and important for Ireland, I think."

"I have colleagues translating into Irish where I work," Antoine said, "They're translating European law. It's difficult for them, because they have to invent lots of terminology," he laughed.

I asked Antoine about the power of literature and art in revolution and social change.

"I firmly believe in the transformative power of art and literature in general, and poetry in particular," he said. "I wrote about this a few weeks ago for *The Sunday Circle* here in Malta. It was an article that came out just before the Malta Mediterranean Literature festival, about the social dimension of poetry. I mentioned different episodes in history, even recent ones, where poetry was actually central to a social event—a protest. For example, in Tiananmen Square during the protests, the crowd was spurred on and emboldened by a poem by Bei Dao, a Chinese poet. It was a poem called 'Answer.' It's a very cryptic poem and one that blows my mind. This poem glued the people together in defiance of the regime. Recently, in Egypt during the revolution, a poet in exile, Tamim al-Barguti, the son of another poet, was faxing in poems from abroad. They were being read in Tahrir Square. A few days later, they installed a makeshift big screen and had a video connection with him; he was reciting his poetry to the masses in the square during the revolution. When Pablo Neruda died, not long after the coup of Pinochet, his funeral—which was very heavily policed—became a protest in itself. People were reciting his verses in front of the police.

"That's what's *visible*. That's what you can see in terms of how poetry can be active in pushing social change.

"On the other side," he continued, "below the surface, on a more individual level, when you're reading a poem, if you're receptive to it then it works on your consciousness. It can have long-term effects that are not measurable, and probably not even followable, because you may have forgotten a certain poem that you read, but it affected you and shifted your perspective somehow.

"Whenever someone says that poetry is useless... okay, you can't open a bottle of wine with a poem, or a can of tuna, but you can write a poem about how to open a can of tuna. Poetry is not useless at all."

I smiled. I liked this, the way Antoine thought about the world, and about poetry. He had great humour and passion, and a sense of hope and defiance despite the reasons we sat at a windswept table together: increasing migration, tighter borders and inflated security.

"The same goes, of course, for theatre and literature in general, but poetry has that performance element, and also the more effective meditative dimension," he said. "It can be louder, and it can also be deeper..."

Before we got up to leave, Antoine and I arranged to go to the Hal Far open centre, and the *Laboratorju tal-Paċi* (the Peace Laboratory) before I was to leave Malta. We had to shout over the wind. I had a lot on my mind by the time we shook hands to say goodbye, waving and smiling a windswept smile at the waitress in thanks.

On the way back home, Antoine's point about the transformative power of poetry still rang inside me. Poetry can be meditative—it can change consciousness, changing one's perspective and thoughts about the world, about oneself too. It could be loud, and it could be deep; and it could be all of these things at once, too. Having played with my voice and watched Dave perform many times over, I knew this. I thought of how words linger, and imagined them loud in our consciousness, waking us up, penetrating deep inside, in our subconscious, perhaps floating there before finally taking shape, changing our state and our ideas about what is possible, making us stop and reflect, calling us into our imagination or another world we previously thought impossible.

I thought of how, sometimes, a poem had come to me in this way when I walked in the forest: I'd had to be receptive to hear it. As though if I hadn't, I might have *heard*, but not understood its meaning.

20.

"If you have heart you come here, across the sea."

I met *Boadi, a tall man from Togo at the Refugee Commissioner's Office in Msida, Malta. He'd been standing across the road, on the side street next to mine. "I want to know what you are doing?" he asked, after he'd seen me observing the comings and goings. "I have two kids here. I can't get social security, can't get nothing. I apply someone to help us. I want to get Humanitarian Protection."

"And will they give it to you?" I asked.

"I have three kids. They will give it to me.

"We went to American Embassy, they gave us a letter. We want money for recording equipment, for music, you know. Then we brought the letter to the Maltese President, and she said it was a good idea."

Boadi had made some money from Russian movies, he said. "They want me, you know, they need blacks. And for another movie they need migrant child—so they take mine.

"Now, they give me these yellow papers; then I try to get this Humanitarian Protection. When I have a case, I apply for a lawyer and have to go the Court. Two times it has happened. When I apply for marriage, they take all my papers, and I got taken into detention again. In prison, every week I paid €100 to the lawyer. The girlfriend, she doesn't work, so I have to pay the lawyer. I lost many things," he said. "I got a car for €8,000, sold it €5,000. I lost many things..."

I could not fully understand everything Boadi told me due to his broken English, but asked him about the difficulty in getting help from the Maltese authorities. He told me that he was in a hip-hop group, and, together, they were trying to raise money to rent a space in a hotel, with recording equipment, which they hoped would come from the American Embassy.

"The Maltese authorities won't give me *one cent.* If you are black, they don't want you get opportunity here. I have to go to the lawyer again. I've spent my money on the lawyer for almost two years now. You are leaving soon?" he asked, indicating he hoped I could give him legal aid.

I nodded. "By the end of the month, yes. But I am not a lawyer. I am a writer, a journalist."

I thanked Boadi for talking to me and asked him if he would let me write his story in more detail. We arranged to meet on Gozo, where he lived, the following week. I was also curious about the hip-hop group he was in with other men from Ghana and the Ivory Coast. I told him about my old classmates, Abisai and Elias, in Leguruki King'ori, Tanzania, who were still creating music together, and had recently sent me some of their latest tunes via Abisai's YouTube channel, Ab Mara. [62] Abisai was in Germany with his record label which he'd been signed for shortly after I'd left Tanzania, and had since lived between the two countries, visa permitting.

Another man, on the steps just behind me and across from the Refugee Commissioner's office, recognised me from the EU-funded cultural exchange storytelling workshop in Mdina months before. "I know you," he said.

We reintroduced ourselves, and he spoke to me briefly of his job as a journalist in Somalia.

"On the boat here, I had my papers and notes; I was writing a book. But they were lost, overboard… Why are you only doing one story?" he asked then, as he'd seen me speaking to Boadi.

I couldn't answer. It was a while before I realised I didn't *have* an answer to his question—I wasn't sure there was one.

The Maltese islands are two, Gozo the smaller. I always enjoyed visiting it as it was quieter and greener than Malta, with less people, less tourism. Some days later, I took the short ferry ride across and met Boadi at the church in Victoria. We walked towards his home; as soon as we'd arrived he began telling me his story.

"After I had my exams in Togo, I got sick," he said. "I stopped school. My uncle was manager in the Department of Transport for the city. He wants someone to make business in the company. 'Got money to sponsor?' he asked me. That was what we needed, to open the communication center. And we did. After the end of two years, we bought mini-buses, then taxis.

"There was a change in Presidency. Companies and businesses, they make a lot of money. With the new presidential government, the police came and locked up the shop, because of companies and businesses making money.

"I bought another shop, but the business came down. If I stay there, then I don't think I can get a good future, so I travel. From Togo, we cannot go directly—there are those kinds of people, they help you if you want to go abroad. The visa is 'try-your-luck.'"

"I wanted to go to Holland. It was almost US$4,000,

and I couldn't get the visa. I stay one, two years more in Togo, then I tried to go to Europe—Spain. I got the visa. When I arrived there, with no documents, the Togolese Embassy came to deport all the people from Togo, so, I was taken back to Togo again. From there, I tried to travel again. My cousin, he came to live here in Malta. He called my uncle. He said, 'You don't spend a lot of money here. If you have heart, you come here, across the sea. If you haven't, you can't cross the sea.'

"After my cousin, I start the journey, Togo to Libya. Two weeks. It's in a truck; it's difficult. We met some people, they die. No water; it's desert. *Real* desert.

"When I came to Libya, they bring people to a camp," Boadi continued. "My cousin, he went with people who work as plasterers—he was already a plasterer. I asked, 'What can I do? I don't have money.' I worked seven months in Libya, then I try to continue on the journey. I spent one month waiting for this boat. We were twenty-nine peoples to cross the sea. We thought... you know, nobody knows God's planning. We didn't know..."

Boadi paused for a moment, and didn't finish his thought. There was no need—I knew what he meant. He and the others in the boat had had no idea whether they would make it to their destination, across the sea.

"But we arrived in Malta, the fifth of September, 2008. They keep us in detention. When you say, 'From Togo,' you get eighteen months. We spent eleven months there.

"After this eleven months, they want to deport us. I thought in my head, I don't know if I survive my life in Europe. When I was in the detention centre, I get bad dreams, so they give me a psychological doctor. Every two days, he came there. I spoke to him about my problems in the office. 'Me, I am from Italy,' the doctor said, 'my country of origin is no problem.' But for me, it's different. So, I try to escape to Italy. If I don't go, they will deport me. I escape, I was the first one. When I escape, when I was outside, I had no more bad dreams. My psychological doctor, he said, 'I am happy with you, but you have to go out!'

"If you're from Togo, the Maltese government has got €5,000 for you," Boadi said. "Two of my friends, they got to go back to Togo. They *take* them back.[9]

"If you want to buy a car, or make a business, or

---

[9] Boadi is referring to the forced deportation of his friends. This is illegal according to international migration law and protection, yet it occurs all over Europe, and is often carried out by those who supposedly uphold justice (the Police) in secret. The options were bleak: stay here, get nothing, or, if you show any of the "talent" the Maltese Prime Minister referred to (see p. 250-1) you receive half the amount. Or, leave with a couple of thousand euros—with persecution, and in some cases, death, likely on the refugee's forced return.

something like that, they give you €2,000. They only give you €5,000 if you're going to go, if you gonna *leave*.

"Sunday evening, I escaped out in the night. They take all of them on Tuesday. All."

"All? Regardless of papers or not?" I asked, angry.[10]

"Nothing. All," he said.

"I stayed with a friend in Malta. He gave me ten euros. I get work, I start. My cousin, he was in Italy, he got documents. He wanted to come visit me, he tried to help me get a ferry to Italy because I don't have papers. But I had this friend in Malta; he was plastering, about four years, working alone. He brought me here, to Gozo. The money is too bad, you know, so one day I went out. They were all Gozitans around me and they don't speak English, and I don't speak Maltese. We talk though. I see they want me, but the communication is difficult. Then one said, 'I have a wife.' She's a teacher, she spoke English—I could speak to her! I said, 'I need work.' And they said, 'Next day, start!'

"I started with €150 per week. It's bad, what can I do with that? One day, construction manager, he see me work.

---

[10] Not having papers does not excuse governments deporting innocent people back to danger, nor should it if an asylum seeker fails the legal checks to be granted Humanitarian Protection, but *mass* group deportations are illegal—this means no interview and no case processing was even begun.

He told my manager, 'I want you to give this man whole flat to plaster.' I said, 'Yes, I can do it. Full flat!'

"You see," Boadi gestured toward the tiled floor, "there is a way that plastering and tiles are done in Malta and I did it different, so they want me. They like to see something different. So from €300 for two weeks, I went to €925 in two weeks. Now, I make six bedrooms, a fence, a *pool*—one of my friends wants to make a party for his son's birthday. I work for them for three years—I wanted to go to Spain, I wanted to get the documents there.

"One of the guys had a Maltese girlfriend. I used to live alone, they came here and I gave them a drink. 'If you want a girl,' the guy said, 'I have someone for you.'

"He wanted me to be her boyfriend. So, I go out with her. She asked me, 'You don't have ID card?' I said, 'No, I don't have documents.'

"I spoke to her about what has happened in my life, and she spoke to a lawyer, who said, 'We can bring you back to Togo, for the marriage, because the girl has documents.' But I don't want that—to go to Togo.

"The girl went to the doctor," Boadi continued some moments later. "'Am I pregnant?' she was asking. But the doctor said there was something wrong with her ovaries and she can't get pregnant.

"Nobody knows God's plan, but I can accept what He wants here, for my life. So, I went—I buy the pregnancy tests. This pregnancy is a miracle, because, you know, she can't get pregnant—and now the baby is coming!"

From this miracle pregnancy as Boadi described it, his daughter was born, now three years old.

"The lawyer talked to the court, and this is helping," he said. "The government gave me a flat here, in Gozo.

"The girlfriend, she didn't want to marry. She had already two sons, and I want to help her boys. Last Saturday, the lawyer called me. I stayed two hours. He wants to ask me about the bigger boy. I have some money in the bank, so he can continue to study. She was happy.

"So, now, I'm half-European—half my family is here. Half of me in Europe, and half of me in Africa.

"When I get documents, I can make business. I went to the lawyer to make passport and ID card photocopies, to apply for that permit. When they give us authority we can go ahead. This is for the music video that we need to make in Paceville," he said.

Boadi gave me a CD of his music as I prepared to leave.

"Us Africans, we have a lot of stories to tell," his friend said a few minutes later, as he drove me to where I was staying with a friend, nearby.

"Yes," I replied.

And this is only the tip of the iceberg, I thought.

When I returned to my flat in Msida, I read about deportation theory, as defined by neoliberal economics. I found a paper by the UNHCR policy institute based in Geneva, Switzerland in which they describe deportation as a concept and a policy that "embodies what one might call the liberal democratic paradox." On the one hand, deportation (or more generally, exercising border control) is "fundamental to liberal democracy" for two reasons, they wrote. Firstly, liberal democracy is linked to the definition and theory of the "state," and fundamental to the notion of the sovereignty of the state is the capacity to control borders. Second, that policy in a liberal democracy must to some measure "reflect the... preferences of its citizens. And, nowhere does a majority of the citizenry support open borders." Allegedly, "in the US, only once... have more than 10% of Americans wanted increased immigration."

It was good to know something of the theory behind border control and deportation, but specific policies or their theories don't excuse the resulting actions or effects of a particular regime. And a government throwing people out, back to where they would be killed or persecuted or otherwise afflicted, attributing their efforts to their citizens' wishes seemed absurd, and especially inadequate given the West's role in the making of the chaos of the countries which refugees are running from.

Forcible deportation because of *democracy?* Spreading fear, and protection of the state—at what cost? What about the protection of *people?* Particularly when people fall through the many cracks in law, becoming our most vulnerable in society, this is essential. It seemed that policy became dangerous when its abstract theory is upheld over those it's supposedly representing, in the name of a "liberal" economic dream.

In principle, if people don't know any of the politics behind migration, the fear of open borders becomes intensified, but this is also because of media scaremongering and scapegoating certain nationalities. In this way we never get at the root cause of the deeper inequalities that lie at the heart of the problem.

I read on: "Forcible expulsion from the national territory requires bringing the full powers of the state to bear against an individual. Deportation severs permanently and completely the relationship of responsibility between the state and the individual." In the end of the same paragraph, there was an acknowledgement of the anguish, indignity and brute force it employs: "physically removing individuals against their will, from communities in which they wish to remain, effectively cuts the social, personal and professional bonds created over the course of residence."

Immigration control implies two capacities: "to block the entry of individuals to a state, and to secure the return of those who have entered. Both of these capacities," the report read, "sit uneasily with liberal principles." [63]

But whether it sits uneasily or not, it *is* happening; and, according to the policy institute's working paper, we allowed it to a degree. We have power as people, as citizens. Our governments are already under pressure and have lost control as finance and corporations rule the roost. We need to ask the question, "What are we doing to embrace integration, to solve inequality, and foster healthy and diverse relationships and friendships?" We need to ask the right questions *and* hold our governments accountable. If something stays sitting "uneasily" with us, we will not prevent further chaos and suffering, and, as the Dalai Lama says, nor can we only pray and hope. "I am a Buddhist and I believe in praying. But humans have created this problem, and now we are asking God to solve it. It is illogical," he said in a rare statement, in response to the #PrayForParis campaign that went viral after the November 2015 bombing.[64]

If ordinary US citizens knew about the fundamentally inhumane and degrading treatment of refugees and asylum seekers, the forcible deportations, and understood something more of the causes of forced migration, I don't think they would stand by what their "preferences" allegedly were previous to that, though of course I cannot say for sure. We have been desensitised yes, but as his Holiness says, "we are *all* human beings and there is no basis or justification for killing others."[65] As Anna Pratt of the Canadian-based NGO, No One Is Illegal (Toronto), writes, "We must challenge the idea that some refugees are more worthy than others; we believe everyone has the fundamental human right to mobility."[66] Avoiding tabloids and impersonal accounts, which only feed stereotypes and adds to desensitisation and sensationalism, is a good start.

We also must realise that, as journalist Dawn Paley aptly expresses it, "Far from preventing violence, the border is in fact the reason it occurs."[67] Having tighter immigration controls and border security will do nothing for the fear some people have of multiculturalism and people of different ethnic origins or migrants—often a derogatory term.

There is an assumption that those who are deported are "undesirables"; asylum seekers who "failed" the designated legal processes to become a refugee or an immigrant. However, an increasing number of asylum seekers are being deported because of structural flaws in the legal framework—or lack of it—in the refugee determination system. For example, in Calais in France, it can be seen that there is nothing efficient about the official government response; instead it is leading to more and more chaos. To quote British campaigner and activist Natasha Walter, "Cases drag on for years, letters are lost, interviews are cancelled, detention is used arbitrarily, decisions are overturned."[68]

In Canada, the refugee system has been termed "a lottery system because acceptance rates can vary from 0-

80% depending on the judge."[69] Some legal avenues in Canada, Pratt writes, have acceptance rates of 3-5% while others *do not have to be processed prior to deportation.* There is also no Refugee Appeal Division (despite its guarantee in the June 2002 Immigration and Refugee Protection Act). Deemed "non-citizens" and held in conditions of imprisonment that are fundamentally inhuman and degrading, in Canada "asylum-seekers are liable to be stripped, shackled and sometimes verbally or physically abused." Confined in maximum-security jails and "often excluded from bail [with] no idea when they will be released"[70]—unlike Canadian citizens, who are actually charged with an offence. Seeking asylum is a right, not a crime, as the Toronto branch of No One Is Illegal stated in their report.[71] (No One Is Illegal is a migrant justice and resistance movement that strives and struggles for the freedom to stay, the freedom to move, and the freedom to return. Its roots are held in anti-colonial, anti-capitalist, ecological justice, indigenous self-determination and anti-oppressive politics.)

Dr Liam Thornton is a lecturer in law and legal education who writes for *KOD Lyons*, a human rights and criminal law firm based in Dublin with expertise in immigration and asylum law. There is no legislative basis for the direct provision system and the derisory payment of €19.10 per week per adult asylum seeker (€9.60 per child) he explains, for the "habitual residence condition" dictates that the Department of Social Protection are legislatively barred from making regular social welfare payments, and the "horrific conditions of enforced poverty" in direct provision are therefore allowed to continue. We have yet to see a situation where the socio-economic rights of asylum seekers are respected by Ireland and an end to the direct provision system, though it is being fought by asylum seekers themselves, human rights organisations, lawyers and other individuals.[72]

To prevent deportation, planes have successfully been stopped or not even taken off when some passengers discovered a forcible deportation was taking place. They stood up and refused to sit in their seat—pilots are not allowed to take off if all passengers are not seated, and in fact many passengers and airline employees do not wish to be complicit in the unjust practices of governments.[73]

I thought of Boadi's friends from Togo who had been deported one Tuesday night. I was glad he had got out, just in time, but he was the only one. He had already been deported from Europe previously, years before. It is perhaps not that he, and many other refugees, even *want* to live in Europe—it is most times out of necessity, because of war, persecution and some international agreements or disagreements which holds power in certain countries and takes it from others.

I wondered at his patience and his thoughts on "civilised" Europe, after being told by his cousin, "If you have heart you come here, across the sea."

21.

The open centre with a closed gate

The day before I left Malta, I visited Hal Far open centre with Antoine. We walked down the road from where he'd parked his car and stood on the other side of the road looking at the massive, institution-like walls. These were new—Antoine didn't remember them being there on his last visit.

There was a smaller gate, a pedestrian one which we could enter, to the left of the main gate which was locked. We went through and turned left to stay out of sight of security.[11] We walked along the... I don't know what the word is, it could hardly be called a street—the *concrete*? There were four rows of containers: 1A, 1B, 1C and so on it went on both sides. There were three of these "streets." Antoine gestured toward one man sitting outside his container, as most people were. "There's nothing to do here," he said. "And this is for the ones who *survive!*"

---

[11] This cannot be done without a letter or invitation, and I do not write to say how easy it is to enter, and therefore unsafe for the people at the open centre. It is normally patrolled by guards and security at the entrance. It was previously allowed to enter with permission; a friend of mine used to go there to provide company for refugees. However, now, as it has become stricter and Antoine and I wanted to enter, we reckoned we had to enter *without* permission.

"Have you read Chris Cleave's *The Other Hand?*" I asked Antoine.

"No."

"It's so wrong it's almost funny. The situation I mean, not the book. I'll read an extract for you later," I said. "It's fiction, but... in here, I can see it. Like all fiction that's found somewhere."

We greeted the people on either side of us, and walked slowly down the row of... containers provided by the European Fund 2007-2013. I still wish I could say houses: that would be the normal, nice thing to say, wouldn't it? But they are not houses, and they are not homes.

"I brought some *Passaports* along," he said as we walked. "I was thinking of giving them out."

We came to a stop at one container about halfway down. We'd got a smile and thought it best to ask, here, to take a photo of the sticker on the containers. The sticker was the EU flag, complete with its twelve stars. By way of making and starting conversation, Antoine tried to point out the irony of this to our new friend, when he said, "Yes, yes," and waved his hand, as if to say "Come in."

We stood there, between two containers, and talked and shook hands for about half an hour. It was men, mostly, that came over to speak to us. The conversation was a little stilted at times, but we managed to communicate. Antoine, of course, had some Arabic, having lived in Malta for seven years of his life and it being his parents' country of origin. This area of the open centre was where Syrian people from the recent boat from Libya were. The girl next to Antoine had ran off as soon as she had three *Passaports*, one of each colour in her hand. "To give to her brothers," one young man said smiling. She came back again, this time accompanied by her older sister, who wanted to know more about the *Passaport*.

"This is a passport with no photo, no ID. It's for any country," Antoine said. "And it's free."

"I want one!" she said.

"*Iswad? Ahmar?*— Black? Red? Blue?"

She chose blue.

"I can go to the airport with this? This is real passport?" one young man said to my right.

Antoine and I looked at each other. "You can try," we said slowly, joking, trying to bring some humour to the situation, "but—"

"You have to be careful," Antoine added.

"It's art," I said. "A poetic passport. We are writers. We're trying, through writing, theatre and art, to show people what's happening in the world, and in here. To say that something's not right."

One man in his early thirties, carrying a folder, spoke up: "I take black—*iswad*—because I am black."

Antoine handed him one.

"What's this?" he said, suddenly, pointing to the inside cover.

"That is the rainbow," Antoine said.

"But, what is it supposed to mean?"

"It is to represent all peoples. You know, it has all the colours of all the flags."

"But... There is another meaning, another rainbow flag... I don't agree with this," he said.

"It is also the symbol of the indigenous peoples of South America, the Aymara and Quechua peoples," Antoine said. "It's also the peace flag, and the International Co-Operative movement flag."

"But people might think is—" he broke off.

"There are *many* meanings," I said. "Probably at least four."

He handed the black *Passaport* back to Antoine. "I don't want it," he said.

I wondered whether Antoine had been asked this before, about the LGBT colours on the inside cover of the

Passaport, by someone who had taken offence. However, as we walked on shortly after, I said, smiling, "Your bag's got a lot lighter!"

We found that most people here didn't want to stay in Malta. They mentioned Sweden, Germany, Italy—wherever family were. For now, though, they had to wait. They didn't know how or when or if they would make it to those countries.

We walked the rest of the way, along the middle of the "street." There was a young girl of about four, and it struck me as deeply distressing how I saw nothing in her eyes. I had minded children since I was fourteen years old, and saw nothing of the innocence or joy normally found in kids. But perhaps it is no wonder, considering the harrowing journey she had undertaken, at such a young age, to get here.

The people at Hal Far open centre didn't seem, as far as we could understand, to have had any interviews or their cases processed; rather, they were simply, waiting. "Yes," an older man said, "We are waiting." At least they were not in detention, and had been taken straight here—Syrians are granted this liberty at least; Sub-Saharan Africans are brought straight into detention.

"You know, I wonder," I said to Antoine, "I stood there trying to be all calm and saying all these things about what we're doing and why we're here. And I wonder, do they know, that actually I'm *boiling* inside! It might be weird, or hard to understand. I mean, the worst that can happen to us Europeans is someone gives out to us and tells us to leave. It's so easy, for us."

I'm waiting; we are waiting—I couldn't get this out of my mind, nor how many times it had been echoed as we walked along the grey street, passing the containers and grim smiles or greetings on either side of the makeshift homes. Apparently, different rules and rights applied here. As other, as number, as statistic. As refugee, something ceased to be the same in the eyes of governments and many, many ordinary people—no longer a person with basic needs and human rights. Therefore, there was no need for a home or comfort, poetry or nutrition, something to do. Containers are okay—you should be grateful to be alive. Our governments, the "civilised" West, are keeping people alive, our paperwork and bureaucratic systems proving our civility, so that refugees and asylum seekers can survive—but not more. Keeping bodies alive, whilst killing souls. And this wouldn't change until our perceptions and governments revisited this prejudice and saw it for what it was and is: racial discrimination and heartlessness, by a culture that claims to be progressive, liberal, embracing equality. Lives would continue to be on hold, in limbo, in suspended animation as it were, as long as this continued. And, despite the high numbers of refugees and asylum seekers fleeing to Europe, the UNHCR stated, as of mid-2014, that *developing* countries hosted eighty-six percent of the world's refugees. In light of this, the inaction and deliberation is embarrassing.

Here, in Hal Far, people can come and go—it's an open centre—but no one gives them a *Lonely Planet* guide. No one says, 'Oh, you could go to Valletta tomorrow, it's beautiful there!' And, at the time of my visit, each person in the open centre received about thirty-five euros *per month*! Here they were, after harrowing experiences and in need of help, all together and hidden away as though they were an eyesore.

Migration was an instrument and a reminder of a problem that ran far deeper and hinted embarrassingly at our colonial past. Pointed to the current failings of our capitalist culture and our imperialism, our oil-hungry and blood-thirsty warfare, our economic sanctions and short-term thinking. Governments in the West that are in for only their own benefit, and out as soon as there's nothing left in it for them.

The countries the West has continued to bomb and impose policy and economic sanctions on, fund and support continued military expansion with more weapons and training, then later abandon, are left reeling in the aftermath and destabilised with a knock-on effect on their neighbours, creating further tension. And all the while media plays into the hands of scare-mongering and a US- or Western-friendly paradigm, sympathetic to our fears and longing for control. We are only the keepers of peace, after all. We must protect our governments, our countries, our values, our progress, our united stance, our borders. Against what? Muslims? The Arab Uprising? Syria? Iraq? Iran? Afghanistan? Al-Qaeda? ISIS?

And then?

It occurred to me that everything we had ever fought against had been our own creation in a way. Our tactics and foreign policies that were inappropriate, reactive and geopolitical in their cause, not to mention the millions of innocent people—men, women and children— who'd been killed. And now, those exact people were running away from the chaos that we, at least partly, had caused. [74] Seeking help, shelter, papers. And answers:

could they move on from here, now? Could they find work? Where were their families?

"Yeah," Antoine said pulling me out of my thoughts, "and for the people here, too. They seem kind of calm, but... who knows, on the inside, what's going on."

Antoine noticed a piece of a jigsaw and bent down to pick it up. We looked at it, turned it over, but both sides seemed to be the same grey-green, other than small blue x's on one side. It was made of some sort of chipboard. I noted with irony that my understanding of migration had just gained a jigsaw piece. Though still what I saw and knew were pieces, the picture was beginning to emerge. It was more bloody and far worse than anything I'd thought I'd find: it was not a picture many would be proud of, or want to look at.

We left through a large hole in the wire fencing. "Up there," Antoine said pointing, "that's where the other nationalities are, those from Sub-Saharan Africa; but we should probably go out this way because the security will see us otherwise."

We went back, along the road, to the *Laboratorju tal-Paċi* (the Peace Lab) and where Antoine had parked his car. On the way I pulled out Amanuel's printed documents. "Here," I said, "Chris Cleave." Just like Little Bee's

284

experience of the London detention centre, the irony at Hal Far was immense and heavy, too.

"Most days I wish I was a British pound instead of an African girl. Everyone would be pleased to see me coming... Of course a pound coin can be serious too. It can disguise itself as power or property, and there is nothing more serious when you are a girl who has neither... A girl like me gets stopped at immigration, but a pound can leap the turnstiles, and dodge the tackles of those big men with their uniform caps..."[75]

"Yes," Antoine said. "They have nothing to lose now, nothing but their life or their families' life. They came by boat—they didn't have time to *pack*."

I noted that the Hal Far open centre is located alongside an old military detention centre and the Peace Laboratory. The change from a war station to a peace centre was the result of direct political action, Antoine later told me.

The founder of the Peace Lab, Fr. Dionysius Mintoff, believed deeply in the need for an open and unrestricted meeting place to form community and support, "where people of all backgrounds and attitudes could mix together." Interestingly, it was perhaps exactly what people had wanted in their home countries which was now, in Europe, also banned or not supported when they arrived: a basic need to mix and congregate, freedom of travel, democracy, basic human rights. The Peace Lab is now, in Antoine's words, "home to a small group of Africans who, after losing the jobs and rented rooms they had briefly managed to secure after leaving the open centre, suddenly found themselves unemployed and without a roof."[76]

On the way, we found a minor's hangout that Antoine had heard about, where young people who had been orphaned on their journey spent their time. Antoine had noticed the word *Bienvenu* on the wall and we'd decided to go and see if this was it. We could see a group of young men in the alley. We couldn't enter as there was a security guard a few metres away, but we spoke to the group standing around outside. I quite enjoyed not returning the security guard's glare and ignoring him. I'd noticed a kind of defiance (re)emerging, like I'd had for many of my early teenage years (though, at that time it was directed more generally toward the world at large and parents). I had little fear of "authority," at least for the kind of authority I saw here.

Antoine's friend Joseph, whom we were looking for, wasn't at the complex; we were told he might be at another minor's centre, so we walked back, along the way passing another EU sign complete with its twelve golden stars: *Constructing & Equipping the Independent Living Centre.*

Later that night, I read an interview with Chris Cleave on his website. He had written about an Angolan man named Manuel Bravo who had fled to England and claimed asylum; he and his family would be persecuted and killed if they were returned, after his pro-democracy activity led to attacks on his family, including the murder of his parents. After four years, still with a pending decision on their asylum application, Bravo and his thirteen-year-old son were seized in a dawn raid in September 2005 and brought to an Immigration Removal Centre in southern England. Here, they were told that they would be forcibly deported to Angola the following morning; this was the first news he received that his claim for asylum had been finally refused. At his initial asylum hearing, his solicitor did not attend and he had been forced to represent himself.[77]

That night, Manuel Bravo took his own life by hanging himself in a stairwell. Bravo, aware of a rule under which unaccompanied minors cannot be deported from the UK, "had taken his own life in order to save the life of his son."[78] An undoubtedly heartbreaking and shocking measure of the absolute failure of immigration policy that it had led to such an ending—to leave a father with no other option than what he'd done that night.

At the time of my reading (mid-September 2014), there had been the tragic situation in which a boat had been rammed by Egyptian smugglers, and, allegedly, between 300 and 500 refugees had drowned. Survivors had testified their story of the boat sinking and the confrontation that had happened;[79] they admitted to having been treated like dogs during their *entire* journey, however, nothing as horrific as this.[80] After the ramming of the boat, the smugglers had stayed just long enough to make sure that the boat sank; that their job had been done. Most, or at least many, were drowned immediately with the boats sinking, and many others during the next few days. The few who survived were found three days later. In one article there was an image of the containers I'd seen that day, and it seemed like the Maltese authorities, indeed Europe, were looking for merit, as though providing containers was enough. As though they were doing "their bit"—but what an inconvenience, a burden, these migrants are on our economy, and Europe and each state's security!

I opened up my laptop and noticed that Antoine had been busy, also:

"For reasons as much social as geographical," he wrote on his blog, "the south-eastern corner of Malta is where the nation-state has chosen to stash its dirty laundry: industry, the power station, a recycling plant, the freeport. Taking Malta and its geographical-form as a fish, at the very chin is a remote area called Hal Far. This literally translates to 'Ratville'... and is where one of the migrant open centres is located."[81]

I spent the entire night writing, as I couldn't sleep. Antoine's words echoed in my mind: *the chin of the fish, Ratville.* It seemed surreal—a military detention centre and the Peace Laboratory, beside a migrant centre.

Welcome. Here's a cabin built on hard concrete.

Nor could I get the image of the little girl or the old man's words out of my mind—*Waiting, waiting, we are waiting.* The desolation and grey-white concrete of the open centre. The momentary hope in the young woman's eyes when Antoine and I had stood there, holding *Passaports*—a call to action around the world, highlighting injustice, but unfortunately not the kind of passport that would get her out, that would grant her the freedom to travel to where she wanted to go. Arbitrary political lines drawn on a map, on the world, offer acceptance and inclusion, or invisibility and exclusion, depending on which side of those lines she had been born.

Part III

"We are all just walking each other home."

– Ram Dass, spiritual teacher and author

22.

"It's only three letters, but the word 'gay' is so powerful."

"There are those who say it's wrong and shouldn't exist."

I was speaking to Lorna via Skype, from the sweltering heat in Malta whilst she walked home from school through drizzly Dublin suburbs. "They didn't believe in it, you know? They say, 'Oh, you're *confused*! You haven't found the right man.' Then there are other people, they're just standoffish about it, and there are people who say that I shouldn't have kids. But if *you* get kids, I get to, too!

"I get different attitudes that I have to brush off. It's mostly ignorance though—they don't understand, yet they argue with me. But I'm sad about it, and it makes me angry because I have to react, just because they don't accept me. It's like someone arguing, 'No, the sky isn't blue!' It *is*! I love someone, you love someone: it doesn't matter who I love."

"What was it like hiding that for several years from your mum and dad?"

"With my mum, well, I was sad that I had to hide that I was with someone. I was not really being myself—I was being *quiet*," she said.

We both laughed.

"Exactly!" Lorna said still laughing. "She said to me one day, 'I need to talk to you, Lorna, for a minute.' We went to my room... and I just broke down in tears. She just came out with it. She said, 'Are you gay?'

"I'd rehearsed it in my head so many times and I didn't think I was going to break down like that. I'd been 'out'[12] with my friends for so many years, and I'd never thought I would cry. With my dad, it was strange. This was just recently. I sat down with him, and I *also* started crying. He's someone who's important to me. I told him that I didn't think it was the right time before then, 'I didn't know how you would react, Dad,' I said.

"When you don't know how someone close to you is going to react to what you tell them... It's only three letters, but the word 'gay' is so powerful. When it's people you really care about, it can mean so much: it's a small word, but it can change a lot.

---

12 Term used to describe telling friends/family/other people that one is gay/lesbian/bi/queer.

"My father, he thinks he's modern, but actually I think he's a bit backwards; I got really nervous. I just hoped that they were going to take it well. But he said, 'Look, I just want you to be *happy*. I'm just scared because your life will be more difficult now.' And yes, maybe it will be a little bit, but I thought, Oh my god, is this really happening? I was shocked that it went so well. We fight a lot, but he was still there for me."

I asked Lorna about the time when she'd realised she was gay. She had told me a little of this before.

"When I was thirteen," she said, "we went on a family holiday cruise. I was concerned about how I looked at that time: how people saw me, and who I was. There was a seventeen-year-old girl there. She was creative and stylish, and I thought, I'd really love to be her. But she liked *girls*, and I was like, Noooo! She asked me did *I* like girls. Then, suddenly one night, she just leaned down and kissed me. I felt dizzy, my head went light, and she said, 'Well, I think I just answered *that* question for you!' I remember I'd gone bright red.

"When I went back home, I researched LGBT on the web. There's an organisation called BeLonG To in Ireland. It's so good, and I got advice there. I got familiar with the whole thing. It got normal, after a while. [13]

"I was freaked out in the beginning and excited, but now it just made sense: I'm never going to need to try not to be myself. I can now find myself *more*—there's a whole new side to myself I haven't met before, I realised. It felt like I was coming home, like I was born there, to be in that group. Like this is where I was meant to be the whole time: I was accepted with no judgements. Something I didn't even know was there suddenly came to the surface. The whole experience was like I was finally finding my own skin. Before, I bought clothes in the latest fashion, wore make-up, and kissed boys that I didn't like. Now, it felt like *me.* I didn't have to put make-up on for boys—something I'd never wanted to do in the first place. I would definitely say it was like coming home.

"I've had two other girlfriends in the past, but I hid that from my parents. When I introduced Laura, my current girlfriend, to my mum, my friend was there too, to deflect the awkwardness. I said, 'So, Mum, you know the way there's this thing about me, and there's this girl. Well,

---

[13] There is a list of LGBTQ support networks at the back of this book. Changes or "questioning" in sexuality can bring up very instinctive and irrational fears and thoughts. Even though it may be very different for each person, it may be a difficult time. Get support from friends you trust, Helpines, LGBTQ Support networks or trained counsellors. For those countries in which being LGBT is illegal or denies rights, there are perhaps international lines you can call.

I'm going to introduce her to you, is that okay?' That was after the conversation we'd had in my bedroom where I'd broken down and told her. She'd already guessed, really, because she'd said to me, 'You don't text someone that much if you're not in love with them,'" Lorna laughed.

"I'm more scared of telling adults about my being gay. Teachers in school is a big thing for me. They all know, but they are—or I think they are—standoffish about it, awkward. I was scared that if they found out, they might mark me harder or grade me unfairly, treat me differently in class as a whole: not let me answer questions, or when I have my hand raised that they wouldn't take my answer.

"I told this one teacher that I was scared my telling her would affect how she taught me," Lorna added, "or our relationship in school. 'I don't want it to change anything,' I said to her, 'it worries me a lot.' But the teacher said, 'That's not how it would be *at all*. I wouldn't ever let someone's sexual orientation affect my work or how I treated any student.' And then she gave me a big hug!

"I didn't want her to not like me because of something that I can't change. Coming out, no longer bi but gay, was a real realisation: *this is who I am for my life.* I'll be seventy-seven and I'll be gay! It's not just for now. There is this fear of people knowing, and altering their perception of me because of it. It's this knowing of one thing, and that this one thing could change my relationship with that person—that freaked me out a lot," she said, coming to a close.

"Thank you, Lorna," I said.

I found her courage and insight remarkable; she was barely eighteen. I could see that Lorna was a great support to many people, as was her story.

23.

"I think I'm a woman," I said

"What are you smiling at?" Fiona asked. I can't remember now if it was verbal or how she looked at me.

I'd come to see her before I went back to Ireland as Fiona had become a go-to for me for healing. I sat down in a large armchair in her bright and airy living room in St. Paul's Bay in Malta, where her healing practice is held. Her eyes seemed to sparkle, and she smiled, her wavy golden hair caught in the light around us, her blue eyes waiting and compassionate. I had been through a lot with Fiona's help, and this was why I felt she always saw right through me, to how I was. Today she saw me very happy—the sunshine was doing me a lot of good and I was excited to be returning to Ireland soon. But there was something that I had just discovered about myself that suddenly made me say, "I think I'm a *woman*."

We both laughed, I a little nervously, but she caught the gravity of what I was saying, and I was beginning to as well. I just stood there and couldn't stop smiling, nor did I really explain what I'd meant as I couldn't yet. I knew that Fiona didn't need me to explain if I wasn't ready.

"I don't know how I can ever thank you enough," I said, my smile now mixed with tears. I thought of the times she'd helped me through a severe illness, my last year of University with my thesis and exams, my break-up with Dave.

"I think it's enough for me to see you now and again, to see what you're doing and where you are," she said.

I understood that, and nodded.

I had first gone to see Fiona sixteen months before, and she had asked me the question, "What does it mean to you, to be a woman?" I had come to her because an old injury from gardening, in my right hip, had flared up again because of my hours spent sitting and studying as a student, and my right arm and wrist had also developed a repetitive strain injury. Yoga did not seem to be helping, and, as I'm very flexible, it seems I can easily strain my joints or muscles, even as a yoga teacher.

I soon realised she didn't want me to *answer* the question, she'd wanted to *give me* the question.

That first time, I'd sat there, thinking. I didn't know, and how could I? I had unconsciously but nevertheless resisted that question as long as I could remember, and so, someone as energetically sensitive as Fiona asking me had touched something inside. I was afraid of it, and of what it might mean. My comment to Fiona about my realising I was a *woman* was because I'd recognised how much of my life I'd spent trying to be compassionate, but masculine in my approach to being in the world, and not allowing myself rest, or the use of my intuition in my work, nor had I really felt the sadness of my research and work as an activist, for years. I had been such a tomboy for many years of my life, with an active lifestyle and upbringing; at the age of six or seven I had actually thought I *was* a boy. Not physically, but in every other way possible—I had even got a boy's haircut to prove it.

Later, I realise, I'd decided that feeling less and being less feminine made it easier to live in a world rife with violence, rape, war, oppression, inequality, injustice and suffering. It also made it more likely, in my view, for many years, that people would be more likely to listen if I was rational and knowledgeable, not emotional or "soft" in my approach—because men were the ones who, mostly, made the big decisions in the world. Decisions that could make the current situation continue, or change it—for everyone's good. The kind of decisions that can, literally, wipe out lives in seconds; that hold women and oppressed minorities in their place, and men, too in a difficult role. Of course, I knew there were women in power, but much less in number than men. This had been my logic and thinking.

About this time, Emma Watson, known to many as "the Harry Potter girl," was campaigning and making the important connection to women's empowerment and equality being about men, too; pointing out how gender inequality affected men, and how they could support this movement toward gender equality to the benefit of *all* of society. In the launch of the campaign, she makes a very moving speech, embracing her vulnerability and newness to this work. [82] I was familiar with professor Brené Brown's work, a bestselling author and researcher on vulnerability and shame [83] and found vulnerability transformative. Perhaps in this case, it was also necessary for Watson to make more of an impact—to emotionally engage those she was asking to join in her vision and campaign, around the world.

I thought that by her doing so, stepping up and sharing what she was passionate about and felt strongly about, she became incredibly powerful. Watson saw that it was a necessity; she saw how her male friends were not allowed express their emotions and how this affected them and their mental health; she recognised that the struggle for women's equality and the long-standing oppression was harmful to *both* sexes.[84] And, isn't it easier for a campaign to succeed if the other half of the population is involved, too?

Both men and women have female sides; both women and men have masculine sides. My own thoughts about how to approach equality, and my activism, resonated with hers and her speech touched me deeply. I began to see how there was nothing to prove; otherwise I was hiding behind an idea that I was less powerful, that my being a woman and owning that made me weak.

This was an *idea*, I saw now, which I had both created and inherited from society or other women who had been brought up with, or taught to believe and act out the same thing. In other words, I didn't need to embrace it. I had been fighting for something I could only find inside: acceptance. The lack of compassion in migration and border control, had been met with an approach of mine that meant more reports, more statistics, more *knowledge*. There is a place for knowledge, but it doesn't sit alone in finding solutions.

I was compassionate over these years, definitely, but I hadn't allowed any of the sadness that I'd witnessed or read about to actually penetrate me, until I'd been in Srinigar, and later also in Delhi, India, in 2013 before making my way to Ladakh. There, poetry was the only form that made sense to me at the time of processing what I saw, as I could not easily Skype anybody and was alone there.

Long and rambling, struck by deep anger and grief at the inequality and suffering all around me, I took to scribbling poems and prose in my notebook, hiding my tears behind my sunglasses at the shock. I knew perfectly well that inequality was everywhere, including Ireland, my home country, but India showed me a heightened example. Here, as I wrote in the poem *A Stolen Childhood*, I felt *"my heart tear apart/like a thousand tiny, sharp/shards of glass."* [85] After several years reading, studying, discussing and fighting against poverty and inequality through grassroots solutions and activism, here it was with no pretences.

In Srinigar, on the way to the bus-stop, I'd passed a small child in a wheelchair (clearly not his own, he sat dwarfed by it) with a big, empty bowl resting expectantly on his tiny lap. He was waiting for money from tourists—people like me. His mother had collapsed and was lying on the pavement with a younger son—only a toddler—by her side. Not fifty metres away, around the corner, was a bank with immaculate lawns, security guards and a monument with a large water fountain. The entire building and its surrounding gardens were *dripping* in wealth, in a country rife with water shortages, poor hygiene and poverty.

I was so angry that I returned to where I was staying in Srinigar (a small and creaky old houseboat on Dal Lake) for the rest of the day, where I lay on the cool floorboards and wrote, at first incapacitated and overwhelmed, but with time beginning to understand and integrate things on a deeper level.

Sometimes, over the years, I'd seen how my more feminine side came through, in my dreams, my work with women, girls, words, and the land. That day, I had reached a limit to individual empathy and my ability to cope with levels of sadness and extreme situations. I had realised, as journalist and activist Natasha Walter did too, that there *was* one.[86] Working through this required my emotions and my poetry, not intellect. It was a privileged Westerner's response, certainly, but at the time it was the only thing I could do.

In Malta that sunny morning, I left Fiona's with the words, "What does it mean to be a woman?" on my lips.

On my last day in Malta, I was given John Green's *The Fault In Our Stars* by the grandmother of twelve-year-old Zoe, whom I'd helped with her writing as she wrote poetry and had ideas for a novel. She was a total bookworm: we got on very well. *The Fault In Our Stars* resulted in the last hour of my plane journey spent with tears streaming down my face as I came toward the closing part in the book.

It was good, really good, both the book and my crying. Just the evening and night before I'd been at Hal Far, and I hadn't processed the fact that I was leaving. Material preparations were real: going to the charity shop, the post office, packing and unpacking and repacking, meeting friends and saying goodbyes, doing final interviews for *Integra*. But preparation on an emotional level hadn't sunk in: I was leaving the island that'd been my home for two years.

Something else had happened that week too, something I'd never thought would in my wildest dreams—what I'd thought was the reason I'd gone to Fiona, but when I got there hadn't felt ready to explain.

I'd been at a public meditation. As I was leaving, I was introduced to a girl next to an old friend, Karl.

I was suddenly temporarily stunned!

Emily was so beautiful she took my breath away. I found her *really* attractive, I realised, as a whirlwind of emotions were unleashed inside of me. It all happened in the space of a few seconds, and I laugh now about how I tried to continue to make conversation. After a few minutes we said goodbye—I had to get my things, go home and continue packing, and prepare for Hal Far. All the time I tried to understand what'd just happened, as the image of her face stayed in my mind. Again and again I realised, shocked: it was not just that I'd *found her attractive*, it was that I was *attracted to her!* That was the crucial difference, to me. The feeling had been really strong, and I kept wondering at labels and what this all meant.

There had been one time when I'd said to Dave, when we'd been annoyed with each other, or our situation, "Well, maybe, I'll just... become a lesbian." It'd been a joke, I hadn't meant it obviously. We both knew one doesn't decide; and then, *voilà.* We'd been talking about our relationship and we'd both laughed when I'd said it. I'd never even considered that it might actually happen—and so suddenly—as I hadn't been attracted to a woman before. Like my passport, which until recently, I'd taken for granted—I'd never considered my sexuality.

Early the following morning, I'd texted Lorna in the midst of confused tears and asked her if we could Skype. She replied, "Of course we can sweetheart! Don't worry, sexuality is always fluid... it'll be fine."

I'd gone to Pieta to say goodbye to the little wood there: a place I'd spent time in when I'd lived in the extended urban zone, near the University. I sat on the warm ground by the scorched grass and weathered trees, talking to Lorna. I was going to Hal Far and the Peace Lab later and wanted to be ready for that, so it helped me enormously to speak to her. I wanted to empty my mind, basically be more receptive when I was there, and calm the treadmill my mind had become. I'd leaned my back against a tree and felt words coming to me. *"You are here. It's okay. You have a life to live and love."*

And it was true.

I'd cried because of how things *were,* not because I wanted them to be different—but that was what shocked me, possibly even terrified me. I knew inside me that it felt *right*. How deeply it had struck me seeing Emily like that... How I could never have known before, but for it to have become what felt like a huge part of me, an important part. The intensity or electric kind of feeling I'd got when I'd met Emily would fade, and already was fading. I was still attracted to men, very much so, but I didn't understand my feelings towards women and the power they had, coming all at once and so suddenly it felt overwhelming.

I had no idea what LGBT labels really meant, and whether there was any point in my associating myself with one. I was fearful of it all, though I couldn't seem to address that because my mind had gone into overdrive worrying about everything. It felt like I was a teenager again with all my hormones and explosive ups and downs, which built up uncontrollably for a day or two until I called Lorna.

I am grateful for the support she was, and to the calm that came later. I had taken a completely unexpected journey into a part of myself I'd never known or thought about.

I lived in a changing world, a Europe and Ireland that would accept me—a privilege that many in the world do not have. Lorna was able to help me because she had been there, and knew her own way through. She also knew and reminded me that there was nothing to worry about and everything to be grateful for and happy about: I had found an unknown part of myself that was unfamiliar but which would become an essential part of myself.

24.

Homecoming and an oval flower-bed

Leaving Malta on the airplane, I had plenty of time to think about my experience in the open centre with Antoine. I had so many questions in my mind: the unexamined idea that a passport grants universal freedom, and which *remains* unexamined as long as we take it for granted. I was in one lane because I'm European; and I was let through—not questioned, squinted or frowned at or detained. The little document I held in my hands says that I am from a country and citizenship that is considered "more human, more valid," by international agreements or disagreements that grant acceptance to a select few.

In Dublin airport, I accidentally almost handed over one of Antoine's *Passports* to the immigration control, as the mauve-colour is the same as the Irish one—I'd been carrying both in my laptop bag and they're also the same size. I wondered what would have happened if I'd handed over a poetic *Passport* instead of my own. I wondered, too, what Antoine's experiences were, carrying many of them across borders for readings and literary events, and whether they had ever been noticed.

My parents picked me up at Arrivals in the early hours of the morning and we drove south, down the motorway to County Kilkenny. I drifted in and out of sleep and wakefulness. Rosie, our dog, an excitable foxy-coloured terrier, jumped up and licked my face as she always does when I get out of the car. I climbed into bed at three in the morning, in my own little room, happy to be in a bed I knew.

Next morning, I was in Kilkenny town, in the Credit Union on the main street. There was a large queue, and a screen depicting the headline news in the centre of the building. I waited in line with the people around me while elsewhere, in Britain, MPs debated whether to join in the bombing against the Islamic State by the US, and Emma Watson's UN #HeForShe campaign for women and gender equality gained momentum.

Back in Ireland, to live this time, I was quickly reminded of how "small" Ireland is. This is the way we explain the connections we have, either through family, friends, neighbours, or any other way—for there is always a way. In fact, I have heard and been a part of conversations in which people have shown admirable perseverance and enthusiasm to find out "where is it you come from": you might be connected to someone who lives in Ireland, right down to a granny's cousin's nephew, or some similar, distant connection. Then, suddenly there is the exclamation of "Ah!" and everything clicks into place— they have "placed you," and that is an important thing here.

People wanted to know where it was I "came from" and I found this hard to answer, not having been in Ireland for five years. Did I "come from" the countryside of County Kilkenny? Did I come from all the places I'd been? It seemed funny, the idea that someone might say "Oh, Ciara, yes, she's from a cottage, by the river in Kells, County Kilkenny." It felt more like I came from all the places I'd been.

I soon boarded a bus to Dublin, and the bus driver was an old family-friend and father of a school-friend of mine. It'd been eight years or more since I'd seen him, but Ireland *is* small, and I liked that. Dublin is only a little different, it is small in its own way too.

I went to the cinema: *The Hundred Foot Journey*, directed by Lasse Hallström. There is an epic scene in the beginning that sets the understanding and poignancy of an Indian family trying to "make it" in another culture, an *entirely* different culture, though both share an interest and appreciation for good cuisine, according to tradition: Indian and French. Their cuisines couldn't be more different, or more established. The family plan to continue their restaurant business except *in France,* after a traumatic fire and loss led to their having to leave India.

The eldest son, walking down a narrow laneway in the French hills, after their old van has broken down, says to his father "Stop! *Stop,* we must stop this wandering! Papa, where is home?" he shouts. The father replies, "Home is where the family is." "Yes, exactly, and where are we?" "France!" "Yes, *France!"* the young man said exasperated.

I spent the next ten days, my first back in Ireland, between Dublin and Kilkenny. I met friends and family, and made new contacts for networking with at an environmentalists gathering.

About this time was also my mother's fiftieth birthday, so I made her a flowerbed and helped prepare for the party. The bed was meant to be a circle, but between the rain and my dad finishing the last bit of digging, it turned into a kind of oval shape that, on one side, missed its roundness. It was great to be outside again, and to be home with my extended family whom I had not seen for a long time, playing music, sharing stories. We were celebrating a big year for my mum: I had always forgotten exactly what age she was after she had turned forty-four; it had turned into a joke of ours that, every year, mum was turning forty-four again. And of course she'd always smile, because she was therefore growing younger each year, in my eyes.

At the party, grandad and I were found standing outside, discussing the garden and plants. Gardening has always been something grandad and I have seen eye to eye on.

He gave instructions about the latest additions to the flowerbed and other plants and saplings that were still in pots. It was so grandad: bringing unusual varieties of plants or grafted saplings, and advice. Alongside his gardening, grandad had been a primary school teacher all his life; his interest and focus in history had led him also to do a degree in archaeology by night and to do some excavating. Nevertheless, it still amazed me, given his age. At the time of mum's fiftieth, he was ninety-one years old. Years before, in his eighties, when briefly in hospital, the doctors had asked him what medication he was on. Not was he on any, but which ones? When he replied he was not on anything, they had asked again, thinking that he *must* be taking medication at his age and that he'd not understood the question. He replied, in Latin, smiling: *"Mens sana in corpore sano."* (A healthy mind in a healthy body.)

I laughed when I heard this story recalled by my mum. It seemed so like grandad: philosophical, educated and calm. And always, always (as an author and primary school teacher) his love of language and literature and history, which shone through.

The morning after the party, a group of us drove to nearby Tullahought and scrambled up the hill, and through a beautiful patch of forest to get back down again. The little fingers of the pine needles danced gently in the breeze as I walked quietly along. On my left was a deep carpet of moss, that vibrant green found in Ireland—a country where we have at least seven words to describe and give variation to the water that pours out of the sky almost every day. As we came back to the car, light rain danced on the surface of a little pond nearby; a homecoming to the Irish weather and the land.

During our walk, I thought often about Sylvia Couterié and how close to here she'd been when she'd lived in Ireland. I'd just finished her book *No Tears in Ireland* that morning. It was strange and sad to think of the loneliness and terror of the war that she and her sister had endured as "aliens" in Clonea, Dungarvan, County Waterford at the outbreak of World War II. These were places not far from where I stood now, on Tullahought Hill, Kilmacoliver, by the stone circle. I wondered how people and their memories were connected across time and space, how a place would always hold what had happened despite the passage of time; and how collective psychological memory is perhaps present in a way I don't normally think about. I wondered about people in times gone by and times of war, alone, isolated, branded as "alien." Their overlapping history could be found in their books and the places they'd visited, their accounts of their inhospitable welcome in Ireland, the trauma of leaving everything behind, and yet, how many had changed Ireland for the better.

Couterié had written about friends she'd had in Clonmel who visited her and stayed in Clonea in her tiny beach hut in the summer months, but whom afterwards she couldn't meet. It was too far, they said. Now, sixty years later, in my dad's car, we travelled easily and fast. Couterié had cycled in and out, in all weather, as an eleven-year-old girl, doing the shopping for her younger sister and governess.

The bravery, strength and forgiveness that Couterié portrays is astounding. Not only because of the war and being separated—stranded, literally—from her parents across the sea in France while the fighting continued, but by the way she and her sister, as Protestants, were treated by rural Ireland and by their governess, a staunch Irish Catholic. There was a stubborn will to survive the life she had suddenly been thrown into, isolated in a country she'd been told was where she and her young sister were going to for a short holiday. Her understanding and portrayal of the discrimination she and her sister faced as "aliens" is heart-wrenching.

Each week, she made the required trip to the police station where she signed a large black book on the counter. On one such occasion, as she'd made her way in, the guard had told her they were on the lookout for foreign spies. She recounts: "I stared at them silently, wondering if at the age of twelve I would make a good spy... I carefully wrote in my childish handwriting my name, age, religion, sex and address..." Couterié recounts how she mumbled to herself about "the great stupidity of grown-up people." The guard who had handed her the pen scolded her, saying, "Nice little girls don't swear." "I'm not swearing and in any case, I am not a nice little girl, I'm an alien,"[87] Couterié replied.

I'd been drawn to the title on the bookshelf in my grandmother's apartment; granny had attended the same Ursuline Convent school as Couterié and remembered her vaguely—a walk they had shared once, she thought, as teenage girls at the outbreak of World War II.

Without any understanding of the reasons for adult's mistakes and world history, it makes suffering harder for children during war, Couterié said. "As we seldom speak about feelings, adults quickly ignore us, saying, "They are young, they will forget." But children suffer differently, as she accounts of her own childhood: "Unlike adults during wars [children] do not understand the reasons for them and no one really explains."[88]

I thought of all the current "children of the war"[89]— displaced so young, living here and there and nowhere, by means of a migration policy that keeps their and their families' lives on hold, often for many generations. Meanwhile, much of their childhood passes by with no indication of any political progress that might offer a different kind of future. The little they have could be taken away at any moment, and, most times, hope depends on a court ruling, a piece of paper. This was liberal economic policy. They ran from what had threatened their parents— murder, prison, war, ethnic clashes, political instability, radicalisation, bombs—and are now... better off?

Liberalism is a political or social philosophy or worldview advocating the freedom of the individual, parliamentary systems of government, and (nonviolent) modification of political, social or economic institutions. Was it the next part of this definition that caught us, and led to its undercurrent of violence? "Assuring unrestricted development in all spheres of human endeavour." Yet, liberalism also implies governmental guarantees of individual rights and civil liberties. Is a government's treatment of refugees and asylum seekers, and their lack of protection, because of their perceived "otherness," their "rights and civil liberties" being waived because they don't belong and are deemed unworthy of any such need? Their being cast, as Harsha Walia had said, as "eternal outsiders."

That same week as my mother's birthday, she had told me I was related, albeit distantly, to the Ryan sisters from Tomcoole, County Wexford. The Ryans (a large family of twelve) were politically active in the revolutionary period prior to the formation of the Irish state. At least three participated in the 1916 Rising, and the sisters were outspoken and had literary interests. Two were married in succession to Sean T O'Kelly, Ireland's second President. His first wife was Mary Kate ('Kit') a professor of French at the newly-formed University College Dublin. Agnes, who attended Gaelic League summer school in Ring, County Waterford, married political activist Denis McCullough. Nell spent time in prison after the Rising and later was a prominent member of Wexford County Council. Another, Josephine Mary (or 'Min'), was a prominent member and founding member of *Cumann na mBan* (The Irishwomen's Council), played an important role in the Rising and later married Richard Mulcahy, Chief of Staff of the Irish Republican Army, Minister for Defence in the Free State government and leader of Fine Gael for a time. Their brother James, a member of the Irish Volunteers and of the Irish Republican Brotherhood, who fought in 1916, was a Sinn Féin TD and later a Minister in de Valera's Fiánna Fáil governments from 1932.

Politics on either side of the fence, during the Treaty negotiations, meant there were family divisions, though they later reconciled these for the sake of their children, as they wanted the children to know all their aunts and uncles. Though they were not close—being third cousins—my grandad and his siblings remembered thinking them too politicised and did not engage in or foster any friendship.

Extracts from their letters and diaries featured in the book *Vivid Faces* by Roy Foster. I loved reading something of my ancestry and heritage, however distant the connection. In an article in the *Irish Times*, entitled "Lives and loves: the sexual side of the Rising,"[90] it was said that the Ryan sisters' correspondence profiled a lively existence of parties, flirtation and romance, particularly revolving around Kit's circle of friends in Dublin. It felt like a claim to my history, something that rooted me to Ireland—these were women in my lineage who had written, who had been outspoken and political. It made sense, to me, and I was glad to know it.

25.

The Collateral Repair Project in Amman

I made contact with Bella Hancock, whom I knew through the Women and Words group I'd started on Facebook several months before—or so I thought until I'd accepted her incoming video call on Skype. Looking into my webcam, recognising her wide smile and wavy blonde hair, I realised we also knew each other from the Earthsong camp. On the Earthsong Network on Facebook, she'd posted one day about her online fundraising campaign for her up-coming work with refugees in Amman. I wanted to know more, particularly as Bella was going to teach yoga there and begin training refugees so that they could teach when she had left. These classes were for those who were currently in Amman and received help from The Collateral Repair Project (CRP) NGO.[91]

Yoga, in this context, can be healing and allow relaxation and peace of mind, in cases of extreme stress or anxiety despite the external circumstances of ill health, grief, and loss. It can also provide much needed rest from the bigger questions and immediate distress of what's led to having to flee, and the journey itself.

"I'll be working for the CRP, teaching classes in the mornings five days per week—that's the training group for a Foundation Teacher Training. Then, in the afternoons, I'll be with the women doing the dance class, and with the men one day per week; on Saturday, the teens, both boys and girls. I'll have a strict schedule and a lot of work to do, but it also feels like an open space. I get the sense that it is a door to something else: I don't think it's going to stop there."

"Have you worked with refugees before?" I asked, curious.

"No. In South America, though, I did work with women and disadvantaged young people. It was in the city, downtown, amidst the noise and traffic, the chaos."

We began speaking about immigration and the recent crisis at Lampedusa.

"The EU says it's Italy's problem, and Italy says it's a European problem," Bella said. "And that made me wonder, what are borders all about, actually? It's a global issue, a political issue. And then there's this whole thing at the moment, about ISIS becoming another state. It's generating extreme fear—the polar opposite of freedom. This is an international problem, and it's not going away.

"I have this friend, she's German and got married to a Tanzanian man. He couldn't get the permit to come over here. He had a passport and was a professional photographer, middle-class you know. But it was just, 'No, no, no...' The Irish Embassy wouldn't even talk to him when he went in there. Now, they are married, but really I learned from the whole thing—it is a race issue. That's what we're dealing with.

"Somebody said to me, 'It's great you're going away to Amman you know, but there are refugees in Ireland and those people are in need of help too.' And I'm aware, really aware of that. I was at a concert recently and met a lovely woman there. She is part of a group that offers support to asylum seekers and refugees in a direct provision centre in Clonakility. She asked would I consider teaching yoga and dance there. Dance—it's so great for these people! Their life, as refugees, is stuck, immobilised, so to move their bodies is just so great. They loved it."

Bella told me that while dancing on her own, she had realised that her being in Jordan and with the women there is a sharing. "I'm the dance teacher, yes, but we're coming together and having fun, and throughout it I'm just holding the space, rather than my teaching a choreographed dance. And that's the amazing thing about it all—we'll flow together."

I asked Bella whether she had reached her target for her fundraising, and heard the happiness in her voice when she responded positively. She spoke about the details of the CRP NGO.

"CRP is a national project, and it was set up by women. It's in a downtown area where the refugees flood to. It was set up about ten years ago, during the Iraq War, by a woman in her sixties called Sasha Crowe. She'd been horrified at what she saw and wanted to do something. She fundraised—it has a real grassroots beginning. The co-ordinator is a refugee from Iraq; he came to Amman and now has his protected status there. Everybody knows the staff and greets them on the street; it's really rooted in the community. It's got that atmosphere, it's not government run; instead it's run by love and dedication, so I think whatever we present will be supported.

"There's also a place where people can come if they have no food or nowhere to sleep and they have just arrived. A teens group was set up, and for the children there's arts and crafts, dancing, music. There was a man who came from Canada who did music and songwriting projects with CRP, whatever makes sense, because this is for reconciliation and wellbeing. These are tools that they can draw on for a sense of safety and home in themselves... and things like yoga and dance too.

"Tell me more about what you'll do there in the classes," I said.

"With the yoga, I'll focus on keeping it simple," Bella said. "Safety, we'll work on that first. 'There might be something that makes you feel safe,' I'll say, 'that you would like to take to the class with you.' That could be anything—like a photo or a word on paper or a headscarf. Something they can have with them in the room so that there is the feeling of this being a safe place, doing yoga, and being together; here. Then I'll work on body-mind awareness. There's probably anxiety, depression, powerlessness that these people are dealing with.

"The women in Salvador, where I have worked before in the Bahia state of Brazil, were beautiful. It's old, colonial, Baroque kind of culture there. The heart of Brazil. It's where the African slaves were brought to. Dark history, but inner light as well. Strong women—drugs, guns, violence—they're coming from a different story than in Amman. In the refugee camp, some of the Iraqis, for example are middle-class; they are displaced and have lost things. But they do not necessarily come from poor backgrounds.

"In Salvador I used the theme of 'offering.' You know, even if we think we have nothing, we can still offer our hearts, ourselves. In Salvador, the people have marvellously big hearts. Gorgeous women. So warm and kind. Life is quite hard in Brazil. The women are very much on their own in terms of their children. It's a 'macho' sort of culture, so the men feel like they have to leave, or are under pressure to leave, and the women are strong, tough. The older women especially are solid, kind, supportive. But between the younger women, they tended to be competitive."

"About what?" I asked.

"To be beautiful, to get the man, that kind of thing," Bella said. "It's a competitive culture, quite sad. Some of them get cosmetic surgery, breast implants for example, even if they have no money for glass in their windows.

"I did a private dance class too. That was very interesting because they had to pay to come along to the workshop. Because it was private, these women had more money and the feeling was like, I want to be the most beautiful girl dancing. So, I had them do all kinds of things, like calligraphy for example, to take them out of that mind-set. To change it, and take another perspective—why am I dancing? Only for myself, or is it something bigger than me?"

Bella paused for a moment, reflecting. Then she smiled, remembering, "The second day of the workshop happened to be International Women's Day. Some of them spent two hours doing their make-up and costumes, hair... I just threw on a very simple thing: I was travelling

"Something very interesting happened that night: a man started drumming, I started to do some improvised dancing, and I called each of the women to join me. We were all improvising and all of the men were like 'What's happening?' My friend said to me after that that had never happened before.

"Something changed, something in the mind-set." she continued, "I told them, 'We are dancing for all the women around the world who cannot dance, who aren't free to express themselves.'

"Another time, with the background of poverty, I taught kids with very poor backgrounds. My friend Marcia, he told me they might be reactive, so I was kind of nervous and prepared for that. But it wasn't like that at all. They got it—and they danced! One beautiful young man said he'd translate for me because I didn't speak Spanish. We had a wonderful time together. 'You are professional dancers,' I said to them, 'and you all have fantastic teachers who can teach you about technique and the perfection of it, but that is not what I'm here for.' We did a dance on joy, and they all did it; they all expressed joy. I think all that was preparation for Jordan."

"So, given all this... tell me about what home means to you, Bella," I said.

"Over the last two years, I left my home. I lived in my studio, I travelled, and wherever that was became my home. It was transient, but it was a safe place that I held wherever I was.

"I love coming home to myself," she said, "And I get it through my yoga practice. Breath is the centre of this, the key to this... Breathing into the lower belly, the breath moving downwards. The breath is the connection to the two—the heart and the body. Hands on self—the contact is important—to be like, 'I'm holding myself, and I am here now.' For the first bit of time in those two years after I'd left home, I couldn't do anything more than sit. I couldn't do any asanas,[14] or pranayama, just had to be with myself,

---

[14] Asanas are the yogic exercises, literally movements or postures, that are normally thought of as Yoga, but are in fact only a part of what yoga means. In Sanskrit, the word *yoga* means union.

and hold that space to be there. Even if it was just one hour it was, 'Okay, I have this space, on my yoga mat, and I'll just sit here... with that feeling of coming home to myself.'

"Another thing I'll do in Amman actually," Bella added, "is yoga nidra,[15] which in a way is like a welcoming home to oneself. But again, very simple.

"This thing about home," she continued. "I'd often thought I was a kind of 'earthy' person. Our family house was beautiful, ecological—we built it, me and my partner. I always thought I could never leave this, you know; but life throws things at you, and sometimes you get no choice. I left, so I began to think it was more like, 'Okay, this is not my home—it's a house. It was my home, but my home is gonna become something else...' and you let go, you know. And it'll be wherever I happen to be travelling. Home could be any hotel room I'd to stay in, but the home inside enables me to do that.

"In Amman, though, people are from Syria, Iraq, Palestine. They've got no choice, they can't go back." Bella stopped for a moment. "No choice; I can't imagine what

---

Pranayamas are breath control, yogic exercises that are done as part and parcel of the wider, eight-limbed yoga practices, normally done before meditation.

[15] *Yoga nidra* (literally yogic sleep) is the practice of mindful relaxation, where one can access deeper levels of conscious states, set intentions and release stress. In the beginning, it is guided, or led.

that's like. And, if they do go back, everything will be different; destroyed. I have choices, it's totally different."

"On the subject of choices and privilege and travel, let me tell you about the *Passaport*," I said. "I'm organising for Antoine to come to Ireland next year with it." I read two extracts into the Skype webcam; Bella resonated strongly with the poem and its message.

"It's interesting," I said, "isn't it? I never gave it much thought, and had a naïve and unquestioned understanding—more of an assumption really—that passports do grant freedom. After all, they are for travel, right? When I met Antoine, it became a whole other thing, and I began to realise that, yes, for me it is a symbol of freedom, or facilitates my freedom of travel, but for many it takes it away."

"Yes, yes," Bella said softly. "I've seen that myself too."

"It was really lovely to share with you my ideas, and hear yours. Thank you. There aren't that many yoga teachers I know who are also activists, or activists taking more holistic approaches to care and supporting those in need of immediate aid."

I sat in the kitchen in Clontarf, Dublin where I lived, by my notes and growing manuscript after Bella and I finished our Skype conversation. As a yoga teacher too, I knew how yoga can create stability and bring us into the moment, provide relief and presence, healing. Each moment is easier as we live from one to the next.

Yoga and meditation training meant that it was a hand-*up*, not a hand-*out*—it was not charity, it was a self-empowering process that would grow of its own accord, particularly as refugees in CRP would be trained. It could be used and taught again and again, and be passed on; it could never be used up. And it was a practice possible anywhere, not dependent on external circumstances. With freedom from reliving the experience in the mind, peace, renewal, and healing can begin.

26.

Clowns Without Borders
and a little girl in borrowed coats

"You've got to follow your dreams," Kim said over the phone to me in my room in North Dublin where I lived by the sea. We spoke this way as she had no internet connection where she was, in County Cork at the time. Her voice was deep, as I remembered it, and somehow mystical—which, I thought, added to Kim's allure as a performer, as well as her startlingly blue eyes.

"I remember six or seven years ago, when I was in University in Galway before I was clowning, I did a little juggling. I heard about Clowns Without Borders[92] and I just said, 'How could I ever meet the people who are as cool as to do this!?'

"I signed up for a training with Raymond Keane, the Irish actor, theatre director, clown and performer, and straight away he told us his brother was working with Clowns Without Borders. It really showed the power of clowning. There was this deep, instinctual feeling that I needed to work with Clowns Without Borders.

"So, Clowns Without Borders Ireland have probably done ten tours now. There were two to Jordan, one at the start and one at the end of the year which I went on," Kim said. "The idea is to go to a place with refugees, to get the children smiling and laughing. We do a show, we perform, and we do a workshop, with whatever little resources are there. Or we just perform if the workshop isn't possible, like among the Syrian community in Jordan, there's mayhem. Jordan was my first tour.

"There had been UN meetings when I went to Jordan, because of the conflict. It's liberal, but Jordan is the fifth driest country in the world as well, and that doesn't help. There are men who'd crossed the border with coal bags on their heads as the only thing they could bring with them: they'd left their parents behind—they were too old to cross."

Kim was uncharacteristically quiet for a moment.

"So tell me more about what you guys do and the need for it, for clowning?" I asked.

"The adults have nothing to do. They're trapped inside. There are rows of teachers and psychologists etc., come to help. And the adults who live there are standing around and just want a *laugh*! Now, this camp was not what I expected—they were not in tents. Instead, there were big, old apartment blocks, built for when the desert road or railway was made in the past.

"It's northern Jordan, bordering Syria. So in our shows, because we speak English, we use no language, and nothing inappropriate. The children laughed—" Kim laughed suddenly, too, explaining, "You see, I was the only girl, and so in our show, I was the girl 'calling the shots'— I was in charge. There is clearly a desperate need for diversion: sometimes even the adults push to the front."

"Is there a time that particularly stands out?"

"One was in a women's shelter. It was in Amman, the capital city, in a tiny walled-garden. Some women were Palestinian and Iraqi, some Arabic. And they were so traumatised that when I came in, they ran away. They were in deep trauma. I talked to the woman in charge, and she said to be gentle, not to approach them directly. It's a little boisterous, clowning, you know, like there might be a kick in the bum, that kind of thing. But we had to be gentle. When we came in, the girls had their hands under their knees, and they were looking down. By the end, they were saying, 'Thanks so much, we needed a laugh, and we got a laugh; we needed this *lightness.*'

"I remember asking some of the children in a camp, 'Where are you from?'" Kim continued. "Their answer was,

'I'm from here.' But their parents quickly intervened—'No, you are not,' they said. 'You are Palestinian, don't ever forget that!'

"They had only been *born* there, in Jordan. And yet, to the children it was true, it seemed, in a way: they were from where they were born.

"After all this time, all this waiting, all this fighting in their home country; there's still this... *hope* about going back. We were in primary schools and playgroups. In one school, there was a map crudely painted on the wall, a large map of Palestine. In Arabic and English: *Never forget this is your homeland,* was written underneath.

"The Clowns Without Borders driver, Abdullah—a taxi driver all his life, he did Arabic translation for us too—had a daughter about twenty-one years old. They were a really liberal family. And they said, 'No, no we're *Palestinian,*'—even though nobody in their family had ever been in Palestine! They told us to go to the Dead Sea at Sinai. 'It's twenty minutes that way,' they said. So, we drove there.

"I stood there, and I looked across the sea: it was Palestine! Abdullah can *look* at Palestine from his café building, but he isn't allowed to go there!

"There are these third-generation families in Jordan; they're lucky enough, they have a house or a building, but there is still this sense of identity: they are a refugee, on paper, in a way, because they cannot go back to where they came from.

"Jordan is a tourist destination, much like Howth or Dun Laoghaire, in County Dublin," Kim said. "So, from Aqaba, on top of the Red Sea, it's ten or fifteen minutes to Eliat in the South of Israel, on the Egyptian and Jordanian border. The locals would say to us tourists, 'Why don't you go there?' And we were like, 'Why, do you go there?' And they'd say, 'No, once we go to Jordan, we can't go back into Palestinian territory.'

"In Palestine, they're trying to get people *out* and not *in*, so if they left, then it'd be impossible to return. The third and fourth generation families in Jordan, they're thinking, 'Is this gonna last another week or month, or am I gonna be here for the rest of my days?'

"I imagine two grandfathers: a Syrian and a Palestinian, finding their feet—as much as they can in a refugee camp—but both looking at each other, and the Syrian grandfather thinking, *You've been here three generations and you've not been back!*

"I remember at one prefab there was this amazing man..." I felt the smile in Kim's voice as she said, "The men were playing volleyball. One of the clown's sandals broke and this man went off and got him another one. They were so shocked to see me, a woman playing soccer. They are super playful, full of fun.

"A man with a gas ring was making coffee. He invited us into the prefab he shared with two other families—I remember all the children's super neat schoolbags lined up inside... He was a beautiful, well-educated man, fluent in German, English and French, from Damascus; he'd travelled in Europe. He couldn't have been any more like us—but here he was, inviting us into his prefab.

"He'd studied engineering in Berlin. He was a successful middle-class Syrian. 'It was such a beautiful country,' he said. 'I'd just finished my travels, I was fine and back in Syria, when everything suddenly hit the fan. But by now I had a wife and two kids, parents getting elderly. If it'd been five years before, I could've gone back to Germany, but I couldn't afford anything more than a coal bag on my head and to walk across the border with my family.'

"What would they be doing, all these people, where

would they be, if the Indian government and the Jordanian government weren't helping out?" Kim added.

"I remember, years ago in West Africa," she continued, "where I learned African dance. And these Senegalese, Gambian and Malian men were asking me 'Madam, can I have your address? I want to be your friend.' And I was like, 'What the fuck is this? This is *insane!*' And I wondered if I was to tell them and they'd put on the visa or sponsor form, 'Oh, Kim McDonnell, from Cavan in Ireland.' And then I realised: they just needed to go to Europe, they wanted to get out. In Ghana, there's a lot of sex tourism. There are white—European—women who get married to local Ghanian men. Then, back at home, these men just... *disappear.* They really needed visas, they needed to get out.

"There is this saying, 'Sex makes the world go round,' but no, I'd say visas do. And when the two get mingled, that's when it's really messy!"

We began to speak about Ireland and Antoine's visit, our hopes for where we would visit when he arrived in a few months time.

"In Salthill in Galway," Kim said, remembering a last thought, "there is an asylum centre. I remember a young Iranian girl, and all she used to say was, 'We had a swimming pool, we had one too!' And here she was, in borrowed coats. Her parents were lawyers, but here, they were ten to a room."

After Kim and I finished our call, I sat in my office chair thinking, her last words about the little girl in borrowed coats still with me; the heartbreaking simplicity of her words, and her loss. *"We had a swimming pool, we had one too..."*

27.

"You are from everywhere?"

We lit our scraps of paper, one from the other, after voicing what was on them and watched as they floated below, into the river. I leaned over and watched mine—a tiny flaming speck, swirling on the surface of the water before it went out and away downstream, or became invisible in the darkness of the Liffey.

As I stood on Bachelor's Walk with my three friends, I knew that I wanted to do something for women around the world. But the women I knew were *Irish* women; the country I'd grown up in was Ireland. This was where my work would start, that was clear. To know what was next and what was needed, given that I had been away for the best part of five years, I needed to find out what were the networks that we (my friends/colleagues and I) could link into and strengthen, and what would need to be created that hadn't already been. We did not want to reinvent the wheel; we wanted to be respectful of our elders and those who had already made milestones.

I prayed for Ireland, and for clarity in what lay ahead, given the support I had in the three women standing next to me, my own strength, and through friends I had. I prayed for women around the world who are oppressed—not only by men, but by other women and themselves too. And I prayed for those homeless in the city in the coming winter. I found the situation of homeless people in Dublin shocking; I had moved there only three weeks previously. It was coming into winter, mid-October; it was cold and wet and there were a great number of people homeless for a variety of socio-economic reasons. The homeless shelters were full, and some were choosing not to stay there as they considered it less dangerous to be on the streets than in the shelters.

I had met my three friends, Leslie, Anca and Rhiannon through Women and Words on Facebook—though I'd known Leslie before that too. We had felt drawn to work with women together, as she was completing her PhD on sex and sexuality education; combined with my interests, activism, and the play I'd put on with teenage girls, we felt a vision for a project beginning to form. All four of us wanted to exchange ideas and get to know each other better before setting up a Women's Group. I thought, and they agreed, that we needed to be a strong group together before we could open our doors—when we had a location—to other women.

That evening, we wrote three wishes and three things we wanted to let go of, either personal or collective. We stood on Bachelor's Walk and went down the wooden walkway toward the Liffey. Climbing over the railing so that we stood closer to the water, we saw where it was dark and moved steadily below us, the streetlights and high-rise buildings reflected on its surface.

My friends and I said goodbye, and agreed that we would continue meeting until we felt ready and clear about extending the Circle, inviting other women and deciding what exactly we were going to do.

The following morning I joined a friend's birthday ramble up the Hill of Tara in County Meath.

Tara is an ancient sacred site, with a history that goes back to 3000BC. It was the seat of 142 Irish Kings where they became the High Kings of Ireland, *Árd Rí na hÉireann,* and the site of The Battle of Tara, 1798. My grandfather, a former archaeologist, had been one of the excavators at the oldest monument on the Hill, The Mound of the Hostages, or *Duma na nGiall* in Irish, during the 1950s. This mound covers a burial monument built in the period just before 3000 BC, which was used as a place to bury human remains for more than 1,500 years. It lies near the northern edge of a large enclosure called *Ráith na Ríg* (Fort of the Kings). The Hill of Tara has long been associated with ritual and spirit, rich in mythology, and is one of the largest complexes of Celtic monuments in Europe. In the words of author Michael Slavin:

> *"Tara's story is Ireland's story. Tara's symbols are Ireland's symbols—the harp, the shamrock, the ancient gold. Prominent in our oldest myths and legends, the hill has been at the centre of things Irish since the earliest times. In some mysterious way, Tara touches the very soul of Ireland. While its regal and heroic identity hark back to a legendary time long gone by, as a symbol, Tara has survived right up to the present. Thus down the centuries great lovers of this land—like the United Irishmen of 1798, or Daniel O'Connell, the Liberator—have used Tara's grassy banks as a backdrop for their dreams and their messages."*[93]

I wandered down the hill to where it was shaded and the sun hadn't yet dried the dew. There was a hawthorn tree with wishes and prayers tied on to its branches, some made with ribbons, some grass or wool, a green soft-toy shamrock, foreign bank notes. I attached two wishes of my own, in the form of small twigs, and watched as two little girls circled the tree and peered into the branches. Then their mother and father called out to them, "What are you doing in there? Not taking things off the tree, I hope! The *faeries* will get you," they said.

I smiled at this—at our connection that hasn't been lost to our pagan and mythological roots in Ireland, even if remembered momentarily, joking.

At Tara, I felt a deep, peaceful energy and strong sense of kinship and connection with the land, stronger than any I'd felt recently, and spent most of the time lying on one of the circular mounds of the hill. In my experience, the memory of land that is sacred, or energetically intact, has healing power that is immensely transformative. Fiona had told me that when I went back to Ireland I was to lie on the Hill of Tara—in the earth, the mud, the history and memory of bloodshed. This was what I did and felt in the land as I lay on the grassy hills, the sun touching my skin. I had full awareness of all that had come before at this ancient site and held it there; it was like the earth throbbed with a heartbeat that had been made and strengthened by the spirit and history of the people who had fought to keep it, their rituals and place here, amongst the hills. As I'd returned to Ireland only a month before, I felt myself beginning to *land* here, to know this was home. I felt a strong connection to County Meath. This is the county where Tara and Newgrange and a number of other sacred sites lie, in their stillness and mystery. Steeped in long-ago dreams and mythology, our dead were previously buried here. Still to this day, it is a place for wishes and pilgrimage.

That evening, back in Dublin, I was doing some grocery shopping when a young man, a tourist, stopped me on O'Connell Street.

"Where is St Stephen's Green?" he asked.

I began to answer, but he said something else.

"Your accent, it's so nice, where are you from?"

"I am Irish," I said. "St Stephens Green is on the southside, we are on the northside, so—"

"But you have been away? You are German, maybe?"

I laughed, I was beginning to see where the conversation was going. "No. Well, half-German, I suppose. I have been in many other places—that's why my accent is different... You see where those buses are going—"

"Where have you been, where did you live? I am Sam," he said offering his hand. "Nice to meet you."

"And I'm Ciara," I said.

"Ah, so you are from everywhere?" he asked.

"Perhaps," I smiled.

Afterword

Amanuel (chapters 2, 4, and 17) was approved for a visa to Canada. After a four-year application process, he awaited final clearance and the stamp on his travel document that would at last allow him to leave Malta, which he received in spring 2016. Canada is his new home.

Bolton House Hostel, Waterford, Ireland where the South East Refugee Information Centre (chapter 8) was held on the floor below, was unfortunately burnt down in an accident—a fire-some months after I had visited it. Through their insurance, Reverend John Rochford plans to move back into the Centre in 2016, where he will continue his work to appeal and prevent deportation orders under (Section 3.6 of the) Immigration Act 1999; until then, his work continues in a lawyer's office just two blocks away from his premises.

Five months after my meeting Leslie Sherlock when we sent our burning paper wishes for women in Ireland, floating down the Liffey in Dublin (chapter 27), we held the International Women's Day Weekend with seventy-five women in Newgrange, County Meath, in March 2015 as part of *Slí na mBan* (Irish for "Way of the Woman") women's collective. After the conference, a vision of local women's circles came forth, and it is now a diverse and active group for all things women-connected and women-in-community (with events and women's circles, and a vibrant Facebook group). *Slí na mBan* networks now extend to twenty-one facilitators and four mentors around the country, under the original ethos. It continues to build and foster women's community in Ireland, and is run by Leslie Sherock (co-founder) with much assistance from facilitators in the *Slí na mBan* network.

Antoine Cassar and the *Passaport Project* (chapters 18, 19, and 21) came to Ireland for a tour in May 2015, in collaboration with Anti Deportation Ireland. For this tour I wrote and performed a piece, *To be Part of the Irish Nation with No Punctuation*,[94] based on the most recent Irish passport and its latent injustices, lamenting the fact that there are children held in a number of the direct provision centres in Ireland, while "my" new and shining, expensive passport (that is not my property at all) is "laced with poetry," the Irish landscape and ancient relics. Each comma and semi-colon felt like a clause, an afterthought, excluding many from citizenship. In the final analysis, there are still children in direct provision, most of which are tucked out of sight in rural Ireland, in harsh and inappropriate conditions. We have let them down, and ourselves, as long as there is *one* still held there. According to a report by the Irish Refugee Council, there are about 1,800 children and young people in direct provision in Ireland; and the time spent there can be as long as seven years.[95]

Antain Mac Lochlainn, Irish writer and academic, translated a section of the Passaport poem which was published in the Irish language magazine Comhar[96],[97] for the tour in May 2015, and which he read extracts from in Dublin. One of his works, 'Journey,' (a translated work from Irish), can be read on the City of Sanctuary website.[98]

Pietro Bonacina, Italian photographer and anthropologist, who asked me to perform at his event, *f'Darhom: At Home*, in Malta, and which marked the beginning of my writing *Integra,* later moved to Senegal where he worked for an Italian NGO. There, he made a photographic portfolio of *talibes*: children who join informal Koranic schools in Senegal, some of whom essentially end up as streetkids, begging by day for handfuls of rice or money. He wanted to show the contradiction of modern society, and deconstruct a congenially accepted meaning—*if you smile you are not suffering.* We normally think that a smiling person is happy, or a smile is synonymous with a good feeling, and "rarely associate it with suffering and pain." His observation was of a society which seemed more concerned with presenting a happy appearance—the *talibes* were encouraged to smile—instead of dealing with the growing problem of *talibes*, who collect money that goes to their spiritual teachers and are often living in dire poverty. Later, returning to the north of Italy, Pietro worked as coordinator and educator in an asylum seekers' centre, portraying some refugees' in "*Mamma mia dammi 100 lire*" portfolio.[99]

Bella Hancock (chapter 25) and other teachers are offering weekly yoga classes in the direct provision centre in Clonakilty, Co. Cork; she also hopes to teach dance there. She has since returned to Amman, in 2016, with a group of yoga teachers to continue training refugees in yoga and meditation to be teachers themselves.

At the time of publication, I haven't yet visited Peter Cowman and his Living Architecture Centre (chapters 10 and 12), but hope to soon and to do one of his courses to create a home and shelter that is my own: alive, living, and with my own hands.

Acknowledgements

People took me into their homes, their lives, their offices, their arms and hearts, to answer my questions and tell me their stories. Thank you from the depth of my heart, for telling me all that you did. Even those who did not make it into the final draft informed my way of thinking and gave me a starting point. You are almost innumerable but this is most of you: *Amal, *Amanuel, *Akeem, *Mark, my grandfather Paul Gerhardt, my German grandmother who wishes to remain anonymous, Dave Rock, Lorna Fox, Colm Gardner, *Danielle, David Patterson, Antoine Cassar, Anna Szabo, Rudi 'Roo' Hunt, Debbie Hunt, Agi Tebarts, *Boadi, Bella Hancock, Kim McCafferty, Stella Mifsud, Maria Pisani, Censu Caruana, Mark Forster, Winston Lneumi, Robert Green, and Ingram Bondin.

Immense gratitude to my family who supported me in many ways while I climbed the mountain that *Integra* sometimes was—this book could not have been written without your help: in particular my mother Rosemary Ryan, for numerous mornings and nights poring over the manuscript; also my father Dieter Gerhardt; my sister, Liadan, for never taking me too seriously; and my grandfather, John A. Ryan, for your love of literature and the natural world. Amy Borg and Natalie Owens, who saw the potential in the beginning of this book, and for innumerable writers chats. Thank you, Antoine, for your support and for your enthusiasm when I hadn't any. Lucy Pearse, for your work on the manuscript at a critical point, and your showing me how to weave it together; Patrick Bridgeman, for proofreading—and more. Thank you to the Dublin Writers Forum, where I aimed(!) to be each Thursday while I lived in Dublin—I have enormously appreciated the critique and feedback and incentive to get organised. Thank you to Young Friends of the Earth and the opportunity to collaborate on presenting the Passport Project in Brussels with Antoine; and to Anti-Deportation Ireland, particularly Mike Fitzgibbon, its Director, for hosting the Passport Project Tour in Ireland. Mary Honan from the Wild Geese radio show in Limerick, for hosting me on air to speak about community, integration and migration in Ireland. I would like to especially thank Jen Christion Myers, PhD candidate, for sharing her research. Marese Hegarty, Richard Hendin, Fiona Lyndley, Keith Perry, Martin Jahn (aka "NoWhere Boy") and other contributors. Melanie Vella, for legal advice. Vanessa Sheehan, even the *idea* of your thesis made me say, "Yes, this is why I write, and always will." Donal O'Farrell, for your awareness of "deep time," as a geologist: "the Earth with its beauty and impossible longevity." Pietro Bonacina, for inviting me to perform at the mixed media exhibition *f'Darhom* on home and intercultural dialogue in Malta, which gave a place for my poems and my anger, and which led to my writing *Integra*.

Thank you to all my mentors, professors, teachers, peers and facilitators throughout my early years and later adult years for your work and your dedication: Astrid Theissen, Margaret Henry, Thomas Partsch, Richard Auler, Jyoti Tyler, Chrysta Faye, Lauren Howe, Hilary Harvey, Sian Cowman, Carmen Sanchez, Martin Hyams, Ruairi McKiernan, professor Tilar J. Mazzeo, Antoine Cassar, Dr Everaldo Attard, Maria Pisani PhD, Censu Caruana PhD, Dr Nick Chisholm, Mike Fitzgibbon PhD, Guhypati (or "G"), Alfred Decker, Helena Norberg-Hodge PhD, Dolores Whelan, Lydia Kiernan, Peter Cowman, Larry Shoemake PhD, Dr David Mifsud, Carin Kooy, Fiona Lyndley, Treacy

O'Connor, Lesley Merriman, Rachel Parry; Eva Ensler, Clarissa Pinkola Estes PhD, Christiane Northrup PhD, and, more recently, Martin Duffy and all at Dunderry Park Shamanic Studies Centre in Meath, Ireland.

Thank you to the many places, homes, desks, cafès and parks where I have written. Thank you to Nicola Winters, Leslie Sherlock, Anca Berindeu, Anna Runefelt, Alison Kingston, Lydia Atkins, Margaret McHugh, Gerry Dalton, Marese Hegarty, Sue Hassett, Grace Wilentz, Masha Duna and Enda Donnellan, for your friendship, your support and kindness.

There were more people who were interviewed for *Integra*, but whose words did not make it onto the final pages—I had started too big, the idea was too big, and I was trying to ask too many questions in one place:

Mark Forster, an outdoors guide and ex-army commander.

Censu Caruana, a good friend, and professor of Environmental Education at University of Malta.

Winston Lneumi, who trained trainers in Holland to work with refugees, and has travelled and worked in a dizzying number of countries.

Robert Green, aka "Greenie," on mathematics and the theory of completeness; Ingram Bondin, PhD candidate, for your thoughts on the theory of wholeness and integration in mathematics.

And another, I'll call her Danielle, who shared her story with me, though she later made the important decision that it must be written by her.

Further Reading - Networks, Groups and Resources

This list has been put together in the hope it proves useful to find more information, reach out to others, or live the life you want to live. Some are cross-sectional, but I have listed them where they're most frequent/appropriate. Also, check the *Endnotes* section.

You can support groups such as Avaaz, SumOfUs, Front Line Defenders, Amnesty, Uplift and others who campaign directly for protection of those who live in countries where it is illegal to be LGBT, and/or there is little or no support. There is an excellent book, released this year, *Queer Wars* (see LGBTQ section) which deals with the growing international polarisation over sexual rights, the complexities of how best to support LGBT activists and tackling homophobia.

Notes on this resources section: 1) In the interest of space, I have placed titles by the same author in one line. I have put the publisher name only at the end, where the publisher did not change across publications. 2) At the end of the section, I have found it helpful to separate them here for ease of reading.

Migration, Borders & Human Rights

Azzopardi, A. & Grech, S. (2012). *Inclusive communities: A critical reader* (Vol. 16). Springer Science & Business Media.

Berghs, M. (2015). Disability and Displacement in times of Conflict: Rethinking Migration, Flows and Boundaries. *Disability and the Global South,2*(1), 442-459.

Cassar, A., various incl. the *Passaport Project, Merhba* 'Welcome'. www.antoinecassar.wordpress.com/ & www.passaportproject.org

Cleave, C. (2009). *The Other Hand/Little Bee.* Hachette UK/Simon & Schuster.
Q&A about the book: www.chriscleave.com/little-bee/the-true-story-behind-my-new-novel/

Collier, P. (2013). *Exodus: Immigration and Multiculturalism in the 21st Century.* Penguin Books.

Crossan, S. (2011). *The Weight of Water.* Bloomsbury Publishing.

HumanKind - www.facebook.com/groups/1686179244987392/

Irish Refugee Council - www.irishrefugeecouncil.ie
Children and young people in direct provision accommodation - www.irishrefugeecouncil.ie/children-and-young-people/children-in-direct-provision-accommodation/two-page-report-summary

Migrant Rights Centre Ireland - www.mrci.ie

No One Is Illegal - www.nooneisillegal.org

Pisani, M. (2012). *Addressing the 'citizenship assumption' in critical pedagogy: Exploring the case of rejected female sub-Saharan African asylum seekers in Malta.* Power and Education, 4(2), 185-195.

Spread Poetry Not Fear - www.facebook.com/spreadpoetrynotfear/?fref=ts

Stalker, P. (2008). *The No-Nonsense Guide to Global Migration.* Verso.

State, Ed. Bosch, S. & Haughey, A. (2011). Project Press (Projects Arts Centre, Dublin, Ireland.)

UNHCR - www.unhcr.org/cgi-bin/texis/vtx/home

Walia, H. (2013). *Undoing Border Imperialism.* AK Press.

Wek, A. (2009). *Alek: From Sudanese Refugee to International Supermodel.* Harper Collins.

Zavella, P. (2011). *I'm Neither Here Nor There.* Duke University Press.

- **Links from the Dublin Calais Solidarity Group (Facebook)**

Volunteer in Calais - www.tinyurl.com/hg9eh57

Get involved with groups in Ireland - www.tinyurl.com/jommolh

Send a letter (template) to politicians demanding action:

(short) http://tinyurl.com/gucmztm

& (long) www.tinyurl.com/jcnrt52

Get local TDs' email addresses - www.tinyurl.com/znwurpq

Educational 'debunking myths' about refugees -
www.tinyurl.com/jt4zwye

Donate: www.gofundme.com/9zwfscys

Travel, Indigenous, Political, Multicultural, Identity

Al Jazeera - www.aljazeera.com

Chengu, G., by Global Research (September 2014). *America Created Al-Qaeda and the ISIS Terror Group*. www.globalresearch.ca/america-created-al-qaeda-and-the-isis-terror-group/5402881

Choquette, S. (2014). *Walking Home*. Hay House.

Dolan, A. M. (2014). *You, Me and Diversity*. Trentham/Institute of Education.

Farren, A. (2014). *Learning to Love Ireland: An Immigrant's Tale*. Original Writing.

Gomo, M. (2010). *A Fine Madness*. Ayebia Clarke Publishing.

Hunt, D. Blog of the wagon - www.gypsyrosed.blogspot.ie/

MacWeeney, A. (2007). *Irish Travellers, Tinkers No More*. New England College.

Macy, J. (2010). *Pass It On: Five Stories that Can Change the World*. Parallax Press.

Marnham, P. (1981). *Dispatches from Africa*. Abacus.

Murphy, D., various incl. (2005) *Between River and Sea – Encounters in Israel and Palestine*. (2002) *Through the Embers of Chaos – Balkan Journeys*. Eland.

Nafisi, A. (2003). *Reading Lolita in Tehran*. Random House.

Rodney, W. (1973). *How Europe Underdeveloped Africa*. Howard University Press.

Satrapi, M. (2004). *Persepolis*. Pantheon.

357

Sen, A. (2009). *The Idea of Justice.* Penguin Books.

McKibben, B. (2005) *Wandering Home.* Crown.

Wilkinson, R. G. & Pickett, K. (2009). *The Spirit Level: Why More Equal Societies Almost Always Do Better.* Allen Lane.

Journalists, Writers, NGOs, Alternative Press – Human rights, Politics, Peace

Anti Racism Network - www.enar-eu.org/

Fisk, R., various incl. (2006) *The Great War for Civilization: The Conquest of the Middle East.* Harper Perennial.

Front Line Defenders - www.frontlinedefenders.org/

Hanh, T. N., various incl. (1999) *Call Me By My True Names,* Parallax Press; (1992) *Peace Is Every Step: The Path of Mindfulness in Everyday Life,* Bantam; (2005) *Being Peace,* Parallax Press.

Le Monde N'est Pas Rond - www.mondepasrond.net/

Metro Eireann - www.metroeireann.com/

New Internationalist – www.newint.org/

Pen International - www.pen-international.org/

Positive News - www.positive.news/

Sex trafficking - http://www.stoptraffick.ie/

Yes! - www.yesmagazine.org/

Environment, Ecopsychology, Climate Change, Geopolitics, Ecological Economics, Sustainability

Capra, F., various incl. (1995) with Pauli, G. *Steering Business Toward Sustainability,* United Nations University Press. (1996) *The Web of Life,* Anchor. (1991) *Belonging to the Universe,* Harper. (1989)

Uncommon Wisdom, Bantam. (1992) 3rd Ed. *The Tao of Physics,* Flamingo.

Carson, R. (1962). *Silent Spring.* Houghton Mifflin.

Caruana, V. (2015). Civic Action for Sustainable Futures: What Role for Adult Environmental Education? In *Integrative Approaches to Sustainable Development at University Level* (pp. 663-674). Springer International Publishing.

Eisenstein, C., various incl. (2013) *The Ascent of Humanity,* Panenthea Productions. (2011) *Sacred Economics,* Evolver Editions.

Hartmann, T. (1998). *The Last Hours of Ancient Sunlight.* Mythical Books.

Hopwood, B., Mellor, M., & O'Brien, G. (2005). *Sustainable development: mapping different approaches.* Sustainable development, *13*(1), 38-52.

Jackson, T., various incl. (2009). *Prosperity without Growth - Economics for a Finite Planet.* Earthscan/Routledge.

Klein, N. (2014) *This Changes Everything.* Penguin Books.

Macy, J., various incl. (2012) *Active Hope,* New World Library. (1998) with Brown, M. *Coming Back to Life: Practices to Reconnect Our Lives, Our World,* New Society Publishers.

Malpas, J. (1999). *Place and experience: A philosophical topography.* Cambridge University Press.

McKibben, B., various incl. (1989) *The End of Nature,* Random House. (1995) *Hope, Human and Wild,* Milkweed Editions. (2004) *Enough,* St. Martin's Griffin.

Schumacher, E. F. (1989). *Small is Beautiful: Economics as if People Mattered.* Harper Perennial.

Watts, Alan W., various incl. (1966/89) *The Book - On the taboo against knowing who you are.* Vintage.

Woodworth, P. (2013) *Our Once and Future Planet: Restoring the World in the Climate Change Century.* University of Chicago Press.

Zarlenga, S. (2002). *The Lost Science of Money.* American Monetary Institute Charitable Trust.

Zero Emissions Research Institute - www.zeri.org/ZERI/Home.html

Homes – Living, Green, Ecological, Alternative

Bell, G. (2005). *The Permaculture Way: Practical Steps to Create a Self-Sustaining World.* Chelsea Green Publishing.

Cowman, P. (2013). *The Sheltermaker's Manual,* Python Press.

Earthships - http://earthship.com/

Creativity, Self-Development & Vulnerability

Brown, B., various incl. (2010) *The Gifts of Imperfection,* Hazelden Publishing. (2013) *The Power of Vulnerability,* Sounds True: Books. (2012) *Daring Greatly*, Penguin.

Cameron, J. various incl. (1992) *The Artists Way,* Jeremy Tarcher (now The Penguin Group). (1997) *Vein of Gold: A Journey to Your Creative Heart,* Tarcher Perigee.

Gilbert, E. (2015). *Big Magic: Creative Living Beyond Fear.* Riverhead Books.

King, S. (2000) *On Writing.* Scribner.

Nafisi, A. (2014). *Republic of Imagination.* Viking.

Women's (health, healing, psychology, self-development, shamanic)

Campbell, R. (2015). *Light Is The New Black.* Hay House.

Carrico, E. (2016). *The Other Side of the River: Stories of Women, Water and the World.* Womancraft Publishing.

Dinsmore-Tuli, U. (2014). Yoni Shakti: *A Woman's Guide to Power and*

Freedom Through Yoga and Tantra. YogaWords.

Ensler, E., various, incl. (2001) New Ed. *The Vagina Monologues,* Virago. (2013) *In The Body of The World,* Metropolitan Books. (2013) Reprint, *I Am An Emotional Creature,* Ballantine Books, Inc.

Hay, L. L. (1984). *You Can Heal Your Life.* Hay House, Inc.

Megre, V. (2005). *Anastasia - The Ringing Cedars Series.* Ringing Cedars Press.

Pearse, L., various incl. (2014) *Moods of Motherhood.* (Out June 2016) *Burning Woman.* (2015) *Moon Time.* Womancraft Publishing.

Pinkola Estés, C., various incl. (1998) New Ed. *Women Who Run With the Wolves,* Rider. (2013) *Untie the Strong Woman,* Sounds True.

Pope, A., various incl. (2001). *The wild genie: The healing power of menstruation.* Sterling Publishing Company. (2013) *The Woman's Quest,* Authors Online Ltd.

Restall Orr, E. (2001). *Kissing the Hag: The Dark Goddess and the Unacceptable Nature of Women.* O Books.

Northrup, C. Dr. (2009). Rev Ed. *Women's Bodies, Women's Wisdom.* Piatkus.

Roth, G. (2011). *Women, Food and God.* Simon & Schuster.

Shinn, F. S. (1925). *The Game of Life and how to Play it.* Penguin.

Shinoda Bolen, J. (1984/2004) *Goddesses in Everywoman.* Harper Collins.

V. Andrew, L. (1983). *Medicine Woman.* Harper Collins.

Schwab, N. (2014). *The Heart of the Labyrinth.* Womancraft Publishing.

Strayed, C. (2012). *Wild: From Lost to Found on the Pacific Crest Trail.* Alfred A. Knopf.

- **Links/Blogs/Videos**

Scarleteen - Sex Education for the Real World - www.scarleteen.com/

Watson, E. Gender equality/feminism advocacy & activism. Speech for #HeForShe campaign - www.youtube.com/watch?v=rymHYhlbBmw

Winfrey, O. Stanford Speech - https://www.youtube.com/watch?v=Bpd3raj8xww

Women's healing - http://womboflight.com/healing-the-mother-wound/

Men's (health, healing, self-development, masculine psychology, sex)

Bly, R. (2001). New Ed. *Iron John: A Book About Men.* Rider.

Campbell, J. various incl. (2003) *The Hero's Journey*, New World Library. (1989) with Bill Moyers *The Power of Myth*, Bantam Doubleday. (2008) 5th Ed. *The Hero with a Thousand Faces,* New World Library.

Chang, J. (1977). *The Tao of Love and Sex.* Wildwood House.

Chia, M. (1984). *Taoist Secrets of Love: Cultivating Male Sexual Energy.* Aurora Press.

Deida, D. (2004). *The way of the superior man;.* (2005) *Wild Nights.* Sounds True.

Gordon, J. S. (2013). *The path of Initiation. Spiritual Evolution and the Restoration of the Western Mystery Tradition.* Inner Traditions.

Hollis, J. (1994). *Under Saturn's Shadow: The wounding and healing of men.* Inner City Books.

Johnson, R. A. (1991). *He: Understanding Masculine Psychology.* Harper & Row.

Moore, R. & Gillette, D. (1991). *King Warrior Magician Lover,* HarperOne.

Lai, H. (2002). *The Sexual Teachings of the Jade Dragon: Taoist Methods for Male Sexual Revitalisation.* Destiny Books.

Odier, D. (1997). *Tantric Quest: An Encounter With Absolute Love.* Inner Traditions Bear and Company.

Some, M. (1995). *Water Spirit Ritual Initiation African.* Penguin.

Shinoda Bolen, J. (1989). *Gods in Every Man.* Harper.

Tsunetomo, Y. (2014). *The Secret Wisdom of the Samurai.* Tuttle.

- **Videos**

Andrez Gomez, C. *How to Fight:* www.youtube.com/watch?v=cKMhp7hpYIs

Williams, S. *Our Father:* www.youtube.com/watch?v=EZt5xQ0IVo4 & www.youtube.com/watch?v=xXDl81V4fjw

Gibson, A. & Wirsing, K. *What Will You Tell Your Sons?* www.youtube.com/watch?v=kt_nWX7iEx8

LGBTQ

All Out – www.allout.org/

Altman, D. & Symons, J. (2016). *Queer Wars.* Polity Books.

Bechdel, A. (2007). *Fun home: A family tragicomic.* Houghton Mifflin Harcourt.

Bornstein, K. (1998). *My gender workbook: How to become a real man, a real woman, the real you, or something else entirely.* Psychology Press. (2012). *A Queer and Pleasant Danger: The true story of a nice Jewish boy who joins the Church of Scientology, and leaves twelve years later to become the lovely lady she is today.* Beacon Press.

Butler, J. (2002). *Gender trouble.* Routledge.

Feinberg, L. (1996). *Transgender warriors: making history from Joan of Arc to Dennis Rodman.* Beacon Press.

Gendered Intelligence, UK - Support and education for transgender young people: www.genderedintelligence.co.uk/

Halberstam, J. (1998). *Female masculinity*. Duke University Press.

PFLAG (formerly known as Parents, Families and Friends of Lesbians and Gays). The largest organisation for parents, families, friends, and allies united with people who are lesbian, gay, bisexual, transgender, and queer - www.pflag.org

Sullivan, N. (2003). *A critical introduction to queer theory*. NYU Press.

- LGBT iconic novels

Feinberg, L. (1994). *Stone butch blues*. Alyson Books.

Waters, S. (2000). *Tipping the velvet*. Penguin.

Proulx, A. (2005). *Brokeback mountain*. Simon & Schuster.

- Ireland

BelongTo LGBT Youth Services, Ireland: www.belongto.org

Gay news on gay Ireland and around the globe
- www.theoutmost.com

LGBT Helpline - www.lgbt.ie

Outhouse (Dublin) - www.outhouse.ie

MeetUp groups, e.g. Running Amach - http://www.meetup.com/

Publications: GCN - http://theoutmost.com/gcn-magazine/gcn-current-issue/current-issue/

PTSD, violence, trauma/abuse & mental health

Kabatt-Zinn, J. (2013). *Full Catastrophe Living (Revised Edition): Using the Wisdom of Your Body and Mind to Face Stress, Pain, and Illness*. Random House.

Kabatt-Zinn, J. (2005). *Wherever You Go, There You Are: Mindfulness Meditation in Everyday Life.* Hachette.

Levine, P. A. (2010). *In an Unspoken Voice: How The Body Releases Trauma and Restores Goodness.* North Atlantic Books.

Lynch, T. (2011). *Selfhood: A Key to the Recovery of Emotional Wellbeing, Mental Health and the Prevention of Mental Health Problems.*

Rosenthal, M. (2015) *Heal Your PTSD: Dynamic Strategies that Work.* (2015) *Your Life After Traum: Powerful Practices to Reclaim Your Identity.* W. W. Norton & Company.

Sandersen, C. (2010). *The Warrior Within: A One in Four Handbook to Aid Recovery from Sexual Violence.* One in Four.

Siegel, D. Dr. (2011). *Mindsight: Transform Your Brain with the New Science of Kindness.* One World Publications.

Thompson, B. (2014). *Survivors on the Yoga Mat: Stories for Those Healing from Trauma.* North Atlantic Books.

- **Links & Support Lines**

Rosenthal, M. - http://healmyptsd.com

Support lines, e.g. - www.befrienders.org & www.samaritans.org

- **On myth, identity, our symbolic, spiritual & indigenous nature**

Ende, M. various incl. (2009) New Ed. *Momo* (or *The Men in Grey*). (2009) New Ed. *The Neverending Story.* Puffin Books.

Meade, M. various incl. (2012) *Fate and Destiny, The Two Agreements of the Soul.* (2008) *The World Behind the World,* Greenfire Press.

Prechtel, M. various incl. (2004) *Long Life, Honey in The Heart: A Mayan Epic.* (2006) *Stealing Benefaccio's Roses* (formerly *The Toe Bone and the Tooth*). (2015) *The Smell of Rain on Dust: Grief and Praise.* (2012) *The Unlikely Peace at Chuchumaquic.* North Atlantic Books.

Williams, S. (1999) *She.* (2003) *Said the Shotgun to the Head.* (2006) *Dead Emcee Scrolls.* MTV Books.

-   **Videos**

Williams, S. incl. *Children of the Night,* slam poem: https://www.youtube.com/watch?v=xXDl81V4fjw

References

INTRODUCTION

[1] Emma Restall Orr. *Kissing the Hag: The Dark Goddess and the Unacceptable Nature of Women*, p. 182. O Books, 2001.

[2] Personal email correspondence with Jen Christion Myers, PhD student in Sustainability Education, Prescott College, Arizona, October 2014.

[3] Christion Myers, J. forthcoming PhD. Likely title *Narratives of Place: Vieques, Puerto Rico.* Prescott College, Arizona. Expected publication date: May 2016.

[4] Christion Myers, J. ibid.

[5] Malpas, J. as cited in Myers, ibid. *Place and experience: A philosophical topography.* Cambridge University Press, 1999.

[6] Author's own, *Migration Pressure Ballistics.* Retrieved from: www.ciara-ryan-gerhardt.com/poetry

[7] Klein, N. *This Changes Everything: Capitalism vs. the Planet,* p. 165, on Glenn Albrecht, "The Age of Solastalgia". US, Penguin Books, 2015.

[8] Nafisi, A. *Reading Lolita in Tehran,* p. 94. Fourth Estate Harper Collins, 2004.

[9] Nafisi, A. ibid. p. 111.

[10] Personal email correspondence with Ingram Bondin, PhD student in mathematics at Leeds University, October 2014.

[11] Alex Assali, Syrian refugee, feeds the homeless in Berlin, November 2015. Retrieved from: http://www.huffingtonpost.com/entry/syrian-refugee-feeds-berlin-homeless_us_5654b766e4b0879a5b0cb708

[12] O'Colmain, G., on the Paris attacks, ISIS, and migration, November 2015. Retrieved from: http://wakeupfromyourslumber.com/political-author-gearoid-o-colmain-discusses-the-paris-attacks/

[13] No One is Illegal (Toronto), Anna Pratt: In *Securing Borders: Detention and Deportation in Canada.* Retrieved from: http://toronto.nooneisillegal.org/node/376

CHAPTER ONE

[14] Ai Weiwei, Chinese artist on art, borders and helping refugees, January 2016. Retrieved from: http://www.theguardian.com/artanddesign/2016/jan/01/ai-

weiwei-sets-up-studio-on-greek-island-of-lesbos-to-highlight-plight-of-refugees

[15] Becky Thompson's account of shipwrecked migrants in the Mediterranean, May 2015. Retrieved from: http://www.elephantjournal.com/2015/05/refugee-relief-firsthand-accounts-of-shipwrecked-migrants-in-the-mediterranean/

[16] Pietro Bonacina, photographer and anthropologist. Web: http://www.pietrobonacina.com/ incl. *f'Darhom:* http://www.pietrobonacina.com/projects/f-darhom-home/?lang=en

CHAPTER TWO

[17] Cleave, C. *The Other Hand*, p. 144. Hachette UK, 2009.

[18] UNHCR website, Statelessness. Retrieved from: http://www.unhcr.org/pages/49c3646c155.html

[19] Klein, N. ibid. p. 154.

CHAPTER THREE

[20] Author's own, *Hwawar u Fjuri,* in Le Monde n'Est Pas Ronde, December 2014. Retrieved from: http://mondepasrond.net/2014/12/27/all-that-matters-and-squid-pancakes/

[21] Integra Foundation, Malta. For more information see: http://integrafoundation.org

CHAPTER SEVEN

[22] Walia, H. *Undoing Border Imperialism*, p. 3. AK Press, 2013.

[23] Personal email correspondence with Richard Hendin, co-ordinator of the *Learning from Ladakh* programme with the International Society for Ecology & Culture (now Local Futures), June 2014.

[24] Author's own, *Stately Cows*. Retrieved from: www.ciara-ryan-gerhardt.com/poetry

[25] Julia Harte, journalist, on life in Ladakh, 2007. Retrieved from: http://www.culturalsurvival.org/publications/cultural-survival-quarterly/india/likir-ladakh

[26] Rizvi, J. *Crossroads of High Asia.* An important and comprehensive book on Ladakh, 'Little Tibet,' India. Oxford University Press, 1998.

[27] Norberg-Hodge, H. *Ancient Futures: Learning from Ladakh.* Sierra Club Books, 1992.

[28] The Students Educational and Cultural Movement of Ladakh. Retrieved from: http://www.secmol.org/index.php

CHAPTER EIGHT

[29] Fitzgibbon, M., & Hirzel, M. *The Sahrawis: Living the Consequences of Earth's Longest Military Wall.* In: Besosa, M., Ragaven, C., Loree Allen, S. & O'Halloran, A (Eds). *Walls, Fences, Borders and Boundaries – Essays on Social Exclusion, Inclusion and Integration.* Iowa: Kendall Hunt Publishing, 2010.

[30] Fitzgibbon, M., & Hirzel, M., ibid.

[31] Nina Munk on Jeffrey Sachs UN Millenium Villages, in interview on her book *The Idealist.* Retrieved from: http://developmentdrums.org/835

[32] Anti-Deportation Ireland board member Joe Moore, Facebook post, Anti-Deportation Ireland, June 2015.

[33] Personal communication with Abbas Ghadimi, August 2014.

CHAPTER NINE

[34] MacWeeney, A. *Irish Travellers, Tinkers No More.* 2007.

[35] Chakraborti, N. & Garland, J. *Rural Racism.* Willan, 2004.

CHAPTER TEN

[36] Ensler, E. *Embrace your Inner Girl.* Retrieved from: http://www.ted.com/talks/eve_ensler_embrace_your_inner_girl

[37] Marx, K. *Capital,* Vol. 3 as cited in John Bellamy Forster, *Marx's Ecology: Materialism and Nature.* New York, Monthly Review Press, 2000.

[38] Klein, N. ibid. p. 177.

[39] Hines, H. (Ed.) *Perfect: Young Women Talk About Body Image.* Livewire, 2002.

[40] Cowman, P. and the Living Architecture Centre: http://www.livingarchitecturecentre.com

[41] Capra, F. *The Web of Life,* 1996.

[42] Hopwood, B., Mellor, M., & O'Brien, G. (2005). *Sustainable development: mapping different approaches.* Sustainable development, 13(1), 38-52.

CHAPTER ELEVEN

[43] Hunt, D. For more information see Debbie's blog of the wagon and artist's page at: http://gypsyrosed.blogspot.ie/

[44] Living Architecture CD:
http://www.livingarchitecturecentre.com/sheltermakers-manual/
[45] Living Architecture CD, ibid.

CHAPTER FOURTEEN

[46] UNCHR, facts & figures about refugees. Report, sub-heading, *Seeking Asylum in Europe*. Retrieved from:
http://www.unhcr.ie/about-unhcr/facts-and-figures-about-refugees
[47] Personal email correspondence with Marese Hegarty, Irish Syria Solidarity Movement member and activist, April 2015.
[48] UNHCR, ibid., facts & figures about refugees.
[49] UNHCR, *Country operations profile - Syrian Arab Republic.* Retrieved from: http://www.unhcr.org/cgi-bin/texis/vtx/page?page=49e486a76&submit=GO 2015,
[50] UNHCR, refugee tally at 26-year low while internally displaced increase, June 2006. Retrieved from:
http://www.unhcr.org/4489294f4.html
[51] *Congo Democratic Republic Foreign Policy and Government Guide,* Volume 1, p. 74. International Business Publications, USA.
[52] Van Reybrouck, D. *Congo: Epic History of a People.* Harper Collins, 2014.
[53] George, S. *A Fate Worse than Debt.* Grove Press, 1990.
[54] Fara, P. *Science: A Four Thousand Year History*, p. 44. Oxford University Press, 2009.

CHAPTER FIFTEEN

[55] Alaskan environmentalists protest the Keystone pipeline, August 2013. Retrieved from: http://www.ibtimes.com/keystone-xl-alaska-pipeline-environmentalists-vs-oil-industry-what-obama-can-learn-nixon-1401601
[56] Gerhardt, K. W. *Problems and contradictions of the transition to socialism in post colonial, peasant based societies and the case of Ujamaa-socialism in Tanzania.* University of Manitoba MA thesis, 1980.

CHAPTER EIGHTEEN

[57] Cassar, A.: http://www.passaportproject.org/ and
https://antoinecassar.wordpress.com/author/antoinecassar/
[58] Cassar, A. ibid.

59 *Solo Andata, 'The Uncountable'*. Retrieved from:
http://www.ohpenproductions.com/project/the-uncountable-canzoniere-grecanico-salentino/. 2014.
60 Walia, H. ibid., p. 6.
61 Walia, H. ibid., p. 6.

CHAPTER TWENTY

62 Abisai Marandu ('Ab Mara') Youtube channel:
https://www.youtube.com/watch?v=OwY6SW5JC30
63 UNHCR Policy Institute, New Issues in Refugee Research Working Paper No. 77. 2003. *Deportation and the liberal state: the forcible return of asylum seekers and unlawful migrants in Canada, Germany and the United Kingdom*, p. 1. Retrieved from:
http://www.unhcr.org/3e59de764.html
64 Dalai Lama, *Stop Praying for Paris*, November 2015. Retrieved from: http://theantimedia.org/the-dalai-lama-just-told-the-world-to-stop-praying-for-paris/
65 Dalai Lama, ibid.
66 No One is Illegal (Toronto), ibid.
67 Paley, D. *Violence Doesn't Spill over Borders, Militarized Borders Create Violence*, Unembedded, May 2012. Retrieved from:
http://dawnpaley.tumblr.com/post/23543672055/violence-doesnt-spill-over-borders-militarized
68 Walter, N. *I admire those who bring clothes and tents to Calais, but their efforts need to be allied to a political response*, December 2015. Retrieved from:
http://www.theguardian.com/commentisfree/2015/dec/30/empathy-policy-refugees-asylum-system-humanity-volunteers
69 No One is Illegal (Toronto), ibid.
70 No One is Illegal (Toronto), ibid.
71 No One is Illegal (Toronto), ibid.
72 Thornton, L. in *KOD Lyons* (Human Rights & Criminal Law firm specialising in immigration and asylum law). *An Assault on Human Dignity, An Assault on the Rule of Law: Direct Provision in Ireland*, October 2013. Retrieved from:
http://www.kodlyons.ie/index.php/news/single/an_assault_on_human_dignity_an_assault_on_the_rule_of_law_direct_provision
73 No One is Illegal (Toronto), ibid.

CHAPTER TWENTY-ONE

371

[74] Garikai, C. Global Research, *America Created Al-Qaeda and the ISIS Terror Group,* September 2014. Retrieved from: http://www.globalresearch.ca/america-created-al-qaeda-and-the-isis-terror-group/5402881

[75] Cleave, C. ibid. p. 1-2.

[76] The Peace Lab, Hal Far, Malta, March 2013. Retrieved from: http://antoinecassar.wordpress.com/2013/03/13/ernesto-cardenal-in-malta/ andhttp://peacelab.org for more information

[77] Manuel Bravo Project. Retrieved from: http://www.manuelbravo.org.uk/index.php/about

[78] A true story of father takes life in order to save the life of his son in Immigration Removal Centre in UK. Retrieved from: http://chriscleave.com/little-bee/the-true-story-behind-my-new-novel/

[79] Bring *"Mediterranean mass murderers" to justice* - smugglers who allegedly deliberately sank a boat causing hundreds of refugee deaths, September 2014. Retrieved from: http://www.ohchr.org/EN/NewsEvents/Pages/DisplayNews.aspx?NewsID=15069&

[80] *Shipwreck Was Simple Murder, Migrants Recall,* October 2014. Retrieved from: http://www.nytimes.com/2014/10/21/world/europe/shipwreck-survivors-recount-a-deadly-journey-from-middle-east-to-europe.html?_r=0

[81] Cassar, A. ibid.

CHAPTER TWENTY-THREE

[82] Emma Watson in #HeForShe campaign, opening video at the UN, September 2014. Retrieved from: https://www.youtube.com/watch?v=gkjW9PZBRfk

[83] Brown, B. various incl. *The Power of Vulnerability: Teachings on Authenticity, Connection and Courage.* Sounds True, 2012.

[84] UN Women #HeForShe campaign. Retrieved from: http://www.heforshe.org

[85] Author's own, *A Stolen Childhood.* Retrieved from: htttp://www.ciara-ryan-gerhardt.com/poetry

[86] Walter, N. ibid.

CHAPTER TWENTY-FOUR

[87] Couterié, S. *No Tears in Ireland,* p. 74. Free Press, 2001.

[88] Couterié, ibid. p. 227.

[89] Couterié, ibid. p. 226.

[90] Foster, R. *Vivid Faces*, article in *Irish Times*, September 2014. Retrieved from: http://www.irishtimes.com/culture/books/lives-and-loves-the-sexual-side-of-the-rising-1.1942917

CHAPTER TWENTY-FIVE

[91] Collateral Repair Project (NGO providing support to asylum seekers and refugees), Amman, Jordan. Retrieved from: http://www.collateralrepairproject.org/

CHAPTER TWENTY-SIX

[92] Clowns Without Borders. Retrieved from: http://www.clownswithoutborders.org/ (USA); http://clownswithoutborders.org.uk/ (UK).

CHAPTER TWENTY-SEVEN

[93] Slavin, M., from *The Book Of Tara* (1996). Retrieved from introduction cited at: http://www.hilloftara.com/history

AFTERWORD

[94] Author's own, *To be Part of the Irish Nation with No Punctuation*. Retrieved from: htttp://www.ciara-ryan-gerhardt.com/poetry

[95] Irish Refugee Council, *Children and young people in direct provision accommodation*. Retrieved from: http://www.irishrefugeecouncil.ie/children-and-young-people/children-in-direct-provision-accommodation/two-page-report-summary

[96] Irish translation of a section of Antoine Cassar's *Passaport* poem, by Antain Mac Lachlainn. Retrieved from: http://www.iriscomhar.com/uploadedfiles/Comhar-june-2015_1.pdf

[97] Irish language magazine, Comhar: http://www.iriscomhar.com

[98] Antain Mac Lachlainn, *Journey,* a poignant story that was written at the time that several governments, including the UK, announced they were pulling funding from Mediterranean rescue ships. Retrieved from: https://cityofsanctuary.org/2014/11/27/story-from-dublin-poetry-evening/

[99] Pietro Bonacina, ibid. and *"Mamma mia dammi 100 lire"* portfolio. Retrieved from: http://www.pietrobonacina.com/portfolio/mamma-mia-dammi-100-lire/?lang=it

Lightning Source UK Ltd.
Milton Keynes UK
UKOW02f0637230816

281288UK00002B/21/P